I0054962

Advance praise for *'Leadership for the Age of Change'*

Three burning questions need to be answered before one can become a highly effective leader. First, what exactly is a leader? Second, why would anyone follow that leader? Third, how will that leader influence positive and responsible growth in her/his organization in a world of lightning speed change? In his highly scholarly, practical, and paradigm-changing book 'Leadership for The Age of Change', Dr. Jan Lourens unties the Gordian Knot formed by those three questions. He also gives practical advice that will help you navigate disruptive changes, markedly improve the level of engagement of all in your organization, and dramatically improve your business results. This book is an important resource for leaders at all levels in the field of leadership and change.

Cedric B. Johnson, *PhD, Senior Executive Consultant, AON Hewitt*

I believe that 'Leadership for the Age of Change' is an important read for leaders of all ages and experience whether you are the leader of a country, a multi-national organisation, an entrepreneurial enterprise or a small team. With his practical frameworks which are based on a clear definition of leadership, the importance of trust relationships and inclusion, Lourens provides an invaluable guide for all leaders in the 21st century. The book is easy to read and applying its common-sense approaches will help you to lead successfully in the face of hyper-change, accelerating global trends and disruptive challenges.

Dr John Howard, *FAICD, International Water Executive Advisor, ICE WaRM (International Centre of Excellence in Water Resources Management)*

Jan Lourens provides a fresh overview of leadership for the 21st century. The book serves as a reminder of the role that leadership plays in bringing about change in a volatile, uncertain, complex and ambiguous world. Leadership is thoroughly defined and a framework is provided that serves as a practical guideline in designing strategies for creating profound and creative change leadership opportunities. The core role that trust plays in principal relationships, collaboration and conflict resolution is addressed. The importance of psychological and emotional factors that play a role in behavioural change management are emphasised. Practical applications are provided, based on firm theoretical foundations to create and cultivate an inclusive change-orientated culture, constructive handling of conflict, and building of collaborative relationships. Change leadership is aligned with the different stages of change, regulated by the accentuation of good governance. Practical guidelines are provided for the design of changed-orientated leadership. These guidelines should lead to greater business performance and the success of change initiatives.

This book is a must read for leaders who are interested in applying fundamental concepts of leadership in an ever-changing environment. Jan Lourens provides easy-to-read, though thorough practical guidelines for proactive and effective leadership in the age of change, based on firm theoretical evidence.

Prof. René van Wyk, *Dept. Industrial Psychology & People Management, College of Business and Economics, University of Johannesburg*

Jan Lourens' perspective on leading in a changing world aligns perfectly with the Code of Ethics principles. It inspired me to elevate my thinking to new heights while taking our team on this exciting journey of discovery.

Rina Visser, *B Prim Ed, B Ed, M Ed Special Education, Bachelor of In-service Early Childhood, Head of Early Learning Centre, Portside Christian College*

Jan Lourens took on a daunting challenge when he decided to look at the enormous subject of Leadership in today's challenging environment. Against this background, he has put together a great mix of practical help supported by the latest in Leadership theory in a thought provoking book. The book is thorough and insightful and allows the reader to understand and implement the lessons included. Lessons that are not just for today's business leaders but are applicable to sport and all areas of leadership endeavour.

John L. Munro, *Founder and Director, The ThoughtConnect Group. John previously held executive roles as State and Regional Manager and has over 30 years' experience in the finance, banking and financial planning industry.*

———————

This book is a must-read for anyone who wants to be 'change-fit' to lead in a time of accelerating transformation of our world and the nature of work. It is a beacon of hope in a world increasingly characterised by a lack of trust in leaders—in business and government. It dispels many of the myths of leadership and provides clear pathways for personal and organisational success. It offers a blueprint for a new generation of leaders on how to master the art of managing escalating complexity, change and uncertainty, in partnership with their people.

Tobias Hills, *MPhil (Environmental Management), Principal Project Manager, Environment Protection Authority*

———————

Dr Jan Lourens comprehensively reviews leadership from both a modern theoretical and practical perspective creating a compelling case for his extensive model which is sorely needed by leaders in the 21st century. This book is recommended reading as it delivers the knowledge, guidance and understanding required to be a successful leader in an era of discontinuous change.

John Doughty, *Director, CANDO PLUS Pty Ltd*

———————

Leadership is about the actualisation of shared, desired futures. The key challenge is how to capacitate leadership to engage insightfully and successfully with the future, especially if that future is changing rapidly, in radical and fundamental ways. The burning need is how to enable leadership to become architects, and not victims, of the future under these conditions.

Jan Lourens's bold intention with his book is to empower leadership to be architects of the futures they desire as the 21st century rushes relentlessly upon them. To this end, he skilfully and comprehensively directs leadership to challenge, in courageous and persistent ways, their existing mind sets about leadership from first principles in order to become truly future-fit.

He offers a revised leadership framework—congruent to the 21st century contextual demands— as key departure point. This framework is crafted carefully around the three critical dimensions of change, relationship and execution. Jan elucidates this framework in detail throughout his book, both conceptually and practically.

If you wish to be challenged as a leader in your thinking regarding 21st century leadership, this book can assist greatly in enhancing your insight and capacity in becoming more future-fit.

Prof. Theo H. Veldsman, *Visiting professor and previous HOD, Department of Industrial Psychology and People Management, Faculty of Management, University of Johannesburg, South Africa. Prof Veldsman is the co-editor of a comprehensive thought leadership book dealing with future-fit leaders.*

Trust: a value expected from leaders and followers alike. However, there is a growing trust deficit in leadership worldwide, with approximately a third of followers not trusting their leadership. Jan Lourens's book engages the reader in how to lead in ways that creates trust, change and prosperity in many contexts. The book describes a new integrated Relationship Dimension that revolves around a core of trust, that also provides the foundation for an Execution and a Change Dimension. Adopting these new dimensions give leaders the freedom to lead and in turn adequately equipping followers to add value to the entity. This is a useful reference and framework that successfully challenges traditional ways by rather facilitating achievement of mutual purposes, moulded through non-coercive trust relationships between leaders and followers.

Edgar H. Johnson, *Professional Engineer, Specialist Consultant:Water Efficiency, GHD Pty Ltd*

Dr Lourens' insight into leadership in a changing world provides a fresh perspective for today's leaders. Based on experience and research in a variety of contexts, this outstanding work equips leaders in all fields to overcome the challenges facing them and brings a new energy and sense of excitement to organisations.

Anton Visser, *B Prim Ed, B Ed, M Ed, Deputy Principal, Portside Christian College*

Leadership for the Age of Change

Leadership for the Age of Change

HOW TO LEAD SUCCESSFULLY IN THE 21ST CENTURY

JAN F LOURENS PHD

IncludeChange Pty Ltd ● Adelaide, Australia

Leadership for the Age of Change

Copyright © Dr Jan F Lourens, 2017

First published by IncludeChange Pty Ltd

Adelaide, Australia

www.includechange.com

All rights reserved under International Copyright Conventions. No part of this publication, electronic or otherwise may be reproduced, copied, transmitted, down-loaded, decompiled, re-engineered, or stored in or incorporated into any information storage and retrieval system, in any form or by any means, whether electronic or otherwise, without the prior written permission of the author and the publisher IncludeChange Pty Ltd.

Any company, product, trade, or brand names mentioned in this book are those of their respective owners. IncludeChange and the author are not associated with any company, product, trade, or brand names mentioned in this book.

The publisher and author have used their best efforts in preparing this book, and make no representations or warranties with respect to the accuracy or completeness of its contents. The publisher and author disclaim any liability or implied warranties or fitness for a particular purpose of the use or application of this book. Neither the publisher nor the author shall be liable for damages or losses arising from the use of this book, in whole or in part. Citations of internet web links used in this book may not be valid at the time of publication.

ISBN 978-0-6481810-0-2 (Print copy)

ISBN 978-0-6481810-1-9 (Ebook)

1. Leadership. 2. Organisational Change. 3. Organisational behaviour. 4. Corporate Governance.

Contents

Prologue

I have been privileged to travel on a journey of an extensively diverse and rewarding career. In this leadership guide I will share the rich experience and understanding I have gained over many decades. I am very thankful for the excellent education I received in a variety of fields such as engineering, business and the humanities. I have also travelled and worked in many parts of the world, in many cultures and in a wide variety of entities ranging from small businesses, education, the military, to large corporate businesses in various industries.

I had the honour to be led by the best leaders as well as by some of the worst. I also had the pleasure to lead many people in many different contexts. This varied experience and education provided me with abundant material to prepare this leadership guide—a guide for leaders in an age of truly unprecedented change... with more change coming.

I grew up on a farm in South Africa, blessed with an extreme dose of curiosity. This is probably one of the reasons why my career has been so diverse. As a young school student, I was fascinated with the concepts and principles of chemistry. The fact that everything around us—the seen world—consist of some form of chemistry, inspired me to understand more about the topic; not only to understand more—I wanted to employ the knowledge, beneficially. That is why I embarked on a career as a chemical engineer.

Shortly after becoming a chemical engineer, and again driven by curiosity, I became interested in the business world behind engineering. That is when I decided to complete a Masters degree in business.

Early in my twenties I noticed stark differences between leaders that seemed to be successful and those that were not. I wondered why. Surely, they had all been picked for their leadership roles because they were good at it? Again, my curiosity pushed me into the direction of leadership. I started to read and study leadership as widely as I could. What is the role and task of a leader? Answers to this question are probably the most elusive of all answers about leadership. The Masters degree in business did not answer many of the nagging questions I had about leadership. These questions remained unanswered until recently, when I began to research and write this guide. Some of the many questions I had at that time were:

- Why are there so many, and often conflicting, definitions about leadership? Why can't we agree on what the role is? Why doesn't a role so important as leadership have at least some agreed generic guideline on what it is? Most other human activities, whether professional or vocational, have clear and precise role definitions.
- Humanity has studied leadership over many centuries—surely by now we must know exactly what works and what does not? Surely, we have all the necessary knowledge and training available to us to be clear on what this familiar role ought to accomplish?
- Why do we experience so many failures with our change initiatives and lose trust in our leaders? Why are people becoming disengaged and getting hurt by entities with apparent good intensions?
- Why do we tolerate leadership failures, yet we do not tolerate the same levels of failure in many other human endeavours? For example, people in the medical or legal professions attract

stern scrutiny regarding their conduct. Yet the effect of bad leadership on our organisations, societies and economies can be profound.

These questions are only a small sample of what I needed answers for, and I am sure you will probably have many similar questions. Clearly, the performance records show that current leadership methods do not deliver the expected results any longer. I was disillusioned and irritated with the alleged tried-and-tested ways of leadership.

Around the turn of the century, another honour befell me. I became part of a doctoral course programme that covered the complete discipline of organisational behaviour. For the doctoral research dissertation, I elected to do confirmatory validation research on the newly discovered theory of Three-dimensional leadership. In the research, we also included work on leaders' emotional intelligence, visionary ability and citizenship behaviour.

Ever since I completed my research I have always wanted to write a book on leadership. I could not find any book that can be used as a guide to lead proactively in a future of constant change, that addresses the role of leadership comprehensively, that is based on both practical experience and sound theoretical principles, and that could be applied in a variety of contexts and entities. So, I decided to undertake this challenge and write a leadership guide that addresses these needs. I have designed this guide for leaders to lead into the future, to provide new leadership mindsets and frameworks, in contexts of exponentially rising change.

I will not be so arrogant as to claim that this guide is the only book you will ever need to read on the topic of leadership. Far from it! I am however optimistic that you will find a lot of value in reading it and I encourage you to apply as much of it as you can, to lead your entity into the future.

Jannie Lourens, *Adelaide, Australia, 2017*

www.includechange.com

Introduction

The purpose of this leadership guide

My aim is to help leaders and their entities be pre-prepared and change-fit for the challenges and vast opportunities that are presented by the age of change

We live in an extraordinary age of increasing change—an age that is often referred to as the VUCA world. VUCA is an acronym that describes a world of increasing Volatility, Uncertainty, Complexity and Ambiguity[1]. The pace of change in the world we lead has made a major inflection, onto what I would call the Mega-S-Curve (Chapter 1). The changes we will experience in the VUCA world, will increase in intensity and momentum. In Chapter 1, I explain how this volatile new context has emerged and what leaders can expect in future.

My purpose for *Leadership for the Age of Change*, is to encourage you to take this age of change head-on — to provide you with new leadership mindsets, frameworks and principles of behaviour that will give you the advantage to lead successfully in a context of exponentially rising change. I designed this guide specifically for leaders who want to lead proactively in the age of change. It is not another book about good leadership.

To lead in this new world, we must stop the commonplace predicable, unilateral and linear approaches we were so used to apply. They belong to previous leadership eras. Those approaches might have worked well in eras past—however, the old ways of leading simply does not work any longer.

We are experiencing major leadership deficits everywhere we look—in businesses, governments, public and private institutions. We continue to see declining levels of trust in leadership, decreasing trends in employee engagement, and the success rate of change initiatives remaining miserably low.

The performance results of our entities—measured as the difference between our agreed objectives and what we have achieved—shows a persistent deficit, globally.

Ultimately it all comes down to how well we lead. Leaders should not accept these poor results as a new norm in the context of increasing change. No! The new context of hyper-change needs new leadership approaches. There are better ways to engage with this new future, a future James Canton[2] calls an "Extreme Future".

In this book, I have provided you with new frameworks that will address many leadership deficits. The frameworks will help you to:

- Positively turn around leadership deficits that are damaging our entities and societies.
- Improve your relationships and the trust you build with your people.
- Increase your entities' engagement through a mindset of inclusion.
- Enhance your entities' execution performance and very importantly;
- Increase the rate of success of all your change initiatives.

Who is this leadership guide for?

Leadership for the Age of Change is for the courageous leader. You could be an experienced or an inexperienced leader—it is immaterial. What is important is that you aspire to lead your entity—whether it is a team, an entrepreneurial business, global enterprise, political party, school or sports organisation—with a clear mutual purpose to conquer the new future in a change context.

You don't have to be a chief executive or a top politician to benefit from this guide. You are a leader, who wants to seize new ideas and use new frameworks to proactively confront the challenges of the new era, wherever you are, right now. You are disillusioned and annoyed with the old so-called 'tried-and-tested' ways—those ways that clearly do not deliver excellent results any more.

You are willing to discover how your personal values and principles lead towards trust, collaboration, inclusion and excellence. You want to lead your entity towards its purpose; you want it to achieve its objectives with excellence. You want to lead an entity where everyone is fully engaged, and has a powerful sense of ownership in what the entity does and where it wants to go with its future.

You will discover how to shape the vision, mutual purpose and culture of your entity in a different manner. You will learn to do so in an inclusive way, through trusting relationships with everyone inside and outside your entity. Your people will then develop a strong, positive sense of belonging and ownership—therefore your entity will not develop engagement deficits. People will feel great about themselves and about the entity they are part of. Jointly they can aspire to the vision and be determined to achieve the mutual purpose.

During your journey through this guide, you will recognise that change is a natural phenomenon—change is something that develops through its own Pre-Life-Cycle, before it reaches a viable life cycle. You use this natural phenomenon of change to the advantage of your entity and you follow the Pre-Life-Cycle to make your entity fit for change. I describe the natural characteristics and the Pre-Life-Cycle of change in Chapter 7.

You will realise that part of your leadership role is to lead change proactively. Change-oriented leaders have different values, mindsets, and they behave differently. You will appreciate that change is not something that can be managed through consecutive psychological stages, because your entity may have to deal with several change initiatives that are at different stages, simultaneously. It is not practical or possible any longer to lead change from one state of equilibrium to another. Instead your people will become change-fit to be able to deal with changes on a continual basis. You will lead your entity towards a state of continuous dynamic equilibrium—equilibrium between continually changing contextual drivers for change and restraining forces against change.

You believe that a fundamental shift is needed in the way we lead change. Leaders' behaviours need to change to render our entities more agile and resilient in the face of change—likewise for opportunities and threats likewise. This requires that our people become co-owners and co-developers of our entities' mutual purposes. This means they will not only accept responsibility and accountability for change, they will drive change proactively. You are of the belief that the way to lead change in your entity is to include everyone at his or her level to become proactive in leading change.

You think differently. You follow diverse mindsets that enable and align your entity to become agile and fit for change, before change occurs. You lead your entity to anticipate changes—good and bad, long before anyone else does, and your entity takes proactive actions in inclusive ways. Therefore, your entity is not only comfortable with learning, innovation and disruption, it is change-fit to such an extent that it ushers the entity into the new future by leading change, innovation and disruptions.

You uphold the value of excellence. In everything your entity does, it strives to deliver excellent performance—performance that has its foundation in the values of inclusion, trust, collaboration and mutual purpose.

You want to lead the execution of your entity's activities differently. You lead your entity through strategic governance and direction setting. You don't follow an exclusive top-down command and control approach—you leave your people to do their work as they are equipped to do. The lifeblood of your entity's execution system is an integrated intelligence network based on the principles of transparency, accountability and proactiveness.

Because you ascribe to these leadership values and principles, you find it easy to implement the principles in this book and you will realise the results you expect in this age of hyper-change.

How will you benefit from this book?

If the values and principles as described above resonate with yours, and you are eager to follow a new leadership framework to lead into the future—a framework that positively addresses the leadership deficits I mentioned before—then this guide will benefit you significantly.

Leadership for the Age of Change is packed with practical advice in many easy to follow leadership frameworks, concepts, processes and principles that you can readily apply to lead your entity into the new future.

The benefits you will gain when you apply this framework for leadership are:

- Practical advice relevant to you right now that also equips you for the age of change.
- A guide you can refer to again and again—a companion you can use in many complex leadership contexts.
- Knowledge applicable for any type of entity, of almost any size, from as small as one person—like yourself—to as large as a nation. You can apply it in teams, organisations, schools, sports organisations, political entities, government and non-governmental organisations, commercial businesses and non-for-profit organisations.
- The concepts, frameworks and principles are designed and integrated around the comprehensive role of the leader. The

guide is based on a substantive definition of leadership, which describes the design purpose of the leadership role and does not favour any specific qualities of 'good leadership'.

- It will increase your power and authority positively, as well as the power base of your entity, founded on inclusively achieving a mutual purpose. You won't have to rely on leveraging power through compliance, command, coercion, manipulation and persuasion tactics.

- The frameworks and models are easy to understand. They do not only focus on, the 'people side' of leadership—they include hard-core purpose driven execution and change-focused leadership behaviours necessary in the age of change.

- This guide is based on sound and proven theories in the domains of leadership and organisational behaviour, enhanced with practical experience, and designed for leading the future.

- Unnecessary academic and theoretical jargon and terminology has been avoided—leaving you with clear undrestandable guidelines.

- This guide makes the theoretical practical—it turns concepts into readily applicable leadership behaviours.

- You will achieve significant improvements in your leadership relationships, through building trust, collaboration and engagement throughout your entity.

- This guide explains how to achieve increased inclusion, accuracy, effective speed of decision-making and execution of decisions.

- Your entity will become ready to execute specific change initiatives—and ultimately your entity will reach a state of change-fitness. (Change-fitness is the capacity to continually take challenges head-on and to steer change initiatives without adversely impacting the entity's resilience.)

- You will achieve better success rates with your change initiatives.
- After reading and applying this guide you will be able to measure improvements in performance, leadership behaviours, culture, etc. with measures and metrics you can design by using the principles in the frameworks.
- You can apply the guide as narrowly or as widely as you like. Use only parts of it, or all of it. (You will get the most value when you use it comprehensively.)
- The guide provides practical examples that can be applied in your context.

The scope of this leadership guide

Leadership for the Age of Change is the result of my search for practical solutions to real leadership problems in real entities over many years. When I designed the leadership frameworks, I integrated my own research on leadership in a rapidly changing world with numerous proven theories on leadership and organisational behaviour. Extensive personal experience gained over many years of practical leadership and managerial involvement across many industries is woven into this guide.

In Chapter 1, I expand on the current and future context within which we lead. I introduce concepts such as the Mega-S-Curve, the VUCA world, and some of the major leadership deficits of our time.

For us to lead effectively in this new era, we need to clearly understand exactly what is required to fulfil our role as leaders. A huge number of definitions exist for the concept of leadership. Some of these definitions are useful, but often they are conflicting, confusing, or narrowly focused on one or two qualitative attributes of 'good leadership'. Since there are so many definitions—which one is most suitable?

In Chapter 2, I introduce a descriptive definition of leadership that explains four substantive fundamentals of what leadership is—not what 'good leadership' looks like. The key principle is; when we lead according to the substantive fundamentals of what leadership constitutes, we will be able to perform our leadership task completely and we will realise the mutual purposes of the entities we lead.

The Leadership Framework is the core concept in this book. I introduce the Leadership Framework in Chapter 3. The principles of the Leadership Framework are based on the integrated theory of Three-dimensional leadership behaviour. There are three new leadership dimensions that form integral parts of the Leadership Framework. The three new dimensions are:

- Relationship Dimension
- Change Dimension
- Execution Dimension

Each of these three dimensions consists of numerous associated leadership behaviours. Three-dimensional leadership theory was discovered shortly before the turn of the 21st century, about the same time when the age of change started to ascend onto a Mega-S-Curve. This theory was discovered by the pioneering work of two Scandinavian leadership theorists. Subsequently many others across the world have validated the theory. My own research, conducted in a large multinational organisation, also validates this theory.

Chapter 4 expands on leaders' soft skills—those interpersonal behaviours necessary to succeed in the age of change. I introduce the Relationship Dimension, which has at its core the building of trusting relationships. From a foundation of trust, the Relationship Dimension is expanded into nine interpersonal leadership behaviours.

The Change Dimension is introduced in Chapter 5. The title of this book, 'Leadership for the Age of Change', indicates that it is designed for leaders to lead courageously in a future of continuous and discontinuous change. A substantial part of this book is dedicated to leading change into this new future.

To provide context to the Change Dimension, I first discuss the nature and key characteristics of change in Chapter 6. Leadership is displayed through behaviours—seen and unseen. What you think, say, do and don't do. Leadership behaviours are influenced by the contexts within which you conduct your task as leader. When the context changes, you adjust your behaviours accordingly. If you don't adjust to the context, you cannot expect repetition of previous successes.

Chapter 7 examines how change affects people, especially when change is led in a traditional linear stepwise method, and how people react to change when they are not change-fit.

The Change Dimension is based on a fundamental natural law. This natural law says that any change initiative follows (or rather should follow), what I call the 'Pre-Life-Cycle'. The Pre-Life-Cycle occurs before any change initiative can reach viability. The Pre-Life-Cycle consists of five stages, namely: Enable, Align, Anticipate, Incubate and Implement. Specific leadership behaviours are required in each of these stages. The Change Dimension describes the leadership behaviours you should follow in each stage to ensure successful change initiatives in your entity. The five stages of the Change Dimension are discussed in detail in Chapters 8 to 12.

Chapter 13 introduces the Execution Dimension, which consists of systematically assembling sets of 'hard core behaviours', or execution elements, designed for leaders to lead entities toward superior performance. The Execution Dimension stands firmly on the fundamental principles in the Relationship Dimension. The integration of the 'soft' Relationship Dimension and the 'hard' Execution Dimension renders leadership as neither 'soft' nor 'hard', but makes it purposefully effective. The Execution Dimension is designed for proactive leadership governance, directing operational challenges and opportunities in your entity's unique context, so that your entity delivers on its mutual purpose, strategy and objectives in the short- and long-term.

How can you use this leadership guide?

I am confident that *Leadership for the Age of Change* will help you to identify innumerable instances and contexts within which you can apply the Leadership Framework and its fundamental principles.

Throughout this guide, I have provided numerous models, processes and principles. You can apply them individually or you can use them in a fully integrative manner. I would recommend the latter approach. I have designed *Leadership for the Age of Change* around the integrative definition of leadership and a Leadership Framework that is comprehensive.

In the final chapter, I provide several practical examples to demonstrate the integrated nature of the Leadership Framework. I chose a number of practical examples to illustrate how you can apply this guide in different contexts. The examples pertain to personal leadership conduct, how you can lead change in your entity to improve its performance, and how you can lead change initiatives more successfully.

Becoming a successful leader in the age of change is a process of constant trial and error, of trying new things and new behaviours. It means that you need to display courage, and persistence to overcome the challenges of old school thinking and grab the opportunities in this bold and extreme new future. The leadership behaviours that you will learn in *Leadership for the Age of Change* will help you do so. This guide will encourage you to win in the age of change.

Every leader's entity—whether it is a team, an entrepreneurial business, global enterprise, political party, school or sports organisation—has its context, circumstances, opportunities and challenges varying daily, and in an age of change this context is becoming more ambiguous and paradoxical compared to previous eras. If you want to become a successful leader in this age of change, then *Leadership for the Age of Change* will help you win.

———

Notes

1. The concept called 'VUCA', emerged in the late 1990's from the military fraternity. They have noticed that more and more initiatives fall victim to several uncertainties posed by drivers and variables of change. The variables of change seem to become increasingly Volatile, Uncertain, Complex and Ambiguous. This phenomenon of change gave birth to a now widely used acronym called VUCA.

2. James Canton, J. 2006, *Extreme Future - The top ten trends that will reshape the world*, Penguin, New York.

1. The New Context

WHY DO WE NEED A NEW LEADERSHIP FRAMEWORK?

"Change is not merely necessary to life, it is life"

Alvin Toffler

"It is not the strongest of species that survive nor the most intelligent, but the ones most responsive to change"

Charles Darwin

Introduction

Do we need a different kind of leadership for the age of change and why?

What I am about to describe may seem unquestionably daunting. Yet, I have no intention to be a gloomy doomsayer. To the contrary, my purpose is to provide leaders with new frameworks and mindsets that will encourage and enable them to lead victoriously in the age of change.

First, I describe the context of the age of change. The new context will show vividly that we need new leadership frameworks—new mindsets that will enable leaders to lead in the new future. Mindsets, that necessitate us to adopt new leadership behaviours that will help us to be successful in an age of unprecedented changes. We need new frameworks that will enable us and our people to follow successful strategies and collaborative initiatives into an uncharted territory. As leaders, we simply cannot continue to lead with the many outdated methods we have been taught—they are simply not suitable for leading in the new future.

One such outdated mindset is: *'Knowledge is Power'*.

The dictum of 'knowledge is power' simply no longer holds true.

The amount of information that is created, available, and accessible to almost everyone is increasing at a rate substantially faster than any leader can absorb and hold as solely theirs. Moreover, the durability of knowledge has decreased substantially. Thus, our ability to absorb and retain relevant information is severely challenged. It is now simply impossible for any individual or a small group to hold ransom over knowledge. Information is truly everywhere. Anyone's ability to obtain and access information is becoming easier. Anything leaders say or do, can be questioned and examined. No more can we hide behind our assumed superior knowledge or our presumed superior positions. Almost everything we do or say can be contradicted.

Whether the knowledge and information available are accurate or not; it almost does not matter. People use public data sources to weigh and judge their leaders' visions and initiatives. This has profound implications on how we will lead in the future, how we will create change in the future, and how we will build trust.

A natural reaction from leaders and their followers is to attempt to contain the constant flood of change. There is a relentless counter attack on complexity and uncertainty. Leaders who 'succeed' on 'simplifying' situations are ostensibly the new heroes. I have some empathy with that sentiment—however, it is pure reactionary behaviour—behaviour that cannot be sustained.

Change has always been part of human life. Yet, the world has truly moved into an era of constant change—a phenomenon that has become known as the VUCA world[1] —that is, a new context where change is increasing in Volatility, Uncertainty, Complexity and Ambiguity.

The world of leadership has moved away from the predictable and simplified approaches we were so used to applying in the previous industrial eras. We are now well and truly within the 4th industrial era—that is, the digital and social era. In the decades before the turn of the century, the world has reached a major inflexion point on what I call the Mega-S-Curve. For the first time in many centuries, we are about to embark on the rising leg of exponential change on a Mega-S-Curve. Complexity and uncertainty will grow, faster and fiercer. Leaders who ignore this will do so at their peril.

The answer for leadership in this new world of change does not merely lie in simplification—it lies in approaching change, complexity and leadership differently. We can lead successfully and in the new uncharted world—but we need different mindsets to conquer the new world.

The New Leadership Context

We have all been introduced to the new world of change. People have experienced the turmoil and anxiety around us over the last three to four decades.

During the last two decades of the 20th century the scene was set for major change. In the following first two decades of the 21st century we were beginning to experience an inflection towards substantially more and faster change that is approaching us with increased uncertainty and volatility.

I illustrate the new context of extraordinary change by explaining several fundamental characteristics that are visible at the start of the new era, namely:

- The Mega-S-Curve
- An extreme future in a VUCA world
- Change deficit remains unyielding
- Increasing trust deficit
- Increasing engagement deficit
- Increasing execution deficit.

Each of these contextual characteristics are summarised below:

Nick Obolensky[2] in his book, Complex Adaptive Leadership, shows a graph that represents the pace of change over four centuries. The graph's x-axis shows time, and the y-axis shows the pace of change. He studied the pace of change as it happened in history, in four areas: Military technology, communication technology, transportation technology and the general level of human education and awareness over a period of 4000 years in western civilisations.

Obolensky says that the graph looks like the bottom of an S-curve. I fully concur with his view.

Mega-S-Curve

Figure 1.1 is my adaptation of Obolensky's graph. I have added his concept of an extreme future on the vertical axis and traced a possible S-curve with a dotted line into the next millennium.

From the graph in Figure 1.1, it is evident that the pace of change has only gradually increased over most of the past four centuries. Subsequently, in all the areas Obolensky studied, an inflection in the pace of change has occurred during the last few decades. This inflection clearly indicates to me that we are at the start of the rising leg on a Mega-S-Curve. It would be presumptuous to forecast how long this rising leg would last before we it reaches a plateau. What is clear to me is that we are about to embark on a major roller-coaster ride. This ride will be exiting, but it will also be risky.

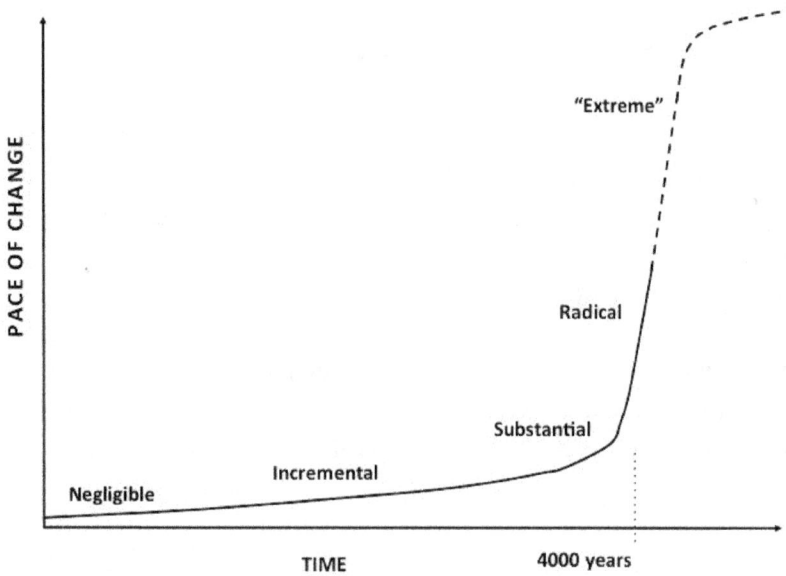

Figure 1.1. The Mega-S-Curve (Adapted from Obolensky)

Obolensky makes a controversial conclusion, which says that we have reached a paradox of information and knowledge:

"The more knowledge there is, the more uncertain we are"

The digital age is fuelling this paradox. For example, the Big Data and analytics industry is feeding an insatiable hunger for more information and more knowledge. It makes exciting business sense, but Big Data, analytics and more information cannot solve the leadership dilemmas of uncertainty and volatility, we are facing.

In their sixth study of the digital universe in 2012, Gantz and Reinsel[3] forecast that from 2005 to 2020, the digital universe would grow by a factor of 300, from 130 exabyte to 40,000 exabyte, or 40 trillion gigabytes. The digital universe will double every year. Yet, only 3%, a tiny fraction of the digital universe has been explored for its analytic value. Therein they say exists the promise of the Big Data industry. The promise lies in the extraction of extraordinary value from this large untapped pool of data.

An Extreme Future in a VUCA world

James Canton (2008)[4] who runs a think tank in San Francisco called the Institute for Global Futures says that leaders must deal with the onset of an *Extreme Future* with its associated destabilising forces that include rapid technological development, changing government regulations, changing demographics and increasing pressure on resources.

Canton's work is part of a long-range strategic forecasting project for Fortune 1000 companies. He identified five major aspects of change that will define our future and how we will experience the new age of change. A new age of change, as Canton calls it: "*The Extreme Future*".

The five attributes of the *extreme future* we will consistently experience, are:

- The Speed of change will increase. The rate of change will be blinding, comprehensive in scope, and will touch every aspect of your life.
- Complexity will increase. Quantum leaps will occur in several seemingly unrelated forces that will have a direct bearing on everything from lifestyles, to work, to personal and national security.
- Risk profiles will change. New risks, higher risks and more threats from terror to crime to global economic upheaval will alter every aspect of your life.
- Change in a variety of life and work aspects will occur simultaneously. Drastic adjustments in our work, community and relationships will force us to adapt quickly to radical transformations.
- Surprise will be the order of the day. Surprises will sometimes

be good, sometimes difficult to imagine. Surprise will become a daily feature of our lives, regularly challenging sensibility and logic.

The scenario Canton describes as an extreme future, supports the characteristics we can see in the intensifying change of the Mega-S-curve I have illustrated.

This increase in speed, complexity, risk, simultaneity and surprise has given rise to another concept of change in the new era. The concept called 'VUCA', emerged in the late 1990's from the military fraternity. They have noticed that more and more initiatives fall victim to several uncertainties posed by drivers and variables of change. The variables of change seem to become increasingly Volatile, Uncertain, Complex and Ambiguous. This phenomenon of change gave birth to a now widely used acronym called VUCA. The meanings of the letters in the acronym are:

- **Volatility** describes the rapidity, frequency and the extent at which a change may deviate from a normal baseline.
- **Uncertainty** describes the level of predictability of a change that occurs, or that is about to occur. The higher the uncertainty is, the higher the associated risks are.
- **Complexity** of change is described by the level of interconnectedness and the number of associated elements in an interconnected dynamic system, as it is the case in most medium and large entities. The more interconnected elements exist within a system, the more complex changes on that system would be. Such changes may not have clear linear causal effects on the system or its elements. The effects of changes will differ across the system and its interconnected elements.
- **Ambiguity** is present when no clear causal relationships, precedents, rules or characteristics of a situation exists. This is

the domain of paradox—there are often no definitive solutions, or there are several valid solutions, or a chosen solution may have to alternate between extreme poles depending on the context.

The VUCA elements describe current and future disruptive changes leaders and entities will face on a continuous basis. The events during the recent financial crises and the demise of several nation-states have intensified our realisation that the world is systemically highly interconnected. Seemingly unrelated changes that occur remotely may have substantial effects on us, no matter where we are on the globe.

John Beddington[5], England's chief scientific advisor, forecasts what he calls the "The 2030 Perfect Storm Scenario". (Note that 2030 is not far away):

He sees the following main developments occurring by the year 2030:

- The global population has increased from 6.8 billion to 8.3 billion.
- Demand for food will grow by 40 percent, but supplies have not kept up with demand.
- Demand for energy has grown by 45 percent, but supplies in recent years have not kept up, and the resulting scarcity has pushed energy prices to record heights.
- Global demand for water has grown by close to 30 percent. Water conservation measures have helped, but close to four billion people are now living in an area of high water stress.
- Efforts to reduce greenhouse gas emissions have fallen far short of the pledges made by countries.
- Shortages of food, energy and water are increasing the number of failed states and enflaming international tensions.

Disruptive changes caused by an increasing VUCA world will not exclusively create adversarial effects on entities.

Disruptive change holds many positive opportunities too. A classic example is the global move to do something positive about climate change. Many reluctant players in, for example, the energy industry have pushed back against climate change and lost their ground. While many others in the same industry have seized opportunities presented by climate change and built huge new industries by following the new trends this move created.

Dobbs, Manyika and Woetzel[6] in their book *"No Ordinary Disruption"*, quote that the economic acceleration we will see shortly will be roughly 10 times faster than the one triggered by the Industrial Revolution and is 300 times the scale. They anticipate a staggering economic force that is 3,000 times as large.

Dobbs, Manyika and Woetzel base their growth forecasts on the fact that it took Britain 154 years to double economic output per person, and Britain did it by starting with a small population of nine million people. The United States achieved the same doubling of economic growth in 53 years; starting with a population of ten million people. China and India have done it in only twelve and sixteen years, respectively, each with about 100 times as many people.

The question is:

Are you and your entity pre-prepared and change-fit to lead both the extreme challenges and opportunities of disruptive change coming your way?

As leaders, we have attempted to deal with this new VUCA world. We use obsolescent toolboxes that were designed to help us lead in previous eras—to little avail. We need new mindsets and leadership frameworks to help as lead the new age of change.

The Change Deficit

Worldwide the success record for change initiatives by entities over the last four to five decades have been disappointing to say the least. Many change initiatives embarked on do not deliver on their intended outcomes. Failed and partially successful change initiatives cost huge amounts in resources: time, money, human energy and lost opportunities.

Despite the vast resource expenditure on change efforts, entities don't achieve what they intended. Instead, often what entities get from failed change attempts are: an incredible loss of trust in leadership, fatigued and disengaged employees, disgruntled customers and performance results below expectations.

On top of this turmoil, leaders are blaming their change consultants for wrong advice to lead changes, while consultants blame leaders for not being fit for the task of leading change.

The simple fact is that both leaders and their advisors are singing from the same hymnbook—both parties are following outdated models and frameworks to lead change. Shifting the blame would not solve the challenges the era of extreme change is posing to us.

Damned if you do change

And damned if you don't change

This blame game is accentuated by an ongoing debate about the success rate of change initiatives. The debate has been narrated in numerous reports and media. For example, Huges[7] published a study that disputes the validity of a longstanding popular cliché that says the failure rate for change initiatives is 70%. He questions the supporting evidence for such a very specific and alarming statistic. Huges reviewed five studies that identified 70% failure rates for change initiatives. In each instance, he highlights the absence of valid and reliable evidence in support of the renowned 70% failure rate.

In a study by IBM[8], *"Making Change Work",* they found that:

- 41% of projects were considered successful in meeting project objectives within planned time, budget and quality constraints
- 44% of change projects missed at least one time, budget or quality goal
- 15% of change projects either missed all goals or were stopped by management.

Another study by Smith[9] looked at 210 changes in entities, ranging across a variety of initiatives, for example, strategy development, business expansions, acquisitions, restructurings, and new IT systems. In Smith's study the success rates varied between 10% and 28%, thus it corroborates the cliché of 70% failure.

Websites such as Calleam.com[10] keeps a current database on major failed change programs worldwide.

What I conclude from this debate on the success of change initiatives and the wide-ranging success statistics, is this:

- Potentially the norm of a 70% failure rate could be overstated—the actual rate may differ depending on different vantage points.
- However, even if the failure rate is as 'low' as 30%, which clearly it isn't, such a low success rate is still too high for any leader to regard as acceptable performance. As leaders, we need to turn this around.

Leaders are in desperate need of new behaviours and frameworks that will guide us to produce far better change results.

The Trust Deficit

Trust provides permanent competitive advantage ...

At zero cost!

There is always huge cost and losses associated with untrustworthy behaviour—especially a leader's untrustworthy behaviour. The price we pay for loss of trust is huge. The deficit created by a loss of trust takes ten times longer to recover than it would have taken to create trust in the first instance. Broken trust causes lost customers, lost loyalty, losses in people engagement, lost talent and performance losses. To recover from the trust deficit, and because we should limit many consequences of untrustworthy behaviours, we increase the rules, regulations, laws and add more bureaucracy.

Yet, it is so obvious, the cost of trustworthy leadership is nil. Trustworthy behaviour provides permanent competitive advantage for leaders and their entities.

While it may be so obvious, the Edelman Trust Barometer[11] tells a sobering story about a growing trust deficit in leadership worldwide.

The Edelman Trust Barometer is an instrument that measures the amount of trust people have in a variety of entities. When Edelman gauged the level of trust people have in leadership in 2013, they found the dismal result that only 43% of people trust CEOs of companies as credible spokespeople (this measure dropped again to 41% in 2015). Only 18% of the general population says they trust business leaders would tell the truth regardless of how complex or unpopular the truth may be. The Edelman trust barometer also shows that trust in leadership is far lower in developed countries.

More astounding however is the difference or gap between the trust people have in business entities and the trust they have in the leaders of those entities. Globally this gap is 32% between the trust in entities and the trust in their leaders, meaning that people would rather trust entities than they would trust the leadership. This trust gap for leadership is 35% in the USA, Australia and China, 34% in India and 29% in Germany.

While only 18% of the global population is saying that they trust business leaders to tell the truth, the gap is even worse for government and political leaders. Only 13% of the world's population trusts government and political leaders to tell the truth.

The Edelman Trust Barometer states that several trends and events have led to the erosion of trust in leadership:

- The democratising trend of recent years. We are experiencing a redistribution of influence—from traditional authority figures such as CEOs and government officials, toward employees, peers and other people with credentials, including academics and technical experts.
- The hierarchical systems of the past are being replaced by more trusted peer-to-peer, horizontal networks of trust.
- The shocks of the financial crises and subsequent recessions and misdeeds by leadership figures have forced people to revisit their expectations of institutions and leaders.
- We have arrived in a new era of scepticism—people need to see and hear something more often and from many different sources before they would believe in it, and they learn equally from traditional and social media.

Building and recovery of trust is probably the most fundamental leadership duty. If we are to survive as leaders in the new era of extreme change we will have to rely significantly more on the creation of solid trustworthy relationships with everyone around us. Building and maintaining trusting relationships will rely on your firm determination to persistently show trustworthy leadership behaviour.

Engagement Deficit

Engaged employees are the lifeblood of their entities and their communities. The level of engagement determines the level of performance.

Several studies have shown that engagement levels of employees in entities have followed similar trends to the trust deficits discussed before. Several engagement measures are available. These measures gauge peoples' engagement levels in entities. For example, Gallup and AON Hewitt[12] are two such entities that gauge engagement on a regular basis.

In their study *"The State of the Global Workplace"*, Gallup measured employee engagement on a global scale during the period 2009 to 2013, and have found that only 13% of employees across 142 countries are fully engaged in their jobs, while a huge percentage; 63%, are not engaged, and as much as 24% are actively disengaged.

On average, this means that people who are negative and potentially antagonistic to their organisations outnumbered engaged employees at a ratio of nearly 2 to 1.

Work units that showed engagement levels in the top 25% of Gallup's study, have shown significantly higher productivity, profitability and customer ratings. They showed less turnover and lower absenteeism levels, and fewer safety incidents than those in the bottom 25% of the study.

Organisations that have an average of about 9 engaged employees for every actively disengaged employee, experienced significantly higher—as high as 147% higher—earnings per share when compared with their competitors in their respective industries. In contrast, those organisations with an average of 2.6 engaged employees for every actively disengaged employee, experienced 2% lower earnings per share, when compared with their competitors during the same period.

This engagement deficit causes a significant drain on the wealth of entities, communities and nations worldwide. Gallup estimates, for example, for the US alone disengagement costs US$450 to $550 billion per annum. For Germany, the engagement deficit ranges between €112 and €138 billion per annum. For the United Kingdom, this figure ranges between £52 and £70 billion per annum.

A study by AON Hewitt focused particularly on the effects of major change initiatives on employee engagement. They found that after a merger or acquisition, the percentage of highly engaged employees tends to fall well below a 10% global baseline. The percentage of highly engaged employees falls further to 5% a few months after a merger or acquisition, and does not recover to the baseline for another two to three years. Furthermore, the negative effects of multiple change initiatives have a cumulative impact on employee engagement. It means that when employees experience several simultaneous changes in their work environment, their engagement level drops considerably, and it takes a longer period for them to regain their normal level of engagement.

AON Hewitt maintains that regardless of the type of change, the degree to which employees can identify with their entity, see a clear future for themselves, and strive toward the entity's mutual purposes, is most significantly at risk during change events.

Imagine you are a leader in one of those entities with such a very low engagement level (the chances are good that you are one, according to the statistics). If you can only double the engagement level (from such a low base) in your entity you will significantly increase the productivity of your people, and you would also significantly create more wealth, resources, and more potential for future change. And on top of that, based on the positive momentum you have created, you can double the engagement level again, because the engagement gap is large enough to deliver double engagement improvements several times.

To recover an engagement deficit, it is not only a matter of achieving more efficient use of the human potential people bring to your entity, such as their talent, time, human energy and experiences. More importantly, proper engagement involves inclusion of every person's full potential. It means aligning their purposes, expectations, dreams and objectives with that of your entity. The more you align and create ownership of the purposes of your entity with the expectations and dreams of your people, the more engagement you will achieve.

When you broaden inclusion of people beyond the execution of regular daily activities, into the entity's purpose and plans for change, you will gain fuller engagement.

Execution Deficit

Entities exists to execute something or to perform certain activities to achieve the mutual goals and purposes of the leaders and people who created the entity in the first instance.

FranklinCovey[13], the creators of the Execution Quotient (xQ) paints a sobering picture about leaders' ability to execute and direct the necessary leadership tasks to achieve entities' goals and objectives—what I would call an 'Execution Deficit'.

The execution deficit is the difference between our agreed objectives and what we achieved. The xQ results shows a persistent deficit, globally.

In *"The 8th Habit"*, Stephen Covey describes the xQ measure. The xQ measures behaviours that are focused on execution and the achievement of results. The measure assesses 31 different behaviours that show the ability of an entity and its leaders to achieve its goals and objectives. Like an IQ test that reveals gaps in intelligence, an xQ test measures the 'execution deficits' within an entity.

Using the Covey xQ measure, Harris Interactive[14] have surveyed around 2.5 million people on the effectiveness of execution within their entities. The results of the xQ studies are sobering, indicating that there is an alarming and persistent execution deficit worldwide, as the xQ execution measures indicate.

The following five measures give a glimpse into the magnitude of the execution deficit:

- Only 37% of employees said they have a clear understanding of what their entity is trying to achieve and why they want to achieve that
- Only 1 in 5 people said they have a clear 'line-of-sight' between their tasks and their team's and entity's goals
- Only 15% felt that their entity fully enables them to execute key goals
- Only 17% felt their entity fosters open communication that is respectful of differing opinions and that results in new and better ideas
- Only 10% felt that their entity holds people accountable for results

Summary

The context of the new era of change may appear to be sobering and a bit daunting. Yet, the new era poses enormous opportunities too. No doubt, we are living in a VUCA world with an extreme future ahead. When leaders understand that we need to change our outdated ways of thinking and behaving, and adapt to the challenges and opportunities posed by the new context, we can collectively make an incredible success of the extreme future.

This new age of change has begun with enormous and often paradoxical opportunities and challenges, such as:

- A Mega S-curve with a very steep and volatile ascent
- Persistently low success rates for change initiatives
- Trust in leadership that is in a disappointing deficit
- Peoples' levels of engagement are getting worse
- Execution deficits in entities that seem to remain static

Yet, as I have said before—I have no intention of being a gloomy doomsayer. To the contrary, we can seize this new era of change and mold it to our advantage. We can lead in all the above challenges to the benefit of mankind.

Before we move on to explore the new Framework for Leadership in the age of change, I will first clarify the true purpose of leadership in the next chapter—what leadership is—and what it is supposed to achieve.

*

Notes

1. The concept called 'VUCA', emerged in the late 1990's from the military fraternity. They have noticed that more and more initiatives fall victim to several uncertainties posed by drivers and variables of change. The variables of change seem to become increasingly Volatile, Uncertain, Complex and Ambiguous. This phenomenon of change gave birth to a now widely used acronym called VUCA.

2. Obolensky, N. 2014, *Complex Adaptive Leadership, Embracing Paradox, and Uncertainty,* 2nd ed., Gower, Surrey, England

3. Gantz, J., & Reinsel, D. 2012, *The Digital Universe 2020, Big Data, Bigger Digital Shadows, and Biggest Growth in the Far East,* https://www.emc.com/leadership/digital-universe/index.htm

4. James Canton, J. 2006, *Extreme Future — The top ten trends that will reshape the world,* Penguin, New York. James Canton runs a think tank in San Francisco called the Institute for Global Futures.

5. Beddington, J. *The 2030 Perfect Storm Scenario,* Population Institute, England.

6. Dobb, R., Manyika, J. & Woetzel, J. 2015, *No Ordinary Disruption,* PublicAffairs, New York

7. Hughes, M. 2011, 'Do 70 percent of all organisational change initiatives really fail?', *Journal of Change management,* vol. 11, no. 4, pp. 451-464.

8. Making Change Work, 2013, *Report by IBM.*

9. Smith, M. 2002, 'Success rates for different types of organisational change', *Performance management,* vol. 41, no.1, pp. 26 – 33.

10. See http://calleam.com.

11. Edelman Trust Barometer (2013) trust results. See http://www.edelman.com

12. Managing Engagement During Times of Change, 2013, *White paper by AON Hewitt.* The State of the Global Workplace, 2013, *Report by Gallup Inc.*(measured employee engagement on a global scale during the period 2009 to 2013). Also see 'Employee Engagement Trends Report', 2011, *Report by PeopleMetrics*, Philadelphia PA.

13. Covey, S. R. 2005, *The 8th Habit,* Free Press, New York.

14. See Covey, S. R. 2005, *The 8th Habit,* Free Press, New York.

2. **What is Leadership?**

DEFINING LEADERSHIP FOR THE AGE OF CHANGE

Einstein once famously said:

"Insanity is doing the same thing repeatedly and expecting different results"

We will continue to lead in the same old ways unless we decide to change how we lead. Leading in the same old ways will not help us achieve our purposes in the new era of change.

You have the power to decide why, when and how to change your leadership behaviours so you can lead effectively in the age of change.

Understanding the fundamental 'design purposes' of the task of leadership will challenge many myths and misconceptions that exist about leadership. This chapter will clarify some of these misconceptions and presents a descriptive definition of leadership. It explains the fundamental elements of the role and task of leadership.

Leadership is a trust relationship among leaders and followers who execute actions and perform change initiatives aimed at achieving mutual purposes.

Defining Leadership

When you read books about leadership you may conclude that leadership is a complex and multifaceted concept. A huge number of definitions exist for the concept of 'leadership'. Numerous and frequently conflicting definitions help to create an aura of mystique, confusion and complexity of what leadership is. It enhances a longstanding mantra that only a few of us are gifted enough to lead, and that people are to be blessed with certain specific traits to be leaders. Adding to the confusion is the fact that many definitions for leadership are often created and based on our personal experience in our specific contexts.

This confused state of defining leadership makes leadership probably one of the most debated and least understood concepts in the human sciences. It is fertile ground for academics and consultants to continually develop and sell new concepts. When you research the meaning or definition of leadership you will find that there are almost as many definitions for leadership as there are people who have attempted to define leadership. Everyone has an opinion and everyone has his own definition of what leadership is.

Because we lack a universal definition of leadership, leadership appears to mean different things to different people. The meaning of leadership might depend on the kind of entity you are in—for example, a team, an entrepreneurial business, global enterprise, political party, school or sports organisation—and on your individual perspective, or some aspects of leadership that is of interest to you individually or to your group. For example, many people form their concept of leadership from heroic characters (either real or fictitious) that are celebrated in the media. Often, their definitions of leadership are formed by people who they have known, trusted or respected, such as former teachers, clergy members, family members or favourite bosses. Others assign the concept of leadership to people who have achieved extraordinary results or something of importance in their contexts, for example a specific political outcome, a remarkable philanthropic act, superior financial results in a business entity, or leading a sports team to significant athletic achievements.

This ongoing mystique and confusion is not helpful, and it is part of the reason why many leaders grapple with what they are supposed to do—what their design purpose is as leaders.

I have concluded that there are two main groups of leadership definitions. The two groups are what I call Qualitative and Descriptive definitions.

Qualitative definitions

Qualitative definitions are describing what 'good' or what preferable leadership is, or should be. They qualify what we want leadership to be, or what leadership is supposed to deliver in specific contexts. Qualitative definitions are therefore often subjective, individualised, emotional, heroic, and highly sensitive to the context. Most leadership definitions are of this kind.

The list below is a small sample of typical qualitative definitions. In brackets are the contemporary leadership theories most relevant to each definition[1].

- A leader must exhibit a variety of 'essential' character qualities, traits or attributes; that is, qualities that usually define the 'best' or most 'desirable' kind of leader or leadership. *(Trait and personality theories made such definitions popular, predominantly in the early 20th century)*
- A leader gives direction to team activities to reach predefined goals. *(Goal directed leadership theory)*
- Leadership is a persuasion and negotiation process between willing and often unwilling parties to achieve the desired outcome of the leader or the entity. *(Transactional leadership theory)*

- Leadership is the creation of a vision and strategy, followed by influencing the entity towards the achievement of their vision and strategy. *(Visionary leadership theory)*
- Leadership is an exercise of personal charisma to achieve the leaders' vision or goals. *(Charismatic leadership theory)*
- Leadership is the performance of transformational changes to move an entity from an undesirable current state to a perceived better future state. *(Transformational leadership theory)*

Many qualitative definitions for leadership are useful and have contributed to our understanding of the concept. Yet none of the qualitative definitions are addressing the *fundamental* aspects of what leadership entails. Qualitative definitions are thus underspecified, context and time specific.

So how can we determine what leadership is? Which one of the above definitions is a complete definition of what leadership is? The confusion creates a real dilemma to lead effectively in the 21st century age of change. We need a definition that summarises what leadership is, what it comprises, and what its reason for existence is. Such a definition must be applicable in any context or at least applicable in as many contexts as possible; and, the definition should not age so quickly that it becomes useless after a short period.

Descriptive definitions

A descriptive definition of leadership explains the substantive fundamentals of what leadership is. It describes its substance, or character, and gives the actual meaning of what leadership is. Descriptive definitions are neutral, fundamental and timeless. Descriptive definitions will stand the test of time until the fundamental reason for the existence of leadership changes.

To move forward in our understanding of leadership and to help leaders perform the role and task of leadership—that is, to lead—we must first understand the core definition of the word 'lead'.

Lead

The verb 'lead' is the foundation of the word 'leadership'.

To lead is to take, or to move something or someone, over a distance, through a period, from a situation to another situation, or from a current position to another position, a new destination, a new future, or a new dispensation, with a specific purpose in mind. In the process of being led, change or transition always occurs, for example, a change of position, location, situation, circumstance, prospects, etc. occurs.

The person leading and the person being led have a mutual understanding and agreement about the purpose for the change or transition, or the new destination that is pursued. For a mutual purpose to exist it implies that a trusting relationship exist between the person who leads and those who are being led. If a mutual purpose does not exist, the process of transition will happen under duress, force, or submission—which is the antithesis of being lead.

Leadership

Linguistically the same fundamental concepts inherent to the verb 'lead' must apply to the concept of 'leadership'. The excellent work on the definition of leadership by the late professor Joseph Rost[2] supports this point.

Like me, Joseph Rost who wrote *"Leadership for the Twenty-first Century"*, had a similar quest to develop an understanding of the prevailing 20th century school of leadership, and to identify a descriptive definition for post-industrial leadership in the 21st century. Rost studied over 300 books on the definition of leadership, some of them written as early as the 1900s. He concluded that all the established definitions reflected the 20th century's industrial paradigm. Rost called the current leadership definitions a 20th century paradigm of leadership—he called it "Leadership as good management".

Rost concluded that the prevailing leadership theories and definitions are individualistic because they focus mainly on the leader, are dominated by goal achievement, are self-interested in outlook, mainly male-oriented, utilitarian and materialistic in ethical perspective, have a mindset of linear thinking, quantitative, and scientific in language and leadership practice.

He also concluded that the same basic paradigm of leadership is apparent in many other disciplines such as anthropology, history, political science, psychology, sociology, theology, business, education, health, military, and public administration.

In his quest to develop a neutral descriptive definition for post-industrial 21st century leadership, Rost[3] created a concise and easily understandable definition for leadership, as follows:

"Leadership is an influence relationship among leaders and their followers who intend real changes, that reflect their mutual purposes"

When one compares Rost's leadership definition with the definition of the verb 'lead', you will see the direct relationships between the parts in the verb 'lead' and the fundamental concepts in Rost's definition. The definition captures the 'design purpose' of leadership—what leadership is, and *not* the kind of leadership that is desired, *nor* what good or convenient leadership could be at any point in time, or in any specific context. It is a definition that stands the test of time in many contexts.

Rost carefully selected the words in his definition to convey specific meanings that contain certain assumptions, which are necessary to lead in the post-industrial 21st century.

Below is an expansion of the elements of Rost's definition:

The leadership relationships are based on influence.

- The influence behaviours are non-coercive and non-directive trusting relationships.
- The influence relationships are multidirectional (between the leader and followers and between the followers and the leader).

Followers include collaborators, constituents, colleagues, and stakeholders

- The followers are active in the mutual relationship.
- There is more than one follower, and there is often more than one leader in the relationship.
- The relationship is inherently unequal because influence patterns are unequal.

Leaders and followers are aiming at real change initiatives.

- It means that the leaders and followers in the relationship purposefully want to realise definite change initiatives.
- 'Real changes' means that the change initiatives are substantive and transforming.
- They intend change initiatives in the present and the outcomes of the change initiatives occur in the future.
- Leaders and followers intend several change initiatives at once.

The leaders and followers execute actions towards achieving their mutual purpose.

- Mutual purposes are executed and achieved through non-coercive relationships between the leader and followers.
- Leaders and followers work towards mutual purposes, not

objectives. Objectives are subordinate to mutual purposes—they support and reflect mutual purposes.

- Change initiatives are aligned with mutual purposes.

The importance of Mutual Purpose

Mutual purpose is the enduring reason for your entity's existence. It is the reason for being, and it must be able to withstand most challenges and changes, whether they are changes to its leadership, the life cycles of its offerings, or ways we execute activities. Yet the mutual purpose cannot be so rigid that it puts the entity's long-term existence in jeopardy.

Mutual purpose focuses the leader's and the entity's efforts, attention and performance towards extraordinary achievement.

Because leadership is about building relationships between leaders and their followers, it follows that the purpose of what they collectively want to achieve must be defined collaboratively. Without inclusion, the relationship between leader and followers will become strained and the achievement of the purpose and underlying goals will be hit-or-miss.

Unlike an overt exercise of power, leadership is inclusive of followers' purposes. Yet leadership is not about achieving consensus at all cost—to the contrary. Inclusive leadership does not favour consensus, but favours engaged decision-making. Inclusive leadership is about constructively challenging and shaping mutual purposes that will endure.

Identifying the mutual purpose for your entity is not about identifying a set of objectives—it is much more fundamental than that. Objectives are essential—yet, they are secondary to the mutual purpose. Goals and objectives must support and align with the purpose, but they are transitory. Mutual purpose is long lasting. Leaders must communicate clear connections and alignment between the mutual purposes and for example, financial or service delivery objectives.

Mutual purposes must be regularly challenged, debated and reviewed to ensure the entity remains agile and resilient within its context. This is particularly necessary in the VUCA world we live in today. In the age of change, an entity's purpose can lose its relevance and confusion will set in. It is your leadership task to regularly communicate and clarify your entity's mutual purpose. Mutual purpose sets the true north on the entity's compass. You must ensure it stays on its course towards achieving its purpose.

Leadership definition for the Age of Change

In the new context of the age of change, I am of the firm opinion that *we need more than an influence relationship* among leaders and followers, as Rost has suggested—*we need a trust relationship.* In Chapter 4, which covers the Relationship Dimension, you will read why and how trust forms the core of leadership relationships. Influence is only one of several essential behaviours that is built on a foundation of a trust relationship between leaders and followers.

Secondly, leaders and followers *must execute worthwhile activities,* as well as future directed change initiatives that reflect their mutual purposes. Leadership without execution won't amount to anything.

Considering that we need the essence of a trust relationship and we must also lead the execution of activities, I have expanded Rost's definition and created one that reflects the essence of the role and task (the design purpose) of a leader in the age of change.

Leadership is a trust relationship among leaders and followers who execute actions and perform change initiatives aimed at achieving mutual purposes.

Management versus Leadership

What is the difference between leaders and managers?

We often come across this continuing debate about the differences between leadership and management. The debate occurs particularly in academic and business texts in the context of business organisations. The debate further obscures the real definition of what leadership is and it is not helpful in this respect.

In my view, the use of simplistic stereotypes to label people as either managers or leaders does little to advance our understanding of leadership. Although leading and managing are separate processes, even this distinction obscures more than it uncovers because the two processes are not mutually exclusive. There is no value in an argument that implies that one can't be both a manager and leader at the same time. It is more beneficial to view leadership and management as different, distinct, and frequently overlapping processes, and not to view leaders and managers as different kinds of people.

I have often found in popular literature and media that leaders are referred to as superior and managers as inferior roles. Such a mindset is negative and harmful. The reality in this age of change is that managers and leaders will have to play both types of roles, from time to time, in his or her specific context. Some of the roles may be 'traditional' managerial roles, while some roles may be 'traditional' leadership roles. Moreover, roles that could be regarded as managerial roles in one context are often regarded as leadership roles in another context. Savvy managers and leaders will know when to switch between roles.

The core argument of the outmoded debate seems to be that managers are deemed to be oriented toward achieving and maintaining consistent predetermined outcomes, while leaders are supposedly more oriented toward visionary change initiatives, innovation and the creative transformation of the entity they lead. Managers supposedly motivate people to continually execute their goals productively, whereas leaders supposedly motivate people about changes and new directions towards new beneficial futures. The designations of 'leader' and 'manager' in contemporary organisations confuse the debate even more. I have experienced on many occasions that the actual roles and role titles often have little in common. I have observed many so-called managers who were performing excellent leader roles as demonstrated by the value they added and the positive changes they led in their entities. Then, on the flip side I have seen many supposed leaders that were hamstrung by their entities through the lack of appropriate accountability and empowerment. This stops them from making significant contributions or achieving real positive change. Hence, having a position or title of 'leader' in such situations is rather ridiculous.

In my view leadership and management are different concepts, yet they are complementary and overlapping. In the 21st century, both leadership and management roles will require behaviours that are substantially more oriented towards creating change and shaping new directions for the future.

It does not matter in which camp you are—the leadership camp or the management camp—the principles in this book will benefit both managers and leaders. Although this book is about leadership, its content is equally beneficial and applicable to managerial and leadership roles in a wide range of contexts.

Summary

The descriptive definition of leadership highlights the significance of building, maintaining and continually enhancing the exchange of people-oriented relationship behaviours between leaders and followers. Trusting relationships that work both ways are a prerequisite for the creation of real change initiatives that are purposeful. Moreover, when intended changes are shared between leaders and their followers, it sets the scene for change initiatives to be executed effectively.

Leaders must lead real changes, whether to recover a situation from a negative state to its previous 'normal' state, or to improve a situation from its current state to a new positive state. Clearly leaders are never engaged by followers or constituents to maintain an unaltered course. We don't need leaders to do that. A leader is almost always required to lead the entity from its current state to another future state. Merely holding an entity in equilibrium, meaning no changes are required, does not require any leadership.

The realisation of a new and better condition through collaborative execution of real changes to achieve the mutual purposes of an entity, determines if a leader and his entity will be perceived as successful.

My substantive definition of what leadership is:

Leadership is a trust relationship among leaders and followers who execute actions and perform change initiatives aimed at achieving mutual purposes.

The definition has four fundamental components:

- **Leadership is directed by the *Purpose***

It is directed by the mutual purposes of the entity—the leader leads and directs the entity towards the achievement of inclusive mutual purposes (not the unilateral exclusive purposes of the leader, or any other individual or group, in or outside the entity).

- **Leadership is firm on *Relationships***

Leadership is built on a solid foundation of healthy and trusting relationships between the leader and his followers.

- **Leadership leads and causes *Change***

Leaders lead change initiatives, aligned to the mutual purpose, to secure growth and survival of the entity.

- **Leadership guides *Execution***

Leaders and their followers achieve the mutual purposes of the entity through leading effective and efficient execution of a multitude of actions and activities.

When any of the above components lack, leadership will be unsuccessful. The rest of this book will show you how to lead in ways that creates trust, change and prosperity in many contexts.

Notes

1. Bass, B. M. 1990, *Bass & Stogdill's Handbook of Leadership. Theory, Research, and Managerial Applications.* 3rd Ed. The Free Press, New York. See also Goethals, G. R., Sorenson, G. J. & Burns, James M. 2004, *Encyclopedia of Leadership*, Sage Publication, London.

2. Rost, J. 1991, Leadership for the Twenty-first Century, Preager, New York. See also Rost, J. 1993, 'Leadership Development in the new Millennium', The Journal of Leadership Studies, vol. 1, no. 1. pp. 91-110. See also Volckman, R. 2005, 'A Fresh Perspective: 21st Century Leadership – an interview with Joseph Rost', Integral Leadership Review.

3. Rost, J. 1991, Leadership for the Twenty-first Century, Preager, New York.

3. A New Leadership Framework for the 21st Century

HOW TO LEAD IN THE AGE OF CHANGE

Over the ages successful leaders have always changed their behaviours to align with prevailing contexts, mindsets and challenges.

The Leadership Eras since the mid 1900s, as shown in Table 3.1 offer a historical portrait of how leaders have adjusted their behaviours over the last fifty to sixty years. I divided the period into four leadership eras. The major inflexion on the Mega-S-Curve as discussed in Chapter 1, has begun during this time frame.

In the 1960s entities experienced contextual circumstances that required them to predominantly make incremental changes to stay in front of their game—small changes were necessary. When globalisation started to intensify during the 70s and 80s, many entities had to undertake major transformations to survive and grow. During this era, transformational and visionary leadership became very popular. From the 80s until the turn of the century, the 4th industrial revolution came into full swing with the introduction of the Internet and the digital revolution.

Period	1960 - 1970	1970 - 1980	1980 - 2000	2000 and beyond
Era	Incremental Change	Managed Transformation	Managed Complexity	Age of Change
Context	Focus on efficient production systems Stable environments Planned incremental change Linear extrapolation Goal setting Internal focus	Focus on competition External focus Globalisation Reengineering Restructuring Downsizing Redesign	Focus on competition 4th industrial revolution begins late 80s Digital revolution begins in 90s Dynamic interactive systems Inflection on S-curve towards rampant change	Focus on customer and innovation VUCA world commences Paradoxical forces Individual-social connectivity Digital super-connectivity Fleeting, instant and transient characteristics of knowledge and relationships
Mindset	Exclusive purpose Planning Goal setting Scientific Analytical	Exclusive purpose Reactive Continuous improvement Change management Transformation Quality	Change management Change processes Learning organisation Flat structures Networking	Inclusive mutual purposes Disciplined and inclusive change leadership Multiple mental models Simultaneous agility and resiliency
Leadership Framework	Hierarchical - top down Exclusive Directive Participative	Visionary Transformational Hierarchical – top down	Flexible leadership Multiple models dealing with complexity	Inclusive change-oriented leadership at center stage

Around the turn of the century, we have entered the age of change. The age of change is characterised by a VUCA world. The focus is on customers, innovation, digitisation, social connectivity and speed of adaptation. We are facing the challenging contextual circumstances I have described in Chapter 1.

In the age of change we require inclusive leadership mindsets—leaders with the following attributes:

- Leaders that lead change as one of their central leadership tasks in a disciplined way
- Leaders who use multiple mental models, and who are comfortable with paradox
- Leaders who will move from the top of the pyramid to a central position, onto the centre stage— leading from within—instead of from up there
- Leaders, who will challenge and shape the entity's purpose inclusively

Nick Obolensky in his book, *Complex Adaptive Leadership*[1], concludes that the pace of change in the last few decades has surpassed the leadership assumptions we hold on to. He states that we are now living in contexts that are changing faster than we can change our assumptions about leadership. I fully agree with this view.

We are already within the age of change, yet many leaders are still leading with mindsets and frameworks from previous eras. We can't continue to behave in the same old ways and expect different outcomes. The leadership deficits in change, trust, engagement and execution would continue and worsen. We should align our behaviours with the prevailing contexts, mindsets and challenges—otherwise we would not lead successfully.

The Leadership Framework for the Age of Change

This chapter introduces a new Leadership Framework that forms the backbone of this book. It is designed for leaders to lead in the age of change—leadership for the 21st century. The Leadership Framework has six elements and includes three core leadership dimensions. It will help you to establish new leadership behaviours—behaviours that are consistent and aligned to the new contextual challenges. Figure 3.1 illustrates the new Leadership Framework.

The Leadership Framework consists of six essential elements. The elements are:

- **Context:** The continually changing contexts within which you lead.
- **Three core leadership dimensions:** The leadership dimensions are based on three-dimensional leadership theory.
- **Leadership Outcomes:** The measurable outcomes of your leadership behaviours

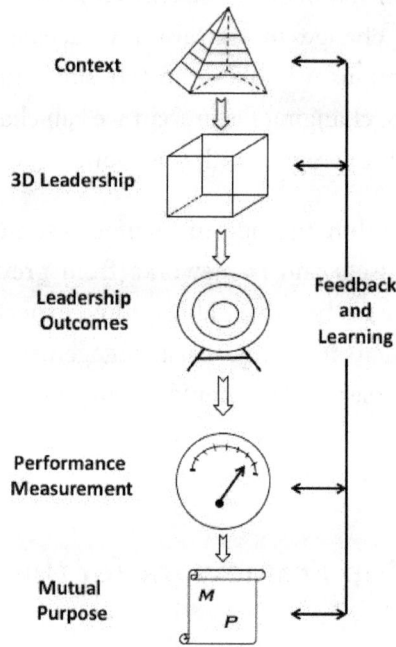

Figure 3.1. The Leadership Framework

- **Performance Measurement:** Measurement of your leadership performance based on your behaviours.
- **Feedback and learning:** Continuous feedback and feed-forward learning cycles that build and reinforce your leadership.
- **Mutual purpose:** The mutual purpose of your entity guides and directs your leadership behaviours.

All the elements in the Leadership Framework are aimed at achieving the entity's mutual purposes.

The Leadership Framework:

- Addresses the contextual environment and issues posed by the VUCA world, as discussed in Chapter 1.

- Is flexible to accommodate changing contexts—the substance of the age of change.
- Is applicable in many contexts, entities and timeframes—it is generically applicable.
- Satisfies the descriptive definition of what leadership is, as discussed in Chapter 2.
- Is grounded in sound leadership and organisation behaviour theories and principles.
- Incorporates practical leadership experience of what works and what does not work in the age of change.
- It can be readily applied by leaders—both novices and experts—so that one can change, establish and measure any new leadership behaviours.

Leadership is about your behaviour. Fulfilling your leadership role, as defined in the descriptive definition of leadership, is through your behaviours. What you do, speaks louder than what you say or think. You display your leadership through your actions, inactions, decisions, verbal and nonverbal communications, mannerisms, habits, presence and conduct, inside and outside your entity. You have the choice to change and show constructive behaviours and eliminate destructive behaviours from your range of typical behaviours. Your behaviour choices will reflect your character, determine your success as a leader, and ultimately the success of your entity. I encourage you to change and establish new leadership behaviours, and to be willing and courageous enough to repeat them until they are consistently positive habits. Your aim is to develop positive behaviours that are constant, until they are part of who you are. Uniformity of behaviour solidifies your character, your relationships and your success as a leader.

The elements of the Leadership Framework

Context

You practice your leadership within specific contexts. The Leadership Framework acknowledges and begins with your assessment of the contexts within which you lead. Your leadership behaviours are influenced by and occur within continually changing contexts. Contexts set the scene for appropriate leadership behaviour choices. Contexts determine the reasons why we behave in certain ways. Your leadership contexts may change numerous times every day, for example, if you are a leader of a global multinational enterprise. Or, it may change once or twice a month, if you are a leader of a small entity. Contexts are therefore role specific.

Contexts describe the background against which you assess leadership issues, i.e. changes, challenges, decisions or conflicts, so that you can make appropriate behaviour choices to address them. Your behaviour choices, and how you apply them within your contexts, determine your leadership outcomes and your success.

The figure that looks like a prism Leadership Framework illustrates the way we would observe different issues in different contexts. Like a real prism, contexts have different faces, levels and vantage points, implying that contexts may be observed differently, depending on the face, the level and the vantage point you choose to observe a specific issue from. When you apply the Leadership Framework and its three leadership dimensions, you will be able to observe changing contexts from different viewpoints on different levels—ensuring that you make better behavioural choices.

The contexts are influenced by continuous changes in your environment and exchanges with the environment—externally and internally. Consequently, your behaviour choices are influenced by the contextual changes that occur in your environment. You and your entity interact with the outside world, and internally with many sub-systems inside your entity. Such interactions and exchanges serve as inputs that influence your perception of the contexts and the leadership issues at hand. Similarly, your choice and application of leadership behaviours will influence your internal and external environments. Consequently, your behaviours may have changing influences on your contexts.

When you perceive and assess leadership issues in their context, the following vantage points are useful:

- Who is involved?
- The level or levels at which the leadership issue occurs
- Complexity of the leadership issue
- Timeframe in which the issue occurs or may occur
- Potential impact or consequences of the issue, if or when it occurs
- Physical location where the issue occurs, i.e. local, regional, or international
- Velocity of progression of the issue
- The situation within the context. (Note that a similar situation, but in a different context, may require different leadership behaviours.)

Three-dimensional Leadership — Core of the Leadership Framework

The core of the Leadership Framework is Three-dimensional leadership theory. The cube in Figure 3.2 named '*3D Leadership*' represents the three dimensions of leadership behaviour. It includes the full range of relationship, execution, and change-oriented behaviours leaders can apply to fulfil their roles.

Your unique leadership behaviours are a combination of your individual traits, qualities, and abilities. All leadership behaviours can be grouped into three major dimensions:

- Relationships
- Execution
- Change

The three dimensions are depicted in Figure 3.2 below.

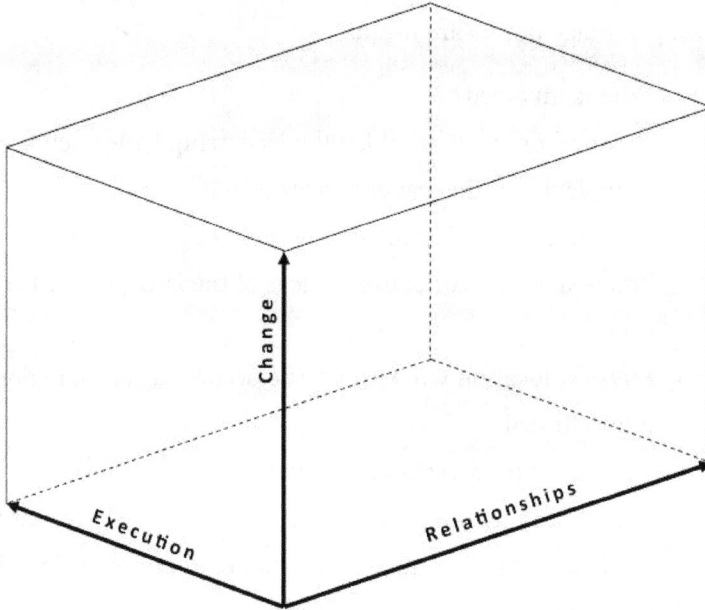

Figure 3.2. The three dimensions of leadership behaviour

Leadership outcomes

Outcomes are the consequences of how you play your leadership role—your leadership behaviours and actions, both positive and negative. The figure that looks like a target illustrates the outcomes you would want to achieve. Your leadership behaviour choices will determine whether you will hit or miss the target, that is, the outcomes you want to achieve as a leader as well as what your entity achieves due to your leadership actions and behaviours. Your desired outcomes must be in alignment with the mutual purposes of your entity. Your behaviour choices will determine how you conduct your relationships, how you lead change, the way you lead execution through your entity, and to what extent your entity achieves its mutual purposes.

Performance measurement

Outcomes of your behaviours determine your leadership performance. The figure that looks like a gauge represents the performance measures and metrics you can design and implement to measure both your own leadership performance and your entity's performance that can be directly linked to your chosen leadership behaviours. Performance measures at the entity level serve only as proxies of your leadership behaviours. Preferably, you should design and use leadership performance measures that are directly related to your behaviour choices. This is a good way to determine the effectiveness and desirability of your behaviour choices, and how successfully you have implemented the Leadership Framework in your role.

Mutual Purpose

Your leadership aim is to work inclusively with your entity to develop and achieve mutual purposes. Mutual purposes are moulded through non-coercive trust relationships between you and your followers. When you follow the principles of Leadership Framework you can form trusting relationships, and lead execution and change initiatives that are focused on achieving the mutual purposes of your entity.

Feedback & Learning

The continuous feedback, feed-forward and learning loop shown in Figure 3.1 illustrates that there are continuous information exchanges between all the elements in the Leadership Framework. It is essential that you learn from, improve, and correct your leadership behaviours, especially when the outcomes and performance you achieve are not in line with preferred relationship, execution and change-oriented behaviours. Likewise, when outcomes and performance deviate from the mutual purpose of your entity, you need to learn from that, realign your leadership behaviours, and redirect your entity towards its mutual purpose.

Theoretical background

The Leadership Framework has been built and conceptualised on several key behavioural theories, amongst others:

- Three-dimensional leadership behaviour forms the core of the Leadership Framework
- Human behaviour models
- Open systems theory
- Learning organisation—especially triple loop learning
- Self-learning
- Action Learning
- Behavioural change
- Integrated leadership

Three-dimensional leadership theory—A summary

Two Scandinavian leadership theorists, Ekvall and Arvonen[2] were the first to identify three independent leadership behaviour dimensions. They named the three dimensions: Change-, Production-, and Employee-orientated leadership behaviours.

The classic leadership behaviour theorists[3] at the time did not identify the third change-oriented dimension in their research work. In leadership theory, until the early 1990s there were only two leadership behaviour dimensions: Task- or production-behaviour and people- or relationship-orientated behaviour. This two-dimensional theory and the distinction between the two dimensions of task and relationship behaviours are still common in leadership literature. Two-dimensional leadership behaviour theory has given birth to an abundance of subsequent leadership theories—most of which are primarily focused on the Relationship Dimension of leadership behaviour.

The lack of the change-orientated dimension in the early theories was primarily because the nature of demands on leaders in the period before the 1970s were well structured, with minimal changes, in predictable industrial-era contexts.

After the 1970s contexts and demands on leaders first started to change incrementally, and then intensified towards the end of the 20th century. Leaders' behaviours had to adjust accordingly. Leadership theories such as Transformational, Charismatic, and Visionary theories have come into vogue to fill the leadership voids in previous eras. We are now well into the 21st century. As I have emphasised in Chapter 1, we need an integrated inclusive change-oriented leadership mindset to lead successfully in the age of change.

After the ground-breaking work of Ekvall and Arvonen in Scandinavia, many other leadership theorists have continued to work on Three-dimensional leadership theory in many other contexts in the USA, Spain, and Australia[4] I have performed confirmatory research on Three-dimensional leadership theory in a large Southern African entity with multinational subsidiaries.[5] In my research I also tested associations between Three-dimensional leadership theory, leaders' emotional intelligence, leaders' visioning ability and citizenship behaviours (Citizenship behaviours are nowadays more commonly referred to as engagement behaviour).[6]

Following the work of Ekvall and Arvonen, Yukl, Gordon and Taber[7], of the State University of New York, did a meta-categorisation of research work done on leadership behaviour over five decades since the 1950s. They integrated all the leadership behaviour theories and research results into a taxonomy of leadership behaviours. Their key finding is that all the theories and results fit into three leadership dimensions—the same three dimensions identified earlier by Ekvall and Arvonen. From this work, Yukl proposed what he called "Flexible Leadership theory", which originated from the Three-dimensional leadership theory. Yukl went further to associate the three leadership dimensions in his flexible leadership theory with organisational effectiveness, performance and situational variables.

The Change Dimension

The new third behaviour dimension found by Ekvall and Arvonen, is called 'Change-orientated behaviour'. The Change Dimension reflects leaders' behaviours that create visions, drive and support new ideas. Leaders with change-oriented behaviours are innovative and prepared to take calculated risks. The Change Dimension includes leadership behaviours that prefer an orientation towards common purposes and new futures for entities. Leaders who have an orientation towards change, are flexible and welcome variations. They create climates that are dynamic, energetic, humorous, and filled with ideas and debate. They stimulate climates in which people's commitment, and engagement are strong. Entities that are change-oriented are agile and temporary changes are often made when and where necessary. Entities with such climates welcome constructive conflict.

The Relationship Dimension

The first leadership behaviour dimension found by Ekvall and Arvonen, was called "Employee-orientation". This dimension is like the relationship-oriented dimension identified by the traditional leadership theorists in the period between the 1950s and 1960s. Then the dimension was also known as: "Concern for people, Employee-centred, and Consideration for people".[8]

For my Leadership Framework, I decided to call the Employee-oriented dimension—the 'Relationship Dimension'. This is because our people-oriented behaviours reach far beyond our direct relationships to cover the important relationships, such as for example, relationships with customers, constituents, stakeholders and the public.

The Relationship Dimension reflects leaders' behaviours that provide people with a sense of belonging and security. Leaders who use relationship-oriented behaviours behave consistently and considerately; they are caring and they moderate conflicts. They encourage co-operation and engagement. They do not act as being superior. They empower people to accept responsibility and experience real inclusion in decision-making. As a result, the climate they create is open and trustful.

The Execution Dimension

Ekvall and Arvonen's second "Production dimension" resembles the traditional task-oriented behaviour dimension. The dimension was called "Initiating Structure" by the Ohio State and Michigan research group in the 1960s. Blake and Mouton, who are also famous leadership theorists, called it "Concern for Production" in their renowned work "*The Managerial Grid*"[9] The dimension is also known as "Task-oriented leadership".

For my Leadership Framework, I decided to call the task-oriented dimension the 'Execution Dimension'. Many leaders are not involved in a 'production' environment. However, all leaders must lead and direct the execution of tasks and objectives to achieve their entity's mutual purpose.

Behaviours in the Execution Dimension are aimed at imposing order, generating consistent methods, structuring tasks and establishing efficient processes. Execution behaviours are oriented towards consistency of actions and conformity to expectations. Leaders who express execution behaviours pursue clear accountabilities and responsibilities. They equip everyone to be able to deliver on the entity's mutual purposes. Execution behaviours include sharing of information about the entity's decisions, performance and results to enhance learning and advance efficient execution.

———————

I provide detailed descriptions, principles and applications of the elements in the Leadership Framework and the three corresponding dimensions in the following chapters:

- Chapter 4 covers the Relationship Dimension.
- Chapters 5 to 12 cover the Change Dimension.
- Chapter 13 covers the Execution Dimension.

Notes

1. Obolensky, N. 2014, Complex Adaptive Leadership, Embracing Paradox, and Uncertainty, 2nd ed., Gower, Surrey, England

2. Arvonen, J. 1995, Leadership Behaviour and Coworker Health – A study in Process Industry, Department of Psychology, Stockholm University, Sweden. See also Ekvall, G. 1991, 'Change-centred leaders: empirical evidence of a third dimension of leadership', *Leadership and Organization Development Journal*, vol.12, pp.18-23. See also Ekvall, G. & Arvonen, J. 1991, 'Change-centred leadership: an extension of the two-dimensional model'. *Scandinavian Journal of Management*, vol. 7, pp.17-26. See also Ekvall, G. & Arvonen, J. 1994, 'Leadership profiles, situation and effectiveness'. *Creativity and Innovation Management*, vol.3, no. 3, pp. 139-161

3. Blake, R. & Mouton, J. 1964, *The Managerial Grid: The Key to Leadership Excellence*. Gulf Publishing Co, Houston: See also Fleishman, E.A. 1957, 'A leader behaviour description for industry', In R.M. Stogdill & A. E. Coons (Eds.), *Leader Behaviour: Its Description and Measurement*. Ohio State University, Columbus. See also Fleishman, E. A., Harris, E.F., & Burt, H. E. 1955, *Leadership and Supervision in Industry*. Ohio State University, Columbus.

4. Gil, F., Rico, R., Alcover, C. M. & Barrasa, A. 2005, 'Change-oriented leadership, satisfaction and performance in work groups, *Journal of Managerial Psychology*, vol. 20, no. 3, pp. 312 – 328. See also Loughman, A., Bowman, K. & Kalia, C. *Leadership Styles amongst the Emergency Services*, UWA School of Medicine and Dentistry, Perth, Australia. See also Barassa, A. 2006, *Integrating Leadership behaviour and climate perceptions in teamwork*, PhD thesis, Universidad Complutense, Madrid, Spain. See also Norris, E. A. 2005, *An investigation of the leadership styles and change styles in a high quality manufacturing organisation*, PhD thesis, University of Phoenix, Arizona.

5. We performed confirmatory research on the Three-dimensional leadership theory in a large global entity with its headquarters in South Africa. See Lourens, J.F. 2001, *Change Centered Leadership and Various Correlates*, PhD thesis, University of Pretoria, South Africa. See Lourens, J.F. & Boshoff, A.B. 2001, 'The Change Cantered leadership behaviour dimension in the South African context'. *Proceedings of the 8th International Conference on Advances in*

Management, vol. 8, pp. 74.   See Lourens, J.F., Boshoff, A.B. & Van Wyk, R. 2003, 'Relationships between Emotional Intelligence and the Three-dimensional leadership Behavior Construct', *Proceedings of the 1st International Conference on Contemporary Management*, 1-2 Sep. 2003, The University of Adelaide, Adelaide, Australia, pp. 49-55.   See Lourens, J.F., Boshoff, A.B. & Van Wyk, R. 2002, 'Change Centered Leadership and various Correlates', *Proceedings of the Pan Pacific Conference XIX*, 28 – 31 May 2002, University of Nebraska-Lincoln, Lincoln, pp. 251-253.

6.   Lourens, J.F., Boshoff, A.B. & Van Wyk, R. 2003, 'Relationships between Emotional Intelligence and the Three-dimensional leadership Behavior Construct', *Proceedings of the 1st International Conference on Contemporary Management*, 1-2 Sep. 2003, The University of Adelaide, Adelaide, Australia, pp. 49-55.   See Lourens, J.F. 2001, *Change Centered Leadership and Various Correlates*, PhD thesis, University of Pretoria, South Africa.

7.   Yukl, G. A., Gordon, A. & Taber, T. 2002, 'A Hierarchical Taxonomy of leadership behaviour: Integrating a half century of behaviour research', *Journal of Leadership and Organizational Studies*, vol. 9, no. 1, pp. 15-32. See Yukl, G. 2003, 'Tridimensional leadership theory: A roadmap for flexible, adaptive leaders'. In R. J. Burke & C. Cooper (Eds.), *Leading in turbulent times*, pp. 75-92, Blackwell, London.

8.   Blake, R. & Mouton, J. 1964, *The Managerial Grid: The Key to Leadership Excellence*. Gulf Publishing Co, Houston. See also Fleishman, E.A. 1957, 'A Leader behaviour description for industry', In R.M. Stogdill & A. E. Coons (Eds.), *Leader Behaviour: Its Description and Measurement*. Ohio State University, Columbus. See also Fleishman, E. A., Harris, E.F., & Burt, H. E. 1955, *Leadership and Supervision in Industry*. Ohio State University, Columbus.

9.   Blake, R. & Mouton, J. 1964, *The Managerial Grid: The Key to Leadership Excellence*. Gulf Publishing Co, Houston.

4. **The New Relationship Dimension**

Solid trustworthy relationships with your followers form the
unshakeable foundation for your leadership.

Your trustworthy relationships create forward momentum to execute
countless activities necessary to reach your entity's mutual purpose.
Your relationships form the foundation upon which many change
initiatives are discovered, shaped and implemented.

Leaders can only lead and accomplish their entity's mutual purposes
through their people. You must therefore collaborate with people inside
and outside your entity to achieve the vision and strategies you mutually
develop. Forming and maintaining trustworthy relationships is critical
to the efficiency, performance, long-term growth and survival of your
entity.

Leadership behaviour theory has developed considerably over the past
seven decades. Since the 1950s many leadership theories have been
developed to help leaders stay abreast with changing demands. The
early theories paid a lot of attention to leaders' relationship-oriented
behaviours. The general aim was to enhance our understanding and
practice of appropriate relationship behaviours.

However, as I have highlighted in Chapter 1, many of the leadership deficits we encounter today, are the consequence of clumsy and insincere behaviours—leadership behaviours that are inappropriate to deal with the challenges in the age of change.

The arrival of the age of change compels us to revisit leaders' relationship behaviours and to use appropriate relationship frameworks. The new Relationship Dimension is a framework for better leadership relationships in the age of change.

Figure 4.1 illustrates the new Relationship Dimension. I designed this new integrated model to comprise the essential relationship behaviours leaders will need to lead in the age of change.

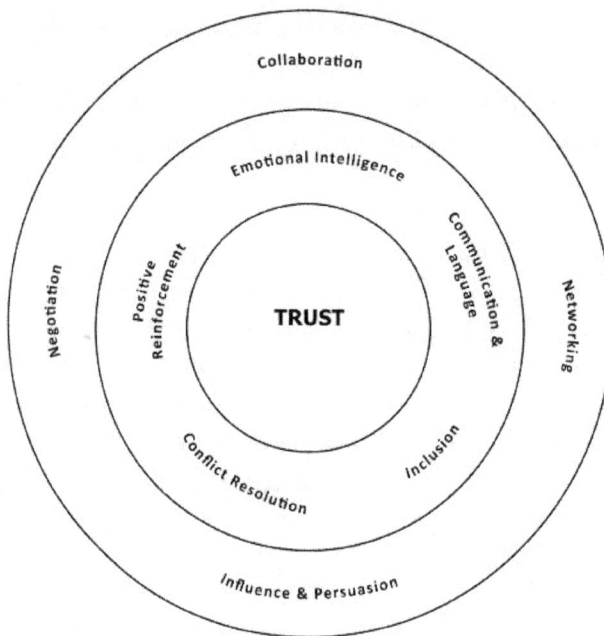

Figure 4.1. The Relationship Dimension

The new Relationship Dimension revolves around trust.

- **Core:** Trust forms the core of all your respected and enduring relationships. When you are insincere, trust can be destroyed in a moment.

- **Principal relationship behaviours:** The internal ring shows the principal relationship behaviours that are vital to effectively lead relationships, inside and outside your entity, irrespective of your level of leadership. These essential relationship behaviours are your emotional intelligence, communication and language, inclusion, conflict resolution and behaviour reinforcement actions.

- **Collaborative behaviours:** The behaviours in the ring on the outside shows the collaborative behaviours you will need to create forward momentum for execution, growth and change. These are essential behaviours to create effective cross-boundary and external engagements, and they are equally important to build internal collaborative relationships. Collaborative behaviours are, for example your networking, influence, persuasion, and negotiation actions, and your judicious use of power and political influence. Leaders use collaborative behaviours to create and enhance relationships between their entities and third parties. Generally, the higher your leadership level, the more competent you would need to be at collaborative behaviours. Successful mastery of collaborative behaviours depends a lot on how skilful you are with the principal leadership behaviours in the middle, and trust building in the core of the Relationship Dimension. Good collaborative relationships begin with building mutual trust.

Trust is the core

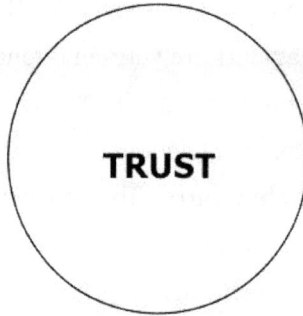

TRUST

Trust is the axis around which the wheel of relationships revolves

Trust is fundamental when leading people and forging relationships. Without trust, viable relationships will not be formed nor continued. You may show off well-groomed relationship-oriented behaviours. However, if you cannot build and maintain trust in your relationships, none of these behaviours will support your leadership role in the long run.

Trust is when people believe that you will do what you said you would, reliably and consistently. Trust is strengthened when you have a reputation of previous trustworthy behaviours, such as when you demonstrate a character of integrity and sincerity, and when you display the necessary capabilities, means and resources to support your promises and commitments.

Trust provides permanent competitive advantage ... at zero cost!

Leaders may not always be able to create value because of forces beyond their control, but they can undoubtedly destroy value through low trust. Fred Kiel who wrote, *"Return on Character"[1]* found there is an obvious and consistent relationship between trustworthy character-driven leaders and better business results. Leaders with stronger morals and principles deliver a higher Return-on-Character (ROC). Leaders who perform high on Kiel's ROC character-assessment scale achieve nearly five times the Return-on-Assets (ROA) for their entities, compared to leaders who score low on ROC.

High trust organisations provide increased value, accelerated growth, enhanced innovation, improved collaboration, have stronger partnerships, perform better at execution, and show higher loyalty. Shochley-Zalabak, *et al[2]* in their study *"Building the high trust organisation"*, showed that high-trust organisations outperformed low-trust organisations by 286 percent in financial returns.

Clearly the price to pay for untrustworthy behaviour is huge, especially when it is the leader's behaviour. The price we pay for a loss of trust translates into lost customers, lost loyalty, reduced engagement, loss of talent, reduced performance, increasing rules, more bureaucracy, and often legal action to mop up the mess. Yet the cost of trustworthy leadership is zero. In fact, trustworthy behaviour is a permanent competitive advantage to you and your entity—it adds considerable value.

Leadership principles for creating and maintaining trust

Say what you will do. Do what you said. Period.
Speak the truth consistently!

Authenticity

Act like the real 'you'. When you are honestly attempting to change

---

your behaviours, keep on trying until you succeed with new habits. Ask for help if necessary. Do not imitate other leaders. Eventually your true character will prevail, and insincere behaviours will discredit the imitated image you were trying to build.

Honesty

Honesty is about the openness you show about yourself. Remember leaders are consistently under observation by their people and their stakeholders—there is really very little you can hide. Trying to hide your mistakes and limitations will eventually catch up with you and reduce your trustworthiness.

Make promises you can keep

Make sure you have the necessary means, capabilities, resources and support available, before you make commitments. Not delivering on what you promised, on time, is an important reason for broken trust relationships.

Keep your promises

Follow through on what you have committed. If you cannot deliver on what you have promised, as soon as possible, with honesty, explain the reasons why you were not able to fulfil your commitments. Do not invent excuses or shift the blame to third parties to disguise your bungles. Act responsibly and admit mistakes.

Integrity

Challenge any unethical behaviour you may observe and push your people to act correctly and honestly—even when it means that you are unable to follow through on commitments made. Take a firm stand and challenge inconsistent behaviours that are against the entity's values and principles, or that are disrespectful.

Transparency

Tell the truth. Never lie. Transparency is about how you manage and share information. Share information honestly. Telling half-truths or supplying only facts that support your agenda is ambiguous and will lead to poor decisions.

Respect

Show respect for people's opinions, values and contributions. Do not break any confidentiality. Absolutely refrain from gossip! When disagreeing with someone, control your temper and stay focused on the issues—not the person.

Credit

Give credit where credit is due—often. Do not take credit for someone else's contributions—that is theft, period! Also, do not make giving credit cheap—give credit when it is deserved.

Nurture

Building trust takes time and patience—especially in an environment notorious for low trust. Nurturing trust is a mutual two-way process. Begin by showing trust and you will get trust in return, little by little. Relate with your mind and heart to others and practice emotional intelligence to become more self-aware, and aware of other's feelings.

Dialogue

Listen sincerely to what people share—their concerns and feedback. Engaging in dialogue (not your monologue) develops mutual understanding and shows respect. Dialogue builds trust, releases people to share more information and solicit honest feedback.

Feedback

Seek and share feedback about your behaviour, respectfully and confidentially. Treat unpleasant personal feedback as valuable information even when it is really uncomfortable. Act sensibly and respectfully when you receive valid feedback. Use it as valuable material for your personal improvement.

The principal relationship behaviours

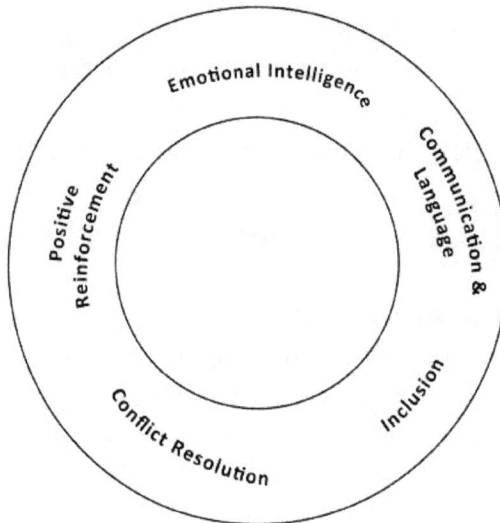

The behaviours shown in the ring in the middle of the Relationship Dimension are the essential leadership behaviours that revolve around the core of trust. They are: Emotional intelligence, inclusion, communication and language, conflict resolution and behaviour reinforcement.

Emotional intelligence

Being authentic and trustworthy when you build your relationships requires that you have a deep understanding of your own and other people's emotions. Ignoring the influence of emotions is a sure way to create distrust and ruin relationships.

For many decades, leading and acknowledging emotions was frowned upon and were considered irrational and non-business like. Discussions about emotions in the work setting were deemed as allowing weaknesses to develop and a sign of poor leadership. Cognitive and technical skills were the quintessential elements of good leadership.

Contrary to this obsolete popular belief that emotions should be excluded from leadership contexts, decades of empirical research has proved that high Emotional Intelligence (EI) is strongly correlated to outstanding leadership and leading of successful change initiatives. In his texts, Goleman[3] goes as far as claiming that the EI competencies for leaders account for close to 90% of the success of outstanding leaders. Our own empirical research[4] has confirmed that there are significant interrelationships between the factors of EI and the dimensions of Three-dimensional leadership.

Salovey and Mayer[5] were the first to coin the term Emotional Intelligence (EI), while Goleman has widely popularised the concept. Since the 1990s many books and articles popularised EI. Daniel Goleman became famous for his books on the subject.

Emotional intelligence for leaders

Your emotional intelligence is your ability to understand and judiciously use emotions—yours and other's emotions. EI is a combination of emotions, behaviours and abilities that benefit your leadership, your relationships and your entity.

Today there are numerous EI models available. Most of the models have four or five primary dimensions. Each dimension is a combination of emotions, behaviours and abilities. Salovey and Mayer's original model has five dimensions. Three of the EI dimensions describe behaviours that focus on the self (you), for example: self-awareness, self-control, and self-motivation. Two dimensions, Empathy and Social skills, are your emotional ability to manage relationships with others.

Emotional intelligence dimensions:

Self-awareness

Your self-awareness means having a deep understanding of your own emotions, strengths, weaknesses, needs and drives. People with strong self-awareness are neither overly self-critical nor unrealistically confident. You are honest about your own behaviours, feelings and emotions. Self-awareness includes a broad understanding of your personal values and goals. People that are self-aware are mindful and comfortable to talk about their limitations and strengths. You will demonstrate openness to constructive criticism. Self-aware people also show self-confidence, but they know their limits. When you have high self-awareness, you will recognise how your emotions influence other people and their performance. You will know when your emotions will be charged under stressful or conflicting situations.

Self-management or self-control

Self-management is about understanding and controlling your feelings and managing your moods. Self-management involves a tendency to suspend your judgement; to think before you act.

Leaders that show a high ability to self-manage, can control their emotional and behavioural impulses and channel their emotions positively. You can control your own disruptive tendencies. You can suppress impulsive pressures. Self-management is your predisposition to reflect on your own emotions and be thoughtful about how they might affect others. You are comfortable with uncertainty and adaptable to change your behaviours. You calmly handle stress and emotionally stressful situations, like interpersonal conflicts.

Self-motivation

Self-motivation is your personal passion to work for reasons that go beyond material possessions. It is your tendency to pursue goals with energy and perseverance. People with high self-motivation want creative challenges, enjoy learning and take pride in achievements. You display determined energy to do things better. You often seem restless with the status quo. You are persistent in questioning predetermined procedures. You are enthusiastic to explore new approaches in your work. People with high self-motivation remain optimistic even in times of adversity. You work steadily towards your goals despite setbacks.

Empathy

Empathy is your ability to acknowledge and understand the emotional behaviour of other people. It involves your compassion with other peoples' emotions. Empathy includes your thoughtful consideration of other peoples' feelings when you make decisions. Empathy is essential in the age of change, to lead teams, and to retain talented people. Leaders with empathy are highly perceptive of the finer nuances in other's body language. You will be able to 'hear' subtle messages beneath the words that are being spoken. You have a keen understanding of how cultural and ethnic differences influence behaviours and emotions.

Social skills

Social skills is the effective use and integration of all the different dimensions of EI. Leaders are very effective at leading relationships when they understand and control their own emotions and when they empathise with the emotions of others. Social skills are your ability to influence and create positive changes in others by using your EI skills. Having good social skills is being effective in your relationships, creating trust, building networks, finding common ground and building rapport. Socially skilled leaders tend to have wide circles of connections, and they can find common ground with diverse people. Yet socially skilled leaders do not socialise continually. They accept that important mutual undertakings are accomplished inclusively through people and not exclusively through individuals.

Inclusion

Instead of hoarding 'power-for-one', inclusive leaders harness and expand 'power-for-many'

Inclusion increases your leadership power and authority. Inclusion goes far beyond expanding the diversity of race, gender, and age in your engagement endeavours. Inclusion also goes far beyond being participative or creating a fully engaged entity. More importantly, inclusion incorporates diversity of mental models, thinking styles, experience and skills sets.

Inclusion is the ultimate form of empowerment. It energises people beyond being engaged—it creates a sense of co-ownership in the mutual purposes of your entity. When people are included, they embrace a shared understanding of long-term mutual purposes and they co-own short-term objectives. Inclusive leaders co-develop a common identity, shared visions, shared values, and change initiatives with their people and stakeholders. Inclusion creates a sense of belonging that make people feel dedicated to the cause of the entity. Their personal goals become aligned to the mission or mutual purposes of the entity.

Inclusion, as you will discover, requires exceptionally courageous and trusting leadership—leadership of a kind that is vastly different to the way we were led in the past. It requires levels of empowerment that means sharing significant amounts of your position power and decision-making authority. It also requires the introduction of new paradigms for leading execution and change (topics I will discuss in subsequent chapters).

Power sharing does not mean abdication of your leadership authority, or the creation of conditions without control. To the contrary, inclusion leads to better alignment, significantly increased value contribution by the whole entity, higher performance, and more successful change initiatives.

Paradoxically leaders who practice inclusion build significantly more power faster, for themselves and their entity, because they mutually create greater and better entities. Instead of hoarding 'power-for-one', inclusive leaders harness and expand 'power-for-many'. Consequently, by being inclusive, you can enlarge the potential of your entity and thus grow the bases of power. An inclusive power base provides the springboard for growth and performance.

In addition, inclusion requires that you shift your mindset to embrace new leadership paradigms that are aligned with the age of change. (I discuss inclusive mindsets in more detail in the chapters on change.)

When you apply the concepts and principles of the *Leadership Framework* (Chapter 3), you will achieve higher levels of inclusion, better strategic governance, more effective power sharing and power building, and correspondingly better performance results.

Shift of leadership paradigms—from autocratic to 21st century fit-for-change

Leadership theories developed over time through a series of eras (Chapter 3). The older leadership paradigms predominantly follow autocratic and hierarchical decision-making styles that do not include active participation, consultation or empowerment. The styles are top-down and communication is usually on a need-to-know basis. At best, people are informed through directive styles such as 'Telling' and 'Selling'. Telling is used to command and control activities, and 'Selling' is used to introduce and push exclusive change initiatives. This paradigm of leadership is predicated on Frederick Taylor's theory of scientific management, which was developed about a century ago. It assumes that leaders and managers have all the information and knowledge necessary to make important decisions, and other people are not able to assist, let alone participate.

Since the advent of the internet, digital communication technologies and the social media revolution are causing a tsunami of information. Information and knowledge that used to be scarce commodities are now available everywhere and anytime. Most people in the developed world can now access vast amounts of information. This level of accessibility, combined with the fact that workforces globally have become more educated and connected than they were only a few decades ago, causes people to demand more inclusion and transparency in decisions. Today knowledge workers generally have far better education than their predecessors, and often better than their leaders.

Within such a complex and dynamic environment, leaders can no longer afford to lead entities reactively with command-and-control styles. Continuously changing contexts demand more proactive, flexible leadership frameworks to help govern entities. Leaders cannot rely solely on a chain of command anymore. New frameworks and models are necessary to cope with the floods of information and change signals. Failing to apply inclusive change-oriented mindsets will ultimately reduce your entity's agility and cause its demise.

Contemporary organisation structures have become flatter, more flexible, and with more elastic boundaries to defend entities against the onslaught of more complexity and dynamism. Some of these new organisation forms are known as networks, boundary-less organisations, horizontal, collaborative, or high involvement organisations. We are implementing better structural designs to cope with the demands of complexity and constant change. Yet the increasing engagement deficits I discussed in Chapter 1, convey a sobering message. The message is that despite these new organisational forms, our current leadership frameworks are still not suitable to lead in the age of change.

The degree of inclusion must lift

While change drivers in our continually changing contexts call on our leadership paradigms to move to new leadership frameworks, so is there a need to shift the degree of inclusion in entities.

Figure 4.2 indicates that as leaders behave more inclusively (perform higher degrees of inclusion), the potential for their people and entities to contribute or add higher levels of value, also increases.

The introduction of behavioural and humanistic leadership theories around the 1950s and 1960s gradually pushed leadership styles away from the old command-and-control, to styles that allow people to become more involved in their entities' decisions. Participative and consultative styles came into fashion. People were allowed to take part in decision-making by leaders who shared some information and solicited opinions from them. Occasionally members' contributions were taken into serious consideration when final decisions were made. Often though, leadership teams did whatever they intended anyway. Due of these exclusive leadership behaviours, participative and consultative leadership got a bad reputation for being insincere ploys to create a haze of inclusion.

Around the 1980s 'Empowerment' became a popular theme after it became apparent that participative and involvement leadership styles

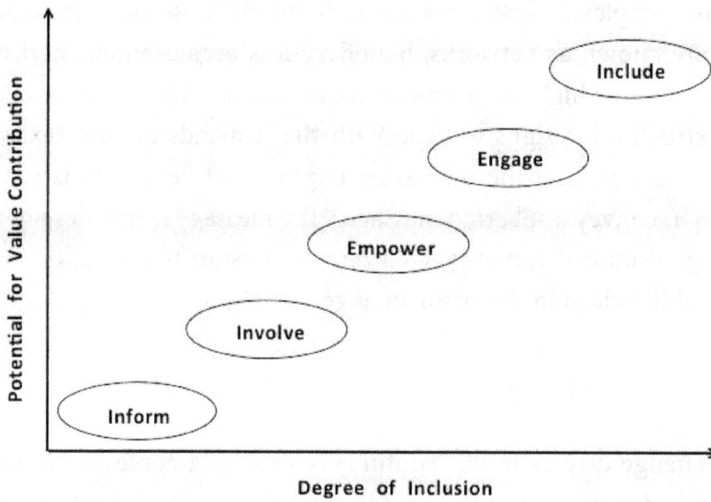

Figure 4.2. Inclusion Drives People's Value Contributions

have delivered suboptimal entity performance improvements. The foundation of empowerment is shared responsibility. Fundamentally the conceptual background of empowerment includes concepts designed to increase members' job- or role-related commitments. The ultimate objective of empowerment is nevertheless to improve achievement of the entity's objectives and performance outcomes.

Presently, the concept of 'Engagement' is in vogue. Engagement is essentially a measure of many outcomes that are related to the degree of empowerment experienced in an entity. In other words, it measures the level at which people feel committed and empowered to do their work, and are willing to put extra effort into it.

Engagement seems like a new behavioural concept. However, it is a popular catch phrase for a vast assortment of established positive behaviours with motivational qualities. Definitions of engagement vary. Generally, the concept comprises many familiar concepts such as:

emotional and rational motivation, performance enhancement behaviours, job satisfaction elements, organisational commitment, improved self-efficacy to enhance job performance, perceived clarity of work roles, and commitment to the entity's objectives and mutual purposes. Engaged people measure positively on these behaviours that are closely aligned towards achieving an entity's objectives.

Yet good engagement is not enough. Given the relentless pace of change, people and stakeholders often perceive opportunities and risks earlier than their leaders. It is unwise to think that in this age leaders can exclusively determine change initiatives that are imminent. The amount of information and contextual viewpoints are too many for one person to form a complete picture of necessary change.

For you to lead effectively in the 21st century, your level of inclusion must lift. The focus of inclusion is quite some distance further than engagement. Where the focus of empowerment and engagement is on the member's job or role, the focus of inclusion is on the sense of co-ownership of the entity's mutual purposes and shared future.

Trusting relationships form the foundation of inclusion. Inclusion is the ultimate form of empowerment. It goes beyond the creation of engagement—it creates a sense of joint ownership with the leaders in the mutual purposes of the entity. People and stakeholders who have a sense of inclusion can co-design and co-create meaningful mutual purposes that have long-term value for the entity. Through inclusion, a leader can co-develop a common identity, shared vision and shared values for his entity.

An inclusive structural design by itself will not solve engagement deficits. So-called flat, flexible, collaborative or open organisational designs require inclusive leadership and cultures too. This will ensure that the entity will viably endure and perform in an environment of continual change. Included people and stakeholders will support you, so that your entity can outperform your rivals and move toward new futures. Your objectives will be mutual—that is to make your entity thrive and perform extraordinarily towards achieving its purpose.

Inclusion principles for leaders

Inclusion starts with you

Traditionally people in entities are referred to as 'human resources'. The association that people are 'resources', like any other resource one would need to complete a task, carries the notion that people can be regarded and treated as means, cost centres, and 'head count'. And so often, as 'objects' that can be shifted in and out of entities at the sole discretion of leaders. Would you regard your close family members as 'resources'? We should relate to people in a considerate, trusting and respectful manner. Every person is different and brings unique values, passions, talents and contributions to share with your entity. Change the mindset—think inclusively.

Share meaning, purpose and contribution

Your key role is to help your people find the connections between their own purposes and the purposes of the entity—to create the sense of belonging and ownership. When people do not experience these connections, they get either frustrated or confused. People want to contribute to and share in meaningful purposes—especially in areas where they feel confident, qualified, experienced and talented. When they feel that they contribute to meaningful mutual purposes, they feel included—they share in mutual ownership of the entity and its future. They will make career progress and contribute to the success of the entity. This can only be achieved through trustworthy leadership.

Share decision-making authority and power

Members also want to feel in control of their roles and want freedom to express themselves in their professions, trades or crafts. Inclusive cultures offer broad participation to all members.

Most inclusive behaviours are relatively easy to implement. Sharing power and delegation of decision-making authority is arguably one of the most difficult personal stumbling blocks for leaders to overcome. Yet it is the most important aspect of inclusion. Leaders are afraid of losing perceived control, positional status, and exposing their weaknesses, by sharing more power and delegation authority. Yet the contrary is true. When you are more confident and trusting, you will share more and include more people; you will co-design bigger and better initiatives faster. Paradoxically, you will gain more control, power, status and increase your self-confidence by becoming more inclusive. It requires your courageous, trusting and collaborative behaviour. It requires that you develop your emotional intelligence and high self-awareness.

In Chapter 13 about the Execution Dimension, I discuss how leaders can maintain better strategic control and governance in an inclusive culture.

Manage expectations and always close the loop

Inclusion is not equal to abdication. Everyone's opinion cannot be accommodated and most entities are not democracies either. You need to articulate the rules of engagement inclusively and then follow them inclusively. Use feedback and feed-forward to communicate decisions to show how decisions are implemented and how peoples' contributions are included in important matters.

Remove any barriers to inclusion

A good method to start being inclusive, enhance your entity's performance and develop worthwhile initiatives is by removing barriers and stumbling blocks. Make it easier for people to become mutual contributors. Get rid of barriers that increase exclusion, such as, unnecessary organisational levels, stifling top-down rules, bureaucratic processes and systems, and old rigid paradigms of thinking. Removal of barriers to inclusion also removes the lack of uptake and follow-through on people's inputs.

Give your people the necessary means and resources

Stop solving problems for your people. Let them come forward with their ideas, options and solutions. But you must ensure that the necessary resources are made available to them to perform effectively. Resources are more than the obvious: It includes among others, the time, organisational capacity, delegated authority, access to information networks, political power and connections, necessary skills development, open communication channels, regular feedback, and very importantly, a safe psychological environment. Your level of inclusion is directly related to the amount and quality of resources you can make available to people. Without adequate resources, engagement drops quickly.

Be the inclusive role model

You must become the leading includer. When you become the role model by demonstrating through your actions how inclusion works, it is very likely that they will follow your lead. You should perform inclusion personally, in your teams, community groups and stakeholder forums to inspire and challenge people to adopt a culture of inclusion.

Clear lines of sight

Everyone in your entity must understand—from the bottom up, and from the top down—how their roles fit into the mutual purposes and objectives of the entity and why their roles are meaningful and important. Understanding the value and meaning of one's contributions and having clarity of your purpose are huge steps towards being included. Clear lines of sight are created by clear role accountabilities and expectations. The topics of enhanced accountability and clarity of expectations is addressed in Chapter 13 about the Execution Dimension.

Communication

"Seek first to understand, then to be understood"   *Steven Covey*

The objectives of leadership communication are fourfold: To create and support mutual purposes, drive behavioural change, enrich engagement, and achieve superior performance results.

The lifeblood of an entity is the knowledge and information currents that flow to and from its leadership. Leaders determine the pulse and flow of this lifeblood in a critical 'life support' system (see Intelligence systems later) through your communication. Your communication skills and actions are key to becoming a successful leader. Communication creates relationships and engagement with the entity and with others.

Successful leaders in the age of continual change communicate inclusively. Yet leaders are often unaware of how their communication actions and inactions directly affects engagement and trust. Leadership communication skills, or the lack thereof, do define your career success as a leader.

Traditionally leaders have cascaded their messages and change directives downwards through a chain of command. Excessive communication energy was spent to 'sell' leadership messages and drive 'buy-in' by the entity. This approach no longer works well. It inhibits employee engagement and stifles entity agility because people feel they are the objects of change, and not part of it. In the age of change, leaders create transparent and inclusive environments through communication that enable people to mutually create new futures.

Collins in his book *'Good-to-Great'*[6] writes that leadership is about creating a climate where the truth is heard and the brutal facts confronted. Good-to-great leaders create cultures in which people have abundant opportunities to be heard, and for the truth to be understood.

Table 4.1 below summarises some of the contrasting differences between leadership communication in traditional ways and leadership communication in an inclusive manner that makes entities change-fit.

Table 4.1. Contrasting Communication styles	
'Old School Leadership'	**Change-fit Inclusive Leadership**
Leader's vision, strategies and directions are articulated vividly to justify the leader's views and decisions.	Entity's mutual purposes are developed inclusively to arrive at co-created visions, strategies, values, etc.
Leader is the sole spokesman	Ownership and alignment to the vision, strategy, and directions through inclusive and interactive communication
Top-down, directive or consultative communication styles through hierarchies	Dialogue, inquiry, feedback and iterative communication styles through networks
Communication on a 'need-to-know' basis—mainly through unidirectional communication means	Leader shares relevance, context, assumptions, trends and future perspectives Frequent dialogue, feedback and feed-forward with varied audiences through diverse channels
Information is well filtered and polished to produce positive public positions	Information is transparent and honest—positives and negatives are shared
Messages are targeted to enhance the public image and maximise perceived value	Messages are focused to create trust and a positive realistic picture of the entity
Achieves 'buy-in' through vigorous and comprehensive 'telling and selling' pitches and campaigns	Achieves mutual ownership through inclusive communication using knowledge networks
Leadership enforces alignment to messages through rigorous structures, directives and compliance measures	Achieves alignment through mutual purposes, inclusive dialogues, clear expectation setting and empowerment

Table 4.1. Contrasting Communication styles	
'Old School Leadership'	**Change-fit Inclusive Leadership**
Leaders communicate from the corner office through a chain of command	Communicates from a centre stage. Use in-person dialogues, informal meetings, and diverse social media
Leaders listen only to inner-circles or loyal groups	Listens to customers, employees, peer-to-peer networks, stakeholders and external parties
Many singular messages targeted at diverse audiences, e.g. customers, entity and stakeholders.	Consistent message content, tailored to different audiences' contexts, needs and interests
Leader communicates exclusive change initiatives, solutions, vision and new directions	Leader catalyses and provokes the use of different mindsets, creativity through questioning, listening and creating climates for open discourse Leader and entity inclusively co-create visions, solutions, change initiatives through collaboration, shared knowledge and networks

*

Communication principles for leaders

Listen! Listen! Listen!

Your communication must start, and end, by actively listening to what is being communicated – verbally or otherwise. Reject the impulse to speak and being heard first. Reject the compulsion to push your solution as the only solution. Listen actively and perceptively to others. Engage your Emotional Intelligence skills when you listen to understand other's contexts, issues, ideas, feelings and interests. Acknowledge and value other points of view and pay full attention. Ask open questions to clarify and show you are actively engaged in dialogue.

Audiences

Know your audiences: customers, stakeholders, members, or third parties. Know what drives each audience—what are their interests and issues? Be clear about the consequences your messages may have on them. They are interested in what is in it for them—not in what is in it for you.

Develop engagement

Create engagement through dialogue, inquiry, reasoning, active listening, openness and transparency. Remember, by not communicating you are 'communicating'—your silence sends certain definite messages. Be mindful of the implicit messages you may send by not communicating.

Create and maintain mutual purposes

Create a shared context in your message and show how it relates to the values, principles and vision of the entity. Create meaning and mutual purpose for the audience by connecting their values and interests to the values and interests of the entity. Where appropriate, bring your authentic values to the table to strengthen the connections. Align the interests of the audience with the entity's mutual purposes.

Drive behavioural change

Drive behavioural change by explaining the context behind your message, providing transparent evidence (pros and cons), and your view of the way forward. Commit to the actions you will take personally. Ask the audience to commit and act on your message. Remember you are the role model that will be cautiously observed. Inadvertent 'bad old' behaviours that may contradict your message will erode trust, engagement, and break the momentum of the change you want.

Results and momentum

Ultimately your message is about achieving superior results in the future. Clearly and concisely state the expectations and outcomes you want to achieve.

Feedback and response

Any responses to your communication: Positive actions, reactions, and inactions—all deserve responses from you. When actions are positive, respond with public and sincere appreciation. When responses are less than positive, solicit open and frank feedback and discussion—again with your EI skills fully engaged.

Catalyse *and* challenge

Abandon the old habits of egocentric leaders—that is, to single-mindedly promote and sell their exclusive ideas as the only solutions. Instead challenge people to come forward and engage. Catalyse and provoke new mindsets by questioning assumptions and suggesting alternative ways of thinking and perceiving issues.

Language, metaphors, stories and signals

Use language, metaphors, stories and signals as powerful tools to effectively convey your messages. When used correctly, people will relate to your stories and metaphors and engage in your communication.

Be careful in the way you use metaphors and new language. For example, the word 'buy-in' has the connotation that someone is 'selling' something to me, and I should 'buy' the thing that is being sold to me. It does not convey the idea that I am willingly engaged in the process. If you use management jargon, for example, 'empowerment', in your message, but people do not observe any matching empowering behaviours, they will consider your message and objectives as insincere.

Consistency

Your messages must be concise, articulate and consistent. Develop different formats for different media channels and different audiences, but keep the message and terminology consistent. If you lose message consistency or use alternative terms (synonyms) you may confuse or dilute your message and lose trust and engagement.

Listen! Listen! Listen!

Your leadership communication must start and end by actively listening to what is being communicated—continually.

Behaviour Reinforcement

There are numerous theories and methodologies available on the topic of motivating people in entities. However, I will limit the discussion to what I regard as the essence of what leaders need to know about motivation. I would like to wrap the topic inside the concept of behaviour reinforcement.

Behaviour reinforcement is a more focussed concept than motivation. Behaviour reinforcement methods are relationship-building behaviours to motivate, develop, encourage, inspire and maintain desirable behaviours. They are methods that align individuals behaviours to the achievement of mutual purposes. Behaviour reinforcement can be applied to strengthen certain behaviours and weaken others, so that desired behaviours can occur regularly and consistently.

I have observed two perspectives concerning behaviour reinforcement:

The first view is the 'human resources' view. This view is a customary interpretation of how peoples' behaviours are reinforced positively or negatively. The human resources view holds that the value people bring to entities are their skills, talents, education, experience, motivation and performance. People pursue success for themselves and the entity they join. In return to the value people add in the entity, they are rewarded, remunerated, and recognised through a variety of intrinsic and extrinsic (material and immaterial) ways. The reward contract in the human resources view can be both formal and informal. It is predominantly a transactional perspective—people are rewarded for contractually agreed outputs.

The second perspective I would call the 'inclusive person' view. This view holds that in addition to the 'human resources view', people also bring to the entity individual purposes, passions, values, and unrealised potential. People want to successfully realise their individual 'inclusive person contracts'. People want to realise their individual purposes, grow their potential, belong, and co-own. When they are offered opportunities that allow them to do so, they become fully engaged, they feel they belong, and they act like co-owners in the entity.

For leaders, it is our opportunity, challenge and duty to use this vast untapped resource of human energy and passion—a resource that can multiply our entity's wealth and performance.

When the 'inclusive person' is not recognised, people become frustrated, disillusioned and disengaged. People would (perhaps) satisfy their contractual obligations according to the 'human resources view'. When we apply behaviour reinforcement correctly, our people will become more engaged and included. They would not only pursue their roles to achieve better material and personal status outcomes for themselves, but they will pursue meaningful joint purposes with passion to the greater benefit of the entity. People become aligned with the purposes of the entity, their performance outcomes multiply and they become fit for change.

In a nutshell, behaviour reinforcement, that embraces the 'inclusive person view', can be achieved through a combination of:

- Correctly aligned remuneration, rewards, recognition and role definitions.
- People development through coaching, training, role and enrichment.
- Continuous development and improvement.
- Learning, knowledge sharing and honest timely feedback.
- Encouraging risk taking and experimentation, without punishment for honest mistakes.
- Flexible work arrangements that encourage creativity.

Aim your behaviour reinforcement actions to achieve the following:

- Align the values, vision, strategy, goals and objectives across the entity.

- Connect and include people into the mutual purposes of the entity, its values and objectives.
- Encourage and maintain desirable behaviours that will take the entity to its aspired future.
- Support and encourage necessary change initiatives.
- Ensure positive future growth of individual people as well as the entity.

Behaviour reinforcement principles

Apply and multiply peoples' passions

Use reinforcement methods and systems to draw your peoples' passions to the purpose, values and vision of the entity. When people understand the relationships between the entity's purposes, their own passion and effort, and the outcomes they produce are appropriately reinforced—they will increase their level of engagement.

Values and reinforcement must match

Leaders often advocate a certain set of values, but reinforce another set of mismatching performance outcomes. For example, an entity may advocate a set of values that endorse quality, risk taking and innovation. Yet the leaders in this example may reward their people for cutting costs, being conservative and sticking to the tried and tested. When you support value mismatches such as the one in the example, it would mean the death knell to building trust, engagement and performance. Value mismatch is a great bugbear when attempting to implement change or winning engagement. Take unconditional precautions to ensure that your stated entity values are

---

reinforced, and not the undesirable espoused values that may creep in over time.

Desired behaviours

Did you identify the correct desired behaviours for each role to align with your entity's values, vision, purpose and goals? On the flip side, did you identify the undesirable behaviours you need to extinguish through appropriate reinforcement methods? When you introduce change initiatives, do you adjust your reinforcement methods to reinforce and align new desired behaviours for each person?

Gratitude and recognition

Your authentic acknowledgement and affirmation of others' contributions is one of the easiest and yet most effective ways to reinforce positive behaviour. How often do you personally express sincere and honest appreciation to people close to, as well as distant in your entity, about jobs well done, about their valuable contributions, valid opinions raised, and positive behaviours that are well expressed?

Role model

What do you do personally to reinforce desired behaviours? Have you changed your own personal behaviours to align with the desired behaviours you want your entity to demonstrate?

Coach

Coaching and mentoring are powerful tools to help reinforce wanted behaviours. Do you provide leadership coaching or mentoring to your direct reports and other people?

Behaviours and outcomes

Do you reinforce positive behaviours as well as wanted outcomes? Most entities only measure and reinforce performance outcomes. Yet it is equally important to measure and reinforce desired behaviours that lead to better performance. Behaviour determines outcomes and performance. When desired behaviours are measured, clear expectations are created and reinforced. Reinforced expectations are followed by desired outcomes.

Roles

Do you have the right people in their right roles? Do they have roles and responsibilities that make the best use of their skills, experience, passions and purposes? Do the roles they have, position and challenge them to strive for excellence, find meaning, and fulfil their potential? Are the opportunities that are available consistent with each member's level of skill, education, and experience?

Balance several methods

Do you rely exclusively on financial remuneration and rewards to reinforce members' behaviours and outcomes? Use a good balance of reinforcement methods—in addition to remuneration and rewards—to give recognition and develop your people.

Continued learning and development

To grow your members' skills, mental models, talents and passions, do you promote continuous learning opportunities and do you follow a continuous improvement mindset with everything you do? Do you provide job enrichment opportunities, learning networks through advanced technology platforms, and communities of practice to advance knowledge sharing?

Feedback

Provide constant and authentic feedback to people on how they perform, how they can improve, and very importantly, when they have done well, and not exclusively through infrequent formal performance reviews.

Corrective action

Use corrective actions in circumstances that unconditionally warrants that—events such as clear behaviour misconduct and unethical and illegal actions. When such misdemeanours occur, apply appropriate corrective actions immediately, and privately. Individuals involved must correctly perceive the corrective actions as appropriate penalties that will prevent a recurrence of their undesired behaviours. When you do not take strict and quick disciplinary action when it is due, you run the risk that such misbehaviours are deemed appropriate. Once such behaviour spreads, it can become part of an unwanted culture, which is not easily eradicable.

In Chapter 12 about delivering change initiatives, I discuss more specific reinforcement behaviours you could use to promote change-oriented cultures.

Conflict Resolution

Conflict occurs in human relationships. Unfortunately, many people have been brought up with a belief that conflicts and disagreements are inherently bad and should be avoided. The media and the entertainment industry also emphasise this idea. However, not only is positive conflict a fruitful source of creativity and innovation, but also, when guided positively, it can foster trust, collaboration and enhance inclusion. Resolution of conflicts, when done constructively, builds stronger relationships.

Conflict resolution is an almost daily occupation for leaders. Effectively resolving conflicts is an essential skill for leaders. Ineffective conflict resolution has derailed many leaders' careers. It is very important in a VUCA world of continual change. Besides, our entities are increasingly becoming cross-cultural, multinational and globally interconnected.

Conflict is a common occurrence in every lifecycle stage of change initiatives. Conflict is more prevalent and resistant, especially when people are not fully included in the change process and development of change initiatives.

Rather that subduing or avoiding conflicts, confident leaders actively encourage positive conflict and inclusive resolution to reach better outcomes for everyone involved. When leaders show avoidance and destructive resolution behaviours, it may be a sign of immaturity to resolve conflicts constructively. When conflict is avoided, it often festers and erupts later in greater proportion. Reactionary solutions then become necessary—often very costly or too late. Smart leaders do not avoid conflicts. With change-oriented foresight you can proactively circumvent potentially unconstructive future conflicts by finding positive solutions inclusively.

Not all conflicts have the potential to be resolved constructively, to be prevented, or to be handled positively. Some conflicts can be personally hurtful, chaotic and costly. I recommend the use of my Conflict Resolution Matrix (Figure 4.3) for resolving and preventing many conflicts constructively. It is also useful to minimise conflicts that have destructive potential.

Elements of conflict

Conflicts can range across a continuum from minor positive

misunderstandings to major destructive conflicts. It is important to understand that conflict usually involves five elements.

The elements of conflict are characterised by:

- Sources of the conflict (objects, differences, losses, or issues)
- Relationships (or people) involved—the relationships that are at risk if the conflict is not resolved. Relationships range from personal one-to-one relationships, to highly formalised third party agreements.
- Emotions of the people involved in the conflict—theirs and ours.
- Interests—material and immaterial, such as scarce resources, assets, status, power, jobs, positions, role, and possessions.
- Needs—usually needs are intangible, such as personal values, identity, purpose, goals, power, control, ambition, respect, perceptions, relationships, and security.

Usually when conflict occurs, leaders tend to focus on the people involved to resolve the issue. Instead, it is important to consider the other conflict elements too, to lead an effective resolution. For example, resolving conflict about peoples' interests only, when their needs are not addressed too, may not effectively resolve the conflict. The conflict elements are also interrelated. For example, people can be highly emotional about differences that may occur to their interests. Therefore, it is so important to appreciate conflict in its interrelated, but separate parts, that is, its relationships, issues, emotions, needs and interests.

Sources of conflict

Most sources of conflict originate from real or perceived differences and losses—differences and losses of interests and needs. However, there are several more complex sources of conflict, such as:

▽ Differences, losses and resistance during change lifecycles

I discuss this source of conflict in more detail in the chapters about the Change Dimension.

▽ Strained relationships

Relationships become strained when trust is broken, roles become incompatible, goals are unclear, standards, measures and rewards are ambiguous or communication is poor.

▽ Paradoxes

Paradoxes often appear to be opposing contradictory positions that cannot co-exist. However, paradoxes require each opposing position to make sense. A paradox exists because of interdependent opposing forces. One cannot have one or the other force—there is always a degree of either present.

Paradox is never permanently solved. Leaders must lead a constructive balance between paradoxical views. The answer to leading paradox is usually that *both* positions must coexist to some degree. Black-or-white, solutions often seem desirable and effective but would seldom permanently resolve a paradoxical conflict.

Examples of paradoxes that often cause conflict in entities are:

- Short-term profits versus long-term resilience
- Speed versus timing
- Quality versus cost
- Agility versus resilience
- Power versus inclusivity
- Centralisation versus decentralisation

▽ Polarities and polarisation

Polarities, unlike paradoxes do not have interdependent opposites.

Examples are: different ideologies, religious beliefs, ethnic cultures, or political views.

Polarities can peacefully co-exist within an entity, if the proponents of polarised views do not determine, or attempt to change, the main characteristics of the entity itself. When that occurs, a polarity can become a source of destructive conflict.

In the age of change there are many polarised views from many stakeholders. Constructive depolarisation is an on-going leadership task.

Conflict resolution matrix

Theories and models on conflict resolution have developed considerably over the past fifty years since Blake and Mouton[7] developed their renowned conflict behaviour styles grid. They identified five personal styles for conflict resolution: avoid, compete, collaborate, compromise and accommodate.

It is useful to know what your preferred conflict resolution style is, when you lead conflict resolution. It is also highly advantageous to know what your counterpart's style is when you deal with individuals. However, the usefulness of knowing which conflict styles exist quickly reduces when you deal with multiple parties simultaneously. Consider for example that you frequently deal with diverse teams, large groups, remotely with people or entities across digital networks. You can't resolve conflicts face-to-face with everyone who is part of a conflict. In situations like these your predominant style may be more of a hindrance than a strength.

Instead of focusing on the personal styles of conflict, I have developed a conflict resolution matrix that considers the relationships between the characteristics of conflict and the appropriate resolution behaviours. The conflict resolution matrix is shown in Figure 4.3.

Conflict characteristics range over a spectrum from very positive to very negative. This is shown on the horizontal axis of the matrix.

Juxtaposed to the conflict spectrum, is the spectrum of conflict resolution behaviours, ranging from behaviours that encourage conflict, to behaviours that prevent conflict (Note the absence of behaviours that suppress or avoid conflict).

Instead of focusing on the personal conflict styles people may use during conflict resolution (us versus them), the emphasis of the conflict resolution matrix is on the features presented by the conflict and the appropriate resolution behaviours (us *and* them, versus the conflict).

The purpose of the matrix is to help you redirect potentially destructive conflict caused by differences, paradoxes, and polarities toward proactive, positive and creative resolution.

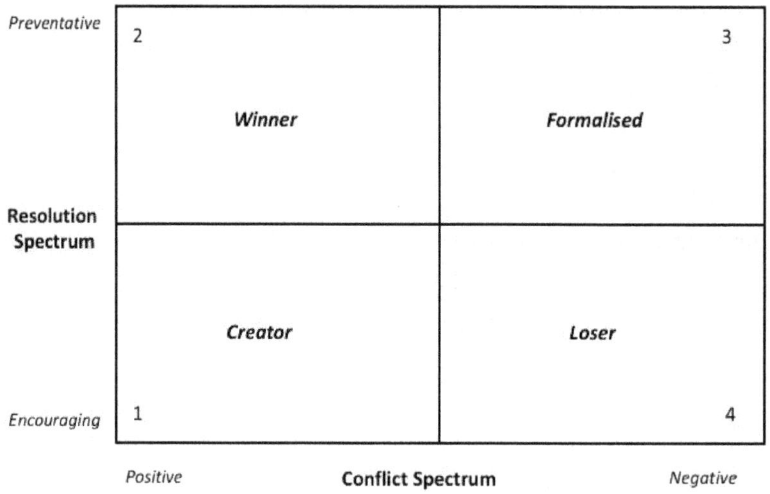

Figure 4.3. Conflict Resolution Matrix

Creators

Quadrant 1 illustrates a positive and encouraging environment for conflict resolution. In quadrant 1 the leader would encourage positive and creative conflicts and create constructive resolutions. You perceive conflict as a creative source, not as a problem. Everyone is encouraged to *create* constructive resolutions—to be 'Creators'.

- The creator's mindset is one of abundance
- High levels of trust and inclusion exist
- Conflict is dealt with immediately and proactively
- Conflict is used as a source of energy and creativity
- Avoidance behaviours are not tolerated—conflict is deemed to be a good source of creativity
- Any avoidance behaviours are monitored to discover signals of lurking conflicts that could become negative
- Conflict is used constructively to catalyse new ideas, new outcomes, and creative solutions.
- Questions about conflicting issues are asked to develop understanding from different member's perspectives
- Disagreements are posed objectively without alienating people
- Leaders encourage opposition to their own positions
- Leaders welcome being challenged
- People are encouraged to voice opposing and diverse views. Open expression makes people more resilient and agile (rather than compliant) to consider different futures.
- People consider wider ranges of perspectives, alternatives, solutions and possible beneficial outcomes.
- Open, honest and heated debate is welcomed
- People voice their values and principles involved in the conflict—without fearing ridicule
- Search for new information and integration of opposing positions
- Leaders and people call attention to and challenge each other's biases

- Paradoxes are sources that can catalyse creative solutions rather than dilemmas that need singular resolutions.
- Resolutions incorporate opposing goals and paradoxical poles
- Paradox is used to incorporate both contradictory positions, rather than 'either-or' positions.

Winners

Winners illustrate a positive and conflict preventing environment. The environment is positive for conflict resolution, and the emphasis is on *preventing* conflict to recur, or escalate.

In quadrant 2 creative conflict resolutions that were developed in quadrant 1 are converted into viable new initiatives. Viable initiatives are further shaped and formed to permanently resolve the conflict. The key feature of the Winner quadrant is that we apply inclusive behaviours to *prevent* a conflict from recurring and we ensure that a positive resolution is locked in, thus creating a 'Winner'. Upon resolution, all parties who are involved accept, adapt and implement the constructive resolution so obtained.

- The winner's mindset is one of abundance.
- High levels of trust and inclusion exist.
- Prevailing styles are collaborative and compromising.
- High levels of emotional intelligence, especially self-regulation.
- Learning environment with information sharing between conflicting parties—sharing facts, concerns and new information.
- People are made part of the resolution and their agreement with the outcomes are more contingent upon the fact that they are included in the process and less on the fact that their ideas should be accepted.
- Open and transparent disclosure that builds mutual trust.

- Decisions on best ways forward, outcomes or resolutions, are reached through inclusive dialogue.
- Active listening and debate
- Different facts, ideas and positions are integrated into solutions, agreements or positions.
- Negotiation and constructive bargaining are often used to resolve differences.
- Joint resolution, direction, or action plans are agreed.
- Change initiatives may result from resolutions.
- Everyone supports the agreed resolution without harbouring negative opinions.
- Final positions and actions are clarified and agreed to leave little ambiguity.

Formalisers

The emphasis of quadrant 3 is on *formalising* preventative mechanisms to prevent recurrence of negative conflict. Formal methods are designed and agreed to prevent possible future conflict. In quadrant 3, constructive resolutions that were *created* in quadrant 1, confirmed and agreed in quadrant 2, are '*formalised*' with appropriate preventative methods.

Formalised conflict resolution methods are designed when:

- Leaders and their people desire more certainty about resolutions.
- Negative conflicts may potentially recur in future.
- Third party relationships need to be endorsed.
- Preventative resolution mechanisms used in Quadrant 2 are deemed inadequate or informal.

Preventative resolution mechanisms used by Formalisers are for example, standards, procedures, frameworks, policies, contracts, legal agreements, and so on. Through proactive creation of preventative resolutions, you can achieve more certainty, clarity, and alignment, mitigate risks, and minimise future conflict. Formalisation may not always be necessary. Especially within trusting cultures, formalised conflict prevention may seem excessive.

In quadrant 3:

- The Formaliser's mindset is that conflict will become negative if not prevented.
- Leaders and stakeholders who are passionate about security, certainty or risk mitigation will call for appropriate preventative mechanisms to be implemented.
- The climate is one of arms-length engagements.
- Avoidance behaviours are replaced with formalisation.
- Trust is balanced, mutual and inclusive.
- Resolutions are often further negotiated before they are finally formalised.
- Formalised and detailed processes are followed to cover foreseeable issues.
- Styles are competitive, collaborative and compromising.
- Agreements, rules, procedures, etc., are proactively designed for areas of potential conflict, conflict prevention and resolution mechanisms.

Losers

Quadrant 4 illustrates a negative conflict environment that encourages conflict escalation. Quadrant 4 is what I call the 'Loser' quadrant. Relationships may have soured to such an extent, that conflict, if not led sensibly, will become destructive. Certain types of entity cultures and behaviours may aggravate negative conflict between parties involved.

If you do not remove or discourage negative resolution behaviours so that the characteristics of the conflict can move across to either quadrant

1 or 3, conflicts in quadrant 4 will make almost every party involved a 'Loser'—except perhaps the lawyers that might be involved to pick up the spoils.

Quadrant 4 has the following characteristics:

- The Losers' mindset is one of scarcity.
- Obvious avoidance behaviours prevail until the conflict can no longer be evaded and must be dealt with.
- Exclusivity, low trust, and low engagement
- Lack of emotional intelligence evident in behaviours, especially lack of empathy for others' concerns.
- Politically charged culture—widespread infighting and gossip
- Conflict seethes below the surface and erupts unpredictably.
- Coercion tactics and threats are used to suppress or coerce parties into agreement and submission.
- Conflict suppressed with command-and-control directives
- More rules, stricter authority and communication directives are mandated.
- Preferred singular views and resolutions pushed—without regard of the effect on relationships involved
- Black-or-white, polar resolutions. Paradoxes are deemed as either-or phenomena.
- Exclusion of divergent views and opinions
- Extremely competitive styles (win-lose)
- Communication and information sharing between conflicting parties trickles down or halts.
- Costly litigation and protracted legal procedures cause time and opportunity losses.
- Damage to productivity, relationships and trust

Leading constructive conflict

The constructive route to lead conflict is to follow a positive path of resolution through Q1, Q2, and Q3. However, when you are faced with a quadrant 4 situation, and presuming that you may already have an inclusive culture in place, you can lead the resolution process by starting at Q3. This will work when you can consider several formalised resolution mechanisms. Sometimes though you may have to move back one or more steps (first Q2 then Q3), before you can reach the final resolution in Q3. Occasionally you may have to move a Q4 conflict into Q1 first, and then resolve it forward through Q2 and Q3.

However, if your entity does not have an inclusive culture yet, you have a more challenging problem at hand. But for leaders that are stuck in a Q4 situation, it may pose an opportunity in disguise. You can demonstrate courage to confront conflict inclusively. Gradually, and deliberately you can change behaviours and influence your culture towards one that regards conflicts as opportunities for growth, innovation and positive change. When you deliberately introduce Creator (Q1) and Winner (Q2) behaviours, your people will eventually become less cautious and wouldn't avoid conflict. Through leading positive resolution rounds, you will begin to move the entity's culture towards inclusion.

Conflict resolution principles for leaders

- Continuously and proactively monitor for the presence of conflicts and conflict avoidance behaviours. When you detect conflicts, apply and insist on immediate constructive resolution. When you allow conflict to fester, or pretend it does not exist, it will act like a spreading infection.
- Always attempt to first resolve conflicts or paradoxes by understanding the reasons and context for the conflict

---

(address the why question). Then realign the reasons and causes of the conflict with your entity's values, principles and agreed mutual purposes. If the parties agree on the values and principles, resolution of conflict would be much easier. Focus on the reasons for conflict first—leave the what, how, and who resolutions for later.

- Avoid focusing on the who-question first—doing so may tempt you to choose the side of your preferred party. Siding with any party, because they may have your preferred views or resolutions, may sound like good tactical leadership, but it is seldom a viable long-term strategy. Turn the focus to the issues first—not to the people involved.

- Gather all the parties involved in the conflict and have them work through their concerns. Face-to-face resolutions, no matter how uncomfortable they are, build trust and relationships. When all the conflicted parties are not present at the same time, conflicts may be protracted, and more distrust could be created among the parties.

- Wear the other party's shoes. To understand conflict often requires that you perceive an issue from the other party's perspective, to have empathy, to challenge the other party, and to be comfortable being challenged on your views. Opposing and alternate views or positions often provoke innovative thinking, and lead to improved resolutions.

- Constructive resolution needs mature emotional intelligence skills to listen considerately and to be emotionally engaged.

- Learn how to identify the difference between a singular

conflict and a paradox (more than one co-existing but conflicting positions). Balancing the co-existing forces of paradoxes is essential. Paradoxes can never be removed completely—paradoxical poles will always exist to some degree. The art is to keep a constant healthy balance. Continuous and constructive inclusion of your people will direct opposing forces of paradoxes toward finding innovative resolutions.

- Use frameworks such as the conflict resolution matrix above to prevent costly, time-consuming, opportunity crushing negative conflicts. Use a deliberate process to direct the energy of differences, conflicts or paradoxes towards positive and creative resolutions.

- Mutually agreed resolutions should be implemented as soon as possible. Delaying implementation of resolutions reduces mutual trust and often exacerbates conflict. This is especially true when the onset of conflict is from within a Q4 conflict situation. While you build goodwill and trust amongst the parties, start implementing resolutions.

- Acknowledge that you may need help to resolve certain kinds of conflicts—especially those in Q4. Sometimes the other party may show no interest in following constructive resolution methods. Or, you may have to follow a predetermined legal course due to regulatory requirements. It may involve mediation, arbitration or litigation. Sometimes you may be at your wits end with a conflict situation. Do not attempt to avoid the conflict—but get the necessary professional assistance as soon as possible.

Collaborative Behaviours

I chose the term 'Collaborative Behaviours' to describe a range of value adding, purposeful behaviours between leaders and other people, across boundaries, within and between entities. Collaborative behaviours are for example, networking, influence, persuasion, negotiation, and the judicious use of power and political influence.

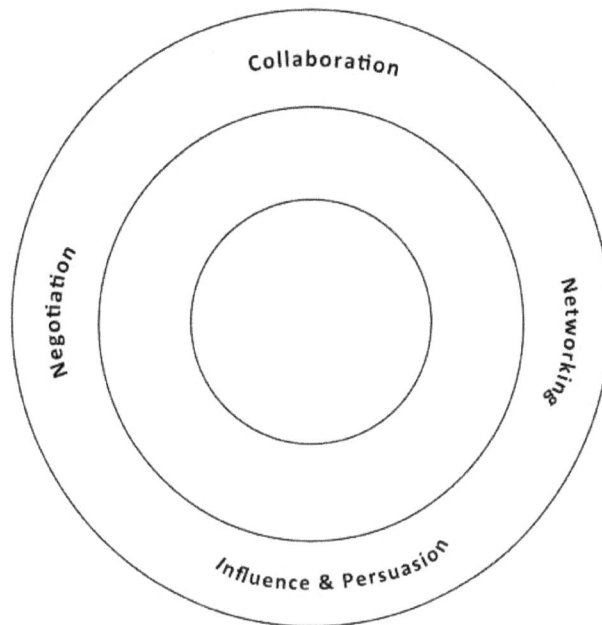

The ring on the outside of the Relationship Dimension shows the essential leadership behaviours you need to form effective cross-boundary and internal collaborative relationships. Effective collaborative behaviours are built on the behaviours in the centre of the Relationship Dimension. The more skilful you are at behaviours in the centre of the Relationship Dimension, the easier it would be for you to apply the collaborative behaviours in the outer ring.

In today's continuously changing contexts, leaders cannot lead ahead of change unless they collaborate with customers, clients, stakeholders and third parties. Successful collaborative relationships are the vehicle to successful change initiatives. Almost every leadership role requires networking, negotiating and influencing of collaborative relationships.

Collaborative relationships are far-reaching

Leaders who are skilled at building and preserving successful collaborative relationships will accelerate their careers. Collaborative relationships are formed through a combination of behaviours that create and achieve common mutual objectives. In collaborative relationships, the different parties will continue with their own interests, however the aim of collaboration is to build on the common interests with each other. For collaborative relationships to be successful, each party must considerately take the other's interests into account when acting on behalf of the relationship.

There are many kinds of internal and external collaborative relationships. Their features vary over different ranges, such as:

- Temporary to permanent
- Public to private
- Contractual to non-contractual
- Two parties to multiparty

Internal collaborative relationships include, for example:

- Change initiatives.
- Cross-functional teams and actions.
- Projects involving more than one function and discipline.
- Processes and value chains that cuts across several organisational structures.

External collaborative relationships include, for example:

- Contractual arrangements with third parties, clients, customers, franchisors, licensors, joint manufacturing, joint research and joint marketing.

- Strategic alliances.
- Private-public partnerships.
- Non-governmental organisations and not-for-profit partnerships.
- Networks and coalitions.
- Social media networks.
- Minority investments and equity swops.
- Joint ventures and consortiums.
- Mergers and acquisitions.

Drivers behind collaborative relationships

Many of your entity's objectives can't be achieved by themselves. You need collaborative relationships to achieve them, to grow and survive. Often change drivers progress so fast that entities are unable to develop the necessary resources and capabilities to grow or survive on their own.

The VUCA world produces many forces for continual change, with huge risks and opportunities—often rapid and surprising. The onset of multiple change drivers may, for example, shorten your entity and its products' lifecycles. Disruptive technologies and the emergence of increasing social connectedness, create the need to obtain access to new relationships, capabilities, capacities and resources. This need pushes leaders to engage in more collaborative relationships to secure and maintain viable enterprises.

The diagram in Figure 4.4 illustrates the point that as change intensifies in the contextual environment, the complexity of collaborative relationships we need to deal with intensifying change, also tends to increase. The collaborative relationships we form are aimed at filling voids in opportunities, capacities, capabilities and resources. As entities become more exposed to continual change, the focus of collaborative relationships progresses from internal partnerships, such as, cross functional teams, project teams, and cross-business unit initiatives, to external collaborative relationships such as, strategic alliances, consortiums and joint ventures.

Forming collaborative relationships is one of many structural options you could use to manage intensifying change. I provide a detailed discussion on structuring your entity in Chapter 13 on Execution. In Chapter 12 on Change Delivery, I provide a detailed discussion on the reasons why we need collaborative relationships as a method to deal with continual change.

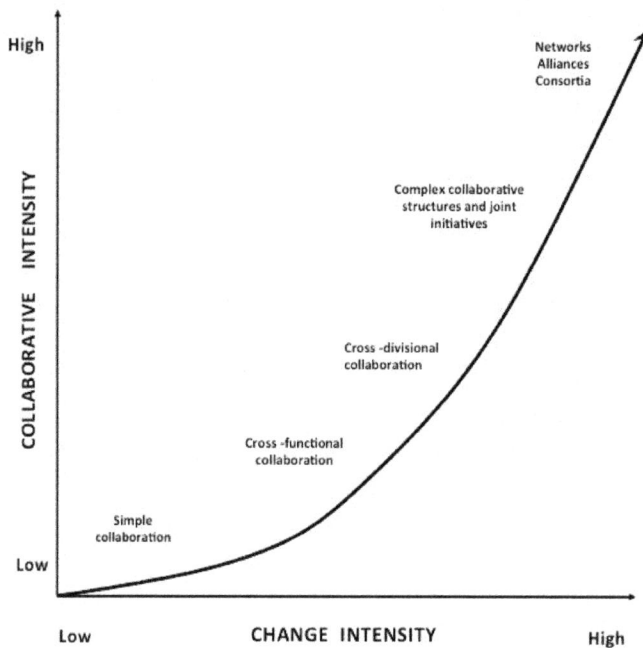

Figure 4. 4. Change drives the Intensity of Collaborative Relationships

Common characteristics of collaborative relationships

The spread and variety of collaborative relationships is impressive. Yet they all share common characteristics and common development stages. Understanding these common characteristics and applying the principles of collaborative relationships will help you to form lasting collaborative relationships.

Most collaborative relationships have the following common characteristics:

- There must exist some common ground or mutual purpose, before an effective collaborative relationship can become viable.
- Trust is vital to the successful creation and continuation of collaborative relationships.
- The parties' contexts, strategies and risk profiles will change with time. Changes in these may cause deviations from the mutual objectives of the relationship, its lifespan, its performance, and so on.
- Interfacial boundaries between party's entities may cause points of potential friction and need to be carefully managed. Boundary interfaces can be for example: technological, procedural or information exchanges.
- Decision-making, accountability and authority in collaborative relationships are shared, split, and often restricted. Mechanisms are necessary to govern decision-making, accountability and authority relationships. Many collaborative relationships are based on reaching consensus on critical decisions.
- Collaborative relationships tend to have shorter lifespans than the founding entities.

Stages of collaborative relationships

Successful collaborative relationships develop through typical stages. See the exhibit below that summarises the stages. Significant collaborative relationships need your leadership for each of the stages. Individual interests of collaborating parties, and the mutual interests of the relationship, often experience opposing driving forces. This common conflict of interest may cause considerable strain on relationships. During the development stages of collaborative relationships leaders often have to judiciously engage their political and influence skills to network and negotiate relationships.

---

1. Pre-collaboration

Network, Influence
Purpose, scope and objectives
Partner review, selection, acceptance
Is collaboration the preferred route?
Risks, drivers and feasibility of collaborative relationship

⇩

---

2. Form Collaborative Relationship

Select, invite, or recruit members
Confirm and align commitments
Negotiate expectations, rules and boundaries

⇩

---

3. Design & Formalise

Agree terms
Agree boundaries
Coordination and control mechanisms
Decision-making rules and procedures
Decide on structure and coordination mechanisms

⇩

4. Governance and Performance

Conflict resolution
Boundary interface management
Perform mutual and separate activities
Measure performance and share feedback

⇓

5. Exit, Change or Revitalise

Exit relationship
Acquire or merge with partner
Change objectives, purpose, structure, scope or format

The stages for developing collaborative relationships are equally applicable to, for example, the formation of small informal cross-functional teams, or the formation of highly complex multinational consortia.

Collaborative relationships *do not* tend to themselves. The stages illustrate a process that needs continual leadership attention to strengthen the collaborative relationships. High failure rates of collaborative partnerships—many sources quote failures between 50% and 70%—means that many collaborative relationships reach the point of exit, at stage five, prematurely. The causes for collaborative failures are many—for example, a failure to realise strategic benefits, or a failure to meet common objectives. Failures of collaborative relationships often cause serious damage to the entities involved. Because governance and performance of a collaborative entity are not always under the control of a singular entity, but may be shared, collaborative relationships need special care. Continual leadership of stages one to four is necessary to maintain lasting and successful collaborative relationships.

*

Principles for leading collaborative relationships

- Be clear about the justification for forming collaborative relationships. Collaborative relationships bring considerable advantages to dynamic contexts, but they can carry opportunity costs and risks beyond your effective control. Carefully weigh the pros and cons.
- Proactively build strong networks by influencing, building and aligning connections, internally and externally. Network to develop knowledge and understanding of possible connections with compatible parties.
- Know what your entity can contribute in collaborative relationships. Present your entity's value propositions in ways that emphasise your benefits to other parties and how you may reduce their potential risks.
- Determine what collaborating parties want, and are willing and able to commit. It is essential to recognise the other parties' real value to your entity. It is equally important that collaborating parties accurately perceive your value to them from their perspective.
- Select parties with complementary skill sets, capacities and resources. Look to balance complementarity and interdependency. Too many complimentary aspects can lead to power and governance imbalances. Too many interdependencies can lead to excessive risks in the relationship.
- Once parties are selected, create and agree the mutual

purpose and objectives. Agree on key interdependencies and complementary contributions. Collaborative relationships include people with different and often competing objectives. Engage parties to align and work toward achieving agreed mutual performance outcomes.

- Engage people in the creation of rules, rights, boundaries and governance frameworks for collaborative relationships. Inclusion leads to common commitments, trust and a code of conduct about accepted behaviours.

- Establish clear rules of accountability. Everyone must have a clear understanding of the mutual purpose of the relationship, the goals to achieve its mission, and the performance measures that apply. Everyone knows each other's responsibilities and accountabilities. The consequences of underperformance by participating parties on the collaborative relationship are clearly understood.

- Be vigilant about new change drivers that can put stress on collaborative relationships. Collaborative relationships and participating parties are dynamic systems in themselves. Consequently, forces of change may influence individual party's interests, as well as the mutual interests of collaborative relationships. It may cause strain on the future viability of the relationships.

- Regularly review the lifecycle of your collaborative relationships. Proactively look to adjust key aspects of collaborative relationships to keep them viable, or to convert them into different forms, or to exit them when necessary.

Summary

The new Relationship Dimension is an integrated model that comprises of the essential relationship behaviours leaders need, to lead in the age of change. The core principle of the New Relationship Dimension is *trust*. Trust forms the centre of all your respected and enduring relationships. Several principal relationship behaviours exist around the core of trust. These behaviours are vital to effectively lead relationships, inside and outside your entity, irrespective of your level of leadership. The principal relationship behaviours leaders must demonstrate successfully are: emotional intelligence, communication, inclusion, conflict resolution and behaviour reinforcement.

Built around the core of trust and the principal relationship behaviours, are behaviours associated with collaboration. These are necessary leadership behaviours to create forward momentum for execution, growth and change in their entities. They are essential to create effective cross-boundary and external engagements and are equally important to build internal collaborative relationships. Collaborative behaviours are: networking, influence, persuasion, negotiation and the judicious use of your power and political influence. Successful mastery of collaborative behaviours depends a lot on how trustworthy you are and how competent you have become with the principal leadership behaviours.

Good collaborative leadership begins with building mutual trust. The new Relationship Dimension shows you how to create excellent relationships by first forming relationships from a platform of trust, followed by enhancing your principal relationship behaviours. Your next level of leader behaviour skills—collaborative behaviours—is developed upon a solid foundation of trusting relations and suitable principal behaviours.

Notes

1. Kiel, F. 2015, Return on Character, Harvard Business Review Press, Boston.

2. Shockley-Zalabak, P. S., Morreale, S. P. & Hackman, M. Z. 2010, Building the high trust Organization, Jossey-Bass, San Francisco.

3. Goleman, D. 2004, 'What makes a leader?', Harvard Business Review, January 2004, pp. 82-91. See Goleman, D. 1996, Emotional Intelligence: Why It Can Matter More Than IQ. Bloomsbury Publishing, London

4. Lourens, J.F., Boshoff, A.B. & Van Wyk, R. 2003, 'Relationships between Emotional Intelligence and the Three-dimensional leadership Behavior Construct', *Proceedings of the 1st International Conference on Contemporary Management*, 1-2 Sep. 2003, The University of Adelaide, Adelaide, Australia, pp. 49-55.

5. Mayer, J.D. & Salovey, P. 1993, 'The intelligence of emotional intelligence'. *Intelligence*, vol. 17, pp. 433-442.

6. Collins, J. 2001, *Good-to-Great*, HarperCollins, New York.

7. Blake, R. & Mouton, J. 1964, *The Managerial Grid: The Key to Leadership Excellence*. Gulf Publishing Co, Houston.

5. **The New Change Dimension**

AN INTRODUCTION

"Change is not merely necessary to life, it is life" Alvin Toffler

In Chapter 1, I explain the context of the age of change. We are living in a VUCA world with an extreme future ahead—a future with enormous leadership opportunities. I also illuminated several major challenges leaders will face in this age of change.

In Chapter 2, I discuss the substantive definition of leadership. You would recall that a key part of the leadership definition states:

'Leaders and followers execute real change initiatives to achieve mutual purposes'

In Chapter 3, I present the new Leadership Framework. The Three-dimensional leadership theory forms the core of the Leadership Framework. The Leadership Framework is built upon the three dimensions, namely:

- The Relationship Dimension (Chapter 4)
- The Change Dimension (in Chapters 8 to 12), and;
- The Execution Dimension (Chapter 13).

Before going into the detail of the Change Dimension, I lay the foundations for change-oriented leadership. Change has several characteristics that can vary and intensify across a continuum. I start with a discussion on the true nature and character of change in Chapter 6, 'The Character of Change'. These important characteristics of change are interdependent. Change, as it occurs, also has several significant psychological, emotional and behavioural impacts on human beings. In Chapter 7, I discuss this very important topic of how change effects our people in our entities. To become an effective leader of change, you must first understand the nature of change and secondly, understand how change impacts your people and the transition processes people have to go through.

In Chapter 6, I also introduce the fundamental concept I call the 'Pre-Life-Cycle'. For any change initiative to be viable and successful, there are natural laws that apply to change that must be followed. The Pre-Life-Cycle of change is a natural law that has been widely ignored. For change initiatives to be successful we must follow this natural law. I have divided the Pre-Life-Cycle into five stages as shown in Table 5.1.

Founded on the five natural stages of change, I designed the Change Dimension (Figure 5.1), which consists of five sets of corresponding leadership behaviours. Table 5.1 shows the links between the Pre-Life-Cycle and the Change Dimension. When leaders adapt these behaviours in the Change Dimension, they can lead change initiatives successfully in the age of change. (see Chapters 8 to 12). The Change Dimension will equip you to lead change initiatives in extreme futures, with your followers.

Table 5.1. The Pre-Life-Cycle and Change Dimension

Pre-Life-Cycle Stage	Corresponding Stage in Change Dimension
Enable	Mindset and thinking is open to change Foster climate and culture to be open to change Remove barriers and resistance to obstacles Comprehensive inclusion of people and stakeholders
Align	Mutual Purpose Change-fit entity Capacities, capabilities and resources Accountabilities
Anticipate	Whole entity is involved in discovering necessary changes Sense, gather, analyse and create actionable intelligence about change
Incubate	Use dialogue to discover options for change initiatives Mutual and inclusive engagement about initiatives Test assumptions for change initiative Pilot, experiment, evaluate Match capacity, capability and resources Decide and select: Go, hold, no-go, etc Optimise timing

Table 5.1. The Pre-Life-Cycle and Change Dimension	
Deliver	Announce, launch
	Engage change management models
	Embed change initiative into Execution system
	Measure change initiative performance
	Match behaviours with benefits and rewards
	Feedback and feed-forward through intelligence system

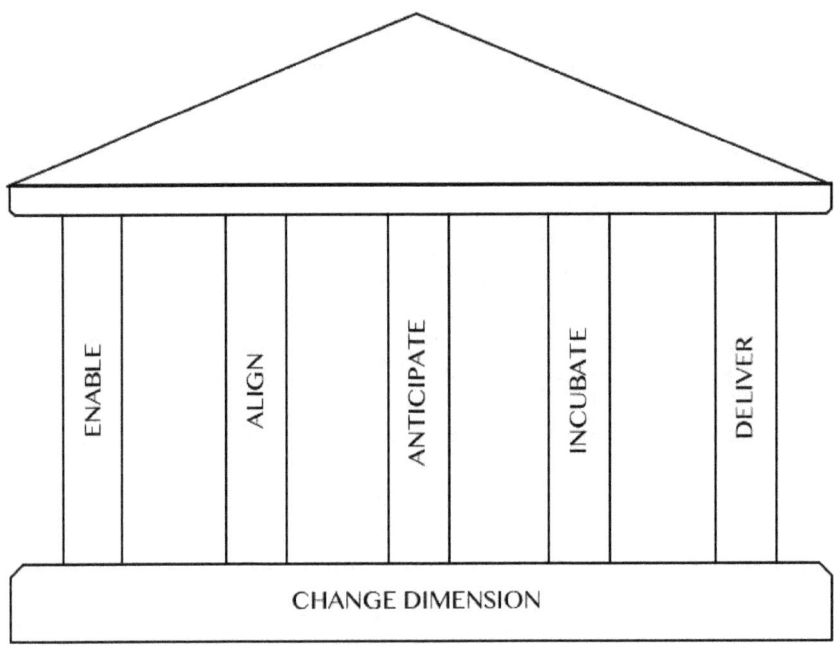

Figure 5.1 The New Change Dimension

The illustration of the Change Dimension in figure 5.1 resembles a building with a solid foundation and five pillars.

- The Change Dimension is built on a foundation of strong leadership relationships, as represented by the Relationship

Framework (Chapter 5). Strong trustworthy behaviours are essential to provide vital leadership support through the full Pre-Life-Cycles of change initiatives.

- The five 'pillars' or stages of the Pre-Life-Cycle form the whole Change Dimension. The five stages are summarised in Table 5.1.
- The five stages of the Change Dimension are discussed in detail in Chapters 8 to 12.

Your relationship behaviours underpin the Change Dimension. Without well-established trustworthy relationship behaviours, you would not lead change successfully. Your people should want to follow you willingly. Willingness to follow leaders is only possible when mutual relationships are strong, inclusive and trustworthy.

Good change-oriented leadership is demonstrated through consistent behaviours that positively exploit change drivers in your contextual environment. Secondly, change initiatives will only be successful when you suitably equip your entity, by providing the necessary means and resources to implement and integrate initiatives. Thirdly, you should ensure that planned change initiatives would not erode the resilience of your entity. Finally, instead of attempting change initiatives exclusively, you would encourage the use of diverse mental models, and create a culture that embraces change, growth, and sound risk awareness. Such a culture will ensure that change initiatives are aligned across your entity, through its structure, systems and stakeholders.

Change-oriented leadership is supported by an entity that is fit for change. The Change Dimension is designed to assist you to create a change-fit entity that is always ready for growth, new opportunities and adverse change conditions. You would be able to lead change as a continuous and normal activity without having to resort to reactive responses. Your people will be able to continuously anticipate changes in advance—changes that will be aligned with the mutual purposes of the entity. Change will not be experienced as discrete events. People will regard changes as routine, like any other operational activities.

Once you have successfully adapted the leadership behaviours I recommend in the Change Dimension, you can expect to see occasions when your people start to push for changes, when they believe progress or advancement in the entity is too slow. When you have created an entity that is continually driven to be proactive, impatient with the status quo, and has available the necessary means to deliver change initiatives, you have successfully created an entity that is fit for change.

When you apply the behaviours in the Change Dimension your change leadership will succeed. Practice the leadership behaviours in each stage to successfully lead change. If one of the stages in the Change Dimension is weak, the 'roof' of the building could fall in (a change failure would likely occur). Deficiencies in change-oriented behaviours in your leadership and entity, in one or more of the stages can stifle the Pre-Life-Cycle and negatively impact the success of delivering change initiatives.

———

6. **The Character of Change**

"It is not the strongest of species that survive nor the most intelligent, but the ones most responsive to change"

Charles Darwin

Introduction

Change can be defined as a movement from a current or 'old' state of something, or someone, to a 'new' state. The new state may be better, or worse than the old state, depending on the success of the transition.

In the age of change we will increasingly experience change of all kinds, ranging from small changes or improvements to chaos and disasters. The phase between the old and the new state can occur in many forms, and include events and initiatives such as growth, development, innovation, improvement, transition and transformation, to name only a few examples.

A leader who is determined to thrive and survive in the age of change must first understand the character of change before he can embrace change to the mutual advantage of the entity. Leadership behaviours and actions that have worked well in past eras will be less effective to lead change in the new future.

Change initiatives can vary significantly in intensity. For example, initiatives intended to stabilise a chaotic situation, or to ensure the survival of an entity, have very high change intensities. Initiatives intended to continually improve performance, or to generate growth, are less intense than the former initiatives. As the leader, you will need the appropriate change-oriented behaviours to lead a variety of change initiatives at different levels of intensity. The principles of the Change Dimension will support you to develop those change-oriented behaviours.

I begin this chapter by explaining the importance of change drivers. All change is proceeded by change drivers. It is vital that leaders can identify and track change drivers ahead of their potential impact. I explain how important characteristics of change intensify for different kinds of change initiatives. I also introduce and explain a new concept, called the Pre-Life-Cycle. Furthermore, I show how the main characteristics of change intensify through consecutive phases in the familiar life cycle (the cycle that follows the Pre-Life-Cycle).

The character of change

The character of change involves several important characteristics. Each characteristic varies in intensity depending on the type and context of the intended change initiative. For you to make the correct choices and designs of change initiatives, it is important to understand the characteristics and how they behave. Change characteristics have significant influence on the performance of your entity. Even when change initiatives seem similar, every change initiative will be different because its contextual environment may be different.

Characteristics of change that are important to understand, are:

- Change drivers
- The Pre-Life-Cycle and the life cycle
- Change stability
- Interdependent complexity
- Modes of change
- Change uncertainty
- Resistance and barriers
- Change intensity.

Change drivers

Change drivers stimulate the need for change. Change drivers encourage movement from old to new states—they are the leads to change initiatives.

How you respond to change drivers will determine how change initiatives develop in your entity, and how your entity's future will unfold. Change initiatives in entities should not happen for the sake of change—valid driving forces in your context must always exist.

Driving forces for change arise from within your entity's external and internal contexts. External change drivers are commonly change trends beyond your control. You should however recognise and understand them early and take the necessary leadership actions.

Fundamentally, external change drivers stem from two major sources: behavioural sources or natural sources.

Behavioural change drivers

Behavioural change drivers occur due to combinations, or accumulations of human behaviours, often over extended periods before change drivers become obvious and produce major consequences on societies and entities.

When one studies different reports on future trends, they all seem to follow different sets of descriptions for contextual change drivers. However, there appears to be general consensus that the main drivers for change in the foreseeable future (at least the next 10 to 30 years), are:

- Rapid technological innovation
- Widely diversifying competition
- Increasing globalisation
- Rising individual expectations
- Population and workforce demographics.

▽ Rapid technological innovation

The age of digitisation and innovation, the almost limitless storage capacity for information with cloud technology and the ability to communicate instantaneously make it possible for anyone that has access to these technologies, to become part of an interconnected global community. This has, for example, sparked the social media revolution we experience today.

We are rapidly progressing from the 'supercomputer' and Internet era to the Internet of Things (IoT). The IoT is a network of internet-connected objects able to collect and exchange data using embedded sensors. Digital technologies are becoming increasingly cheaper and pervasive. The IoT consists of digital systems that enable mechanical and electronic devices to systematically interact online with minimal human interaction. Such rapid technological innovations will impact more parts of our lives and increase the potential for disruptions—in our work, social lives, and entities.

▽ Widely diversifying competition

Digitisation and innovative technologies encourage a globally mobile and skilled labour force to become a diversified economic force. Large numbers of low cost and highly skilled workers are available in developing countries, with access to ever-cheaper digital technologies. This causes the proliferation of innovative competition. The number of players is rising in many industries and institutions, amounting to unprecedented levels of competition with ever-lower production or services costs, offering an abundance of choices to consumers. Players who do not change their business models to keep up with new competition are quickly pushed out.

▽ Increasing globalisation

Digitisation and lower trade barriers provide interconnectedness and fuels globalisation. Globally mobile and skilled workforces combined with the rise of developing countries that supply abundant cost-effective labour, products and services, increase the threat of new competitors and concurrently provide opportunities for new markets and new entities.

▽ Rising individual expectations

The digital and social revolution made it possible to obtain almost instantaneous delivery of services and information. Physical products are increasingly sourced and delivered through the same technologies. This new world of instantaneity has caused people to expect and demand almost immediate access to services, service delivery and immediate satisfaction of their expectations. These rising expectations from employees, voters, learners, customers, patients, and social institutions, for an ever-increasing choice of benefits, products and services put pressure on entities to deliver better, faster and more efficiently. All kinds of enterprises are impacted by this social phenomenon. Entities that are change-fit will be qualified to read the trends before their competitors and seize opportunities.

▽ Population and workforce demographics

The world's population is projected to grow by 20% over the next 20 years to 8.3 billion people[1]. This will bring about 1.4 billion new customers to the global market place. Most of the population growth will occur in developing countries, as their populations will grow seven times faster than the developed countries, ultimately reaching 7 billion people by 2030.

The world's age distribution is increasing. The global population is expected to become about 5 years older mainly due to increased life expectancy. The global median age could increase by 5.1 years to 34 years in 2030. Especially in the developed countries, where the median age is reaching 44 years, and the age group of 60 and over, will gain more importance as a customer group. The developing countries are expected to age by 5.5 years, reaching a median age of 32 years in 2030.

About 300 million young people, which accounts for over 25 percent of the world's youth population, have no productive work, according to World Bank estimates[2]. An unprecedented 'youth bulge' brings more than 120 million young people into the job market each year, mostly in the developing world. Youth unemployment on this scale threatens economic progress and can create a vicious cycle of less economic activity and more unemployment. It also raises the risk of social unrest by creating disillusioned generations who are vulnerable to criminal activities.

A global war for talent will become a major factor of competitive advantage, pitting nations, individuals and entities against one another, as talent grows scarcer. Carton[3] states that the future and composition of the workforce would not be defined by geography, but by talent. Finding high-tech skilled employees from a global talent pool could be the greatest challenge for many entities in many contexts. Necessary innovation then becomes a major determining factor for much needed new workforce skills, requiring education systems to be completely remodelled.

More than half of the world's population is now urbanised. By 2050, the urban population will have nearly doubled to an estimated 6.4 billion. While urbanisation provides important economic and social benefits, it substantially increases risks related to ecological disruptions, pollution, climate change and environmental disasters.

Around 1 billion people, or one-third of the world's urban population, live in slums. This growing population of urban poor is vulnerable to rising food prices and economic crises, posing significant risks of chronic social instability.

Natural change drivers

Natural change drivers are for example:

- Environmental disasters such as tsunamis, earthquakes, or famine.
- Epidemics and health risks such as bird flu, swine flu, Dengue fever, Ebola virus, and locust storms.
- Severe weather conditions, such as hurricanes, fire storms, droughts, or tornados.

Final thoughts on change drivers

This short summary on global future trends and natural change drivers is only a glimpse of what we can expect about future change. I strongly advise leaders to subscribe to reports on future trends. Watching, studying, diagnosing and understanding future trends are essential behaviours that stimulate change-oriented leadership. Diverse sets of analyses on current and future external drivers are available in many reputable publications[4]. These services and reports provide detail on major change drivers and potential threats that will shape the globe. Their perspectives provide valuable views of the wider context within which you should lead change successfully. They cover major expected changes in the external context, from many perspectives, such as economic, environmental, geopolitical, societal, health, climate, security, energy and technological risks. They provide platforms for dialogue and forearm businesses, governments and societies on how leaders, entities and institutions should prepare for imminent change, mitigate risks, and increase the resilience of their entities.

Life cycles

Lifecycles of almost everything—people, living organisms, change initiatives, organisations, businesses, products, services—follow a natural pattern of change that is also known as the Sigmoid curve (or S-curve for short). The lifecycle is also known as the logistic growth function, as illustrated in Figure 6.1. Jerry Harbour wrote an excellent discourse on this natural law of life cycles in his book: "*Performance Paradox*"[5].

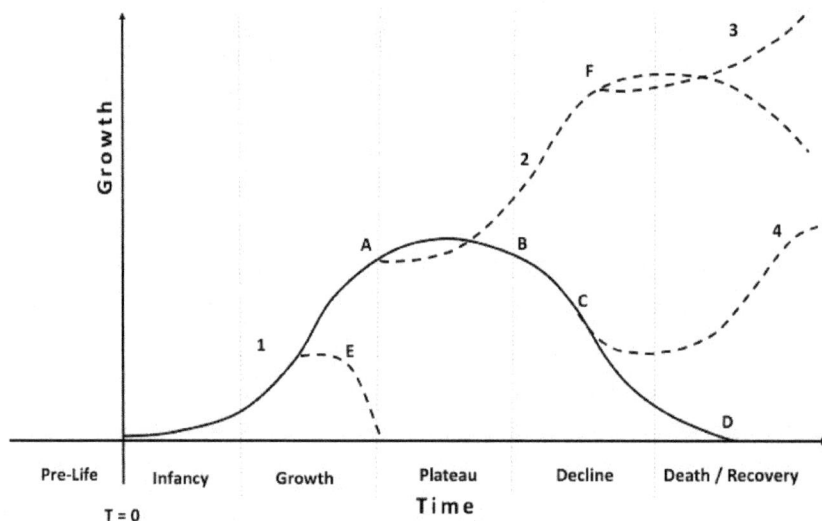

Figure 6.1. Life Cycle

The S-shaped curve can be clearly seen in the left-hand half of curve 1, up to the peak of the curve. From the peak to point D, the S-curve follows a mirror image of the S-curve. The complete lifecycle curve consists of the 'S' on the left and its mirror image on the right-hand side.

The S-curve, or logistic growth function, is a well-known natural phenomenon. Mathematician Pierce Verhulst first described the logistic growth function in 1845[6]. The logistic growth function is derived from the natural law that states:

"The rate of growth is proportional to both the amount of growth already accomplished and the amount of growth remaining to be accomplished"

The S-shaped lifecycle obeys this strict law, founded on the fundamental principle that there is a finite growth ceiling for almost everything. Irrespective of where an object is on its life cycle, there is a finite amount of growth remaining, given enough time.

It is important to note that current literature about life cycles consistently refers to the beginning of a life cycle as the moment when time equals zero (T = 0). That is the moment when we 'push the start-button'—when an initiative begins its new beneficial life. Typically, this moment is after the initiative has been implemented and is ready to go. It is the start of the viable initiative and the beginning of its useful life. T = 0 is the 'go-live' moment. At this instance, the initiative is operational and planned activities can commence to achieve its intended purpose.

The Pre-Life-Cycle

However, there exists a very important characteristic of change—the existence of the Pre-Life-Cycle. The Pre-Life-Cycle is a natural process that occurs before the actual life cycle of something begins. We have overlooked this vital natural law of change, to the disadvantage of the entities we lead.

In Figure 6.1. you would notice that the Pre-Life-Cycle occurs before T = 0. That is the period before a change initiative goes live. During this critical preceding period, change initiatives should go through a pre-life process—a series of stages—to become viable.

It is essential that leaders understand what happens—or rather what should happen—before time zero (T = 0). Before T = 0 we should follow this natural process of change to ensure we create viable and successful change initiatives. Viable change initiatives do not start at 'birth' or at the launch of something new. Viable change starts long before time zero. A positive proactive change initiative would not necessarily be sustainable if we do not prepare the initiative and the entity for it, before it 'goes live'.

The Change Dimension I have designed to lead change in the 21st century is built on the law and principles of the Pre-Life-Cycle. In today's complex, ambiguous and turbulent world, leaders need a framework for change-oriented behaviours to prepare their people to become continually vigilant, agile and fit for change. Leaders with a change-oriented mindset helps to prepare your people and the entity to become aligned as best as possible—before, during and after change initiatives. Your people will be enabled to grow and change course in prosperous and adverse times, at a moment's notice. You will create an entity that is continually fit for change. The new Change Dimension is designed to develop your ability to lead in the age of change.

The Pre-Life-Cycle that is built into the Change Dimension follows an inclusive process. The Pre-Life-Cycle has five stages and ends when a change initiative has been fully implemented—at that moment of implementation, it goes live. The initiative then continues with its actual life cycle, represented by the usual S-curve.

Leading change initiatives viably and successfully on a continuous basis, requires that you proactively lead the Pre-Life-Cycle stages—that is key to successful change initiatives.

A useful way to follow and understand how the Pre-Life-Cycle process works is by way of a gardening metaphor. The right-hand column of Table 6.1 shows metaphorical descriptions of each of the five Pre-Life-Cycle stages. I have used the metaphor of preparing soil to grow plants, to illustrate the Pre-Life-Cycle.

Table 6.1 The Pre-Life-Cycle		
Pre-Life-Cycle Stage	Natural Metaphor	Corresponding stage in Entity
Enable	Cultivate the soil Add fertiliser	Create a change enabling environment and culture that makes the entity fit for continual change
Align	Irrigate soil, apply pesticides, remove weeds, adjust climate controls	Align the entity to become agile and resilient to respond proactively to change drivers
Anticipate	Find the best seeds Plant the seeds	Anticipate change forces that drive change initiatives
Incubate	Seeds start to germinate, weak seedlings die off	Create necessary conditions to develop, test, experiment, pilot and select change initiatives that show potential
Deliver	Transplant viable seedlings into prepared soil and start growing	Take selected initiatives, use change management processes, implement and integrate initiatives

The Pre-Life-Cycle is indicated on the left-hand side of Figure 6.1. The illustration in Figure 6.2 is an expanded version of the Pre-Life-Cycle, showing the five stages that occur before the Infancy stage of the life cycle. The figure with the five pillars (stages) represents the new Change Dimension.

The Pre-Life-Cycle is summarised as follows:

1.   **Enable:** The leader creates an enabling environment in his entity so that change forces can be anticipated, change initiatives can take root, and be viably established.

2.   **Align:** The leader, the people, and entity are aligned with the

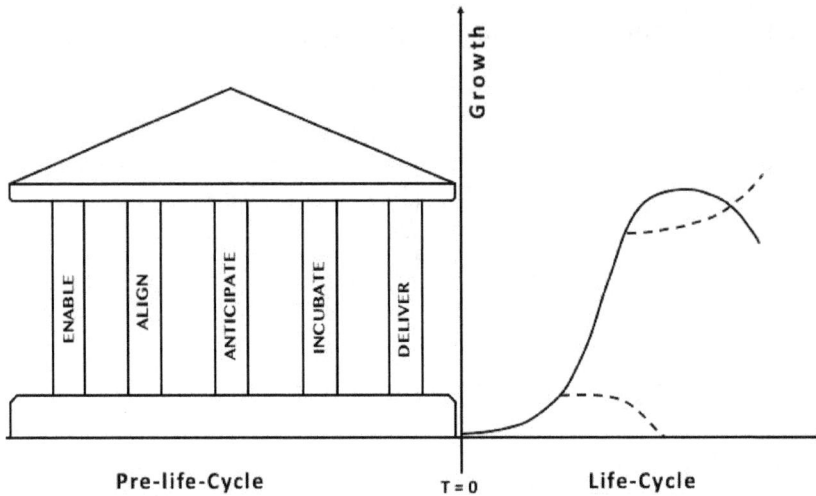

Figure 6.2. The Pre-Life-Cycle

context for change. The entity and the people are equipped for continual change.

3. **Anticipate:** When an enabling environment is in place, the entity is aligned, and fit for change. The leader and the entity proactively sense and anticipate forces for change and new change initiatives.

4. **Incubate**: Anticipated forces for change that are analysed, evaluated and selected for development into viable options for change initiatives, are incubated. Incubated change initiatives are tested and their viability and chances of success confirmed. Change initiatives that are viable are selected for further development or implementation.

5. **Deliver:** Change initiatives that passed the Incubate stage are prepared and executed in the Deliver stage—after this stage it goes live and starts a new life cycle.

When you apply the change-oriented leadership behaviours in Change

Dimension in an inclusive manner, you will prepare your people and entity to become fit for change, so that they will welcome and push change. In the age of change, we need leaders who embrace a change-oriented leadership mindset to create entities and people that are agile and resilient, who anticipate change drivers, and who will survive adversarial changes.

In the following chapters I expand on how leaders can follow the natural process of the Pre-Life-Cycle by applying the new Change Dimension.

The Life Cycle (or 'S-curve')

After the Pre-Life-Cycle has followed its course and when an initiative has been implemented— 'at go live'—the familiar life cycle begins (Figure 6.1). The life cycle starts at Infancy and then grows with a rapidly increasing pace, until growth steadies and plateaus, and eventually waxes and wanes into decline, and finally fades into demise.

The way one leads a change initiative during its life cycle can be either **proactive, or reactive.** Whether you lead change initiatives proactively to catch the next new life cycle, or reactively to curb the decline of the current life cycle, depends a lot on your timing of new change initiatives. Where on the S-curve do you start to lead change initiatives? When you embark on new S-curves during the upward momentum phase of an existing S-curve, you are leading change **proactively**. You use the upward growth momentum of the current lifecycle to *proactively* initiate change initiatives that could spur other new S-curves. When you attempt change initiatives during the plateau or descending phases of an S-curve, you are **reacting** against the natural declining momentum of the life cycle. You are trying to play 'catch-up' and attempt to stem an inevitable downward momentum of declining growth.

Infancy and Growth

Drivers for growth are most intense in the beginning phases of a new initiative, entity, or business—the period after T = 0. You and your followers are pushing to exploit opportunities and overcome obstacles in the internal and external context to establish new initiative.

New initiatives with new life cycles as indicated by curves 1, 2, 3 and 4 in Figure 6.1 are all preceded by Pre-Life-Cycles. Figure 6.3 illustrates how the Pre-Life-Cycle precedes every new initiative. For example, at point A the infancy stage of initiative 2 starts, and at point F, the infancy stage of initiative 3 starts, and so on.

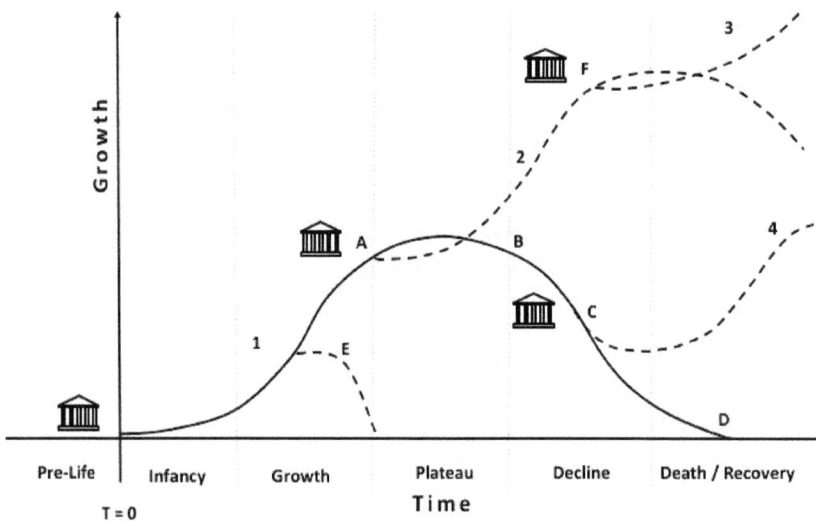

Figure 6.3. Continuous Evolution — Pre-Life-Cycles followed by Life Cycles

New initiatives (Curves 1, 2, 3 and 4 in Figure 6.3) typically display a butterfly-effect. Growth starts small and focused and then gradually spreads wider with more force and momentum. The leader's attention is spread wider and thinner and your entity's resources are becoming severely stretched—often beyond its viable capacity. When you do not follow restraint, a sudden path of demise, such as path E, can occur.

Apart from demands caused by thinly spread resources, many other internal drivers for change can also be at play, such as:

- Establishing essential support from key stakeholders
- Obtaining the correct intelligence to avoid false or overconfident assumptions about the viability of the new initiative
- Recruiting necessary people
- Developing capabilities and capacities
- Securing and allocating essential resources
- Overcoming resistance to accept the new initiative.

Often during the infancy and growth phases, resources available to the initiative may be significantly stretched. You should be able to adjust your behaviour and expectations to ensure your entity and your people are not pushed beyond reasonable limits and consequently jeopardise the viability of the initiative. Your objective is to keep the initiative on the growth path towards point A, and not let it slip prematurely down a curve like curve E.

Renewal

During the plateau and decline stages of an entity's lifecycle, the entity will be constantly pushed to revitalise its growth (from point A to B in figure 6.1). This pressure will intensify when it goes through a period of declining performance, when competitors are showing better performance, or when competitors threaten to capture your hard-earned market share. Point A is the optimal time to take proactive renewal initiatives.

Examples of proactive change initiatives to achieve renewal are:

- Improvements
- Innovations
- Turnarounds
- Recoveries
- Re-engineering.

Optimal decision points to embark on renewal initiatives are, for example, around points A and F in the illustration—just before a current life cycle progresses into its plateau phase. Round about those points your entity has the requisite amounts of resources, human energy and opportunities to get the current lifecycle onto another growth path before it plateaus or dies off. This seems obvious but it is difficult in practice. For example, how does a leader know when it is the right time for a change, when the entity seems to be performing at its best—usually right in the middle of its plateau phase—and there seems to be no good reasons for renewal?

Thus, to succeed in the long term, you need to inclusively anticipate and commence new initiatives ahead of time. Too often leaders wait too long—they reach point B on the entity's or product's lifecycle before they make renewal changes. By that time, you may lack the necessary resources for renewal or recovery, and often demise is the only inevitable outcome (curve D).

Internal drivers for renewal can occur at any stage of a lifecycle. There is no guarantee that the lifecycle of an entity, product, or service will follow the usual and familiar S-shape as depicted in Figure 6.3. Severe external change forces may threaten your entity. Drivers for change can be so strong that the lifecycle follows curve E into sudden demise.

Encouragingly though, forces for growth can be highly advantageous, so much so, that your entity may experience exponential growth—as many entities in the digital age have enjoyed. The growth trajectory may then skyrocket past point A and take a longer time before plateauing eventually sets in, making the prediction of when to start renewal more challenging.

Drivers for renewal often occur when the entity, or its offerings, no longer perform adequately in its markets. To take advantage of proactive renewal, you should:

- Launch a renewal strategy for the current lifecycle while it is still on the upward and growing success path—before, or at point A.

- Accumulate resources and build the entity's resilience from the reserves generated by the current growth lifecycle. This will enable you to initiate new life cycles with adequate capacity and capability resources.

- Pursue actionable intelligence, which is gathered through knowledge of trends, new ideas, innovations, product development, experimentation, and pilot tests, in parallel with current lifecycles. Continuously work on ideas for new lifecycles.

- When the timing is optimal, switchover from the current lifecycle—curve 1, to a new life cycle—curve 2 or 3. The switchover from the old lifecycle can occur gradually while you follow a well-planned exit strategy from curve 1. The exit strategy, if necessary, is performed at or before point B, to harvest maximum value from the old lifecycle.

Realign

When your entity has missed the most opportune points to initiate renewal initiatives, such as points A or F, you have entered realignment territory—which requires *reactive* change initiatives.

Drivers for realignment cause reactive behaviours since the entity did not anticipate external change drivers on time, and were caught unawares. Realignment initiatives are *reactive*, because they are designed to reposition an entity back onto its former growth trajectory.

Applying the correct change initiatives may prevent the decline from B to C, and might return the entity to a success trajectory (curves 2 or 3) again. Realignment interventions are generally more pervasive and drastic, depending on the severity of the change initiative. The number of barriers and sources of resistance are also much more than in the growth and plateau stages.

Firstly, because of inattentiveness and overconfidence, the entity might have drifted from its mutual purpose, or it did not follow its strategy, or it may have pursued non-viable opportunities. When your entity has veered off course for a while, you can determine where dis-alignment occurred and initiate the necessary initiatives to put it back on its course. You will have to engage reactive change initiatives to realign the vision, strategy and execution system.

Alternatively, in more desperate realignment situations, you may have to revise the entity's vision and strategy altogether. After you and your followers have realigned to a new direction, change initiatives such as re-structuring, re-organisation, re-engineering, or consolidation may be required to prevent the entity from falling rapidly down the S-curve—from C to D.

Another reason might be that your entity may have suffered a downturn in demand for its offerings, or it may have underperformed against stakeholder expectations. Key performance indicators may show disappointing results. Costs of execution may have risen too high, or key resources may have become constrained. All these are potential causes for decline in performance and a drive to realign.

Reactive initiatives that are customarily applied during plateau and decline phases are, for example, re-structuring, re-organisation, re-engineering, management moves, downsizing, and consolidation.

Survival

When a lifecycle has reached points C or D, it has moved into 'survival mode'. You will need drastic *reactive* change initiatives to rescue the entity from demise to recover it onto a new lifecycle. The drive for survival is mainly triggered by external forces for change we did not pay considered attention to, or did not anticipate. Generally, if your entity paid persistent attention to contextual changes, it would have detected strong signals of those impending forces long before a decline phase commenced.

Sadly though, survival modes often follow some leaders' conscious decisions to ignore warning signals and write them off as inconsequential.

"Success contains the seeds of its own destruction"

Andrew Grove, author of "Only the Paranoid Survive"

Some causes of rapid decline in the life cycles of entities, products and services are:

- Market collapse
- Threats of, or actual acquisitions and take-overs
- Economic disasters, e.g. the Global Financial Crisis
- Changes in legislation
- Sovereign and risk events
- Natural disasters.

During survival, you must take extra care not to weaken your entity's reserves of agility and resilience. When you lead your entity to be agile and resilient in its affairs, you would likely have the necessary defensive reserves and capacity to withstand unforeseen circumstances.

However, entities that do not follow a robust agile and resilient discipline, often cut too deep to become too lean and save costs, and consequently, struggle to survive during adverse times. Such defensive moves (to boost short term financial outlooks) are often the beginning of a downward spiral. By cutting into the entity's long-term resilience capacity, leaders may cut into its ability to survive and bounce back again. When another shock hits the entity, its ability to recover is severely jeopardised, and demise is inevitable.

Inappropriate cost cutting and 'leaning' is often done indiscriminately across the board. The optimal proactive approach to being lean and to build resilience, is by:

- Being lean from the outset—during the growth and plateau phases—when the life cycle generates surplus wealth resources, to build your entity's resilience reserves and capacity.
- Being lean on uncompetitive, low value-adding offerings and markets, which are unlikely to grow.
- Proactively divesting non-core offerings, or activities, which are not essential for growth or survival.

Survival initiatives are normally extensive and drastic and do not guarantee success.

Typical reactive survival initiatives are:

- Downsize and deep cost cutting, with lay-offs in parallel
- Restructure and down-size
- Sell the entity at a fire-sale value
- Merge with a white-knight rescuer
- Take-over by a black-knight acquirer

Once survival interventions have gone their course and the entity has been revived, albeit in another form, further change initiatives can be expected. Entities that have succeeded to survive round one, often experience years of painful subsequent changes, putting extra demands on employees' ability to cope with many change initiatives.

Change stability

Change stability is related to the consequences and outcomes caused by change initiatives. For example, when the result of change is smooth and predictable, the change is assumed to be stable. When the outcomes are erratic and volatile, the change is described as unstable. Change stability is also associated with the dynamic interconnectedness of systems and subsystems within entities. The more interconnected systems and subsystems are, the more one can expect that change would cause instability in some parts of systems, often unexpectedly.

Change and its resulting outcomes over time can be depicted as in Figure 6.4 below. The figures show a smooth transition from a steady state, State 1, to a new state, State 2.

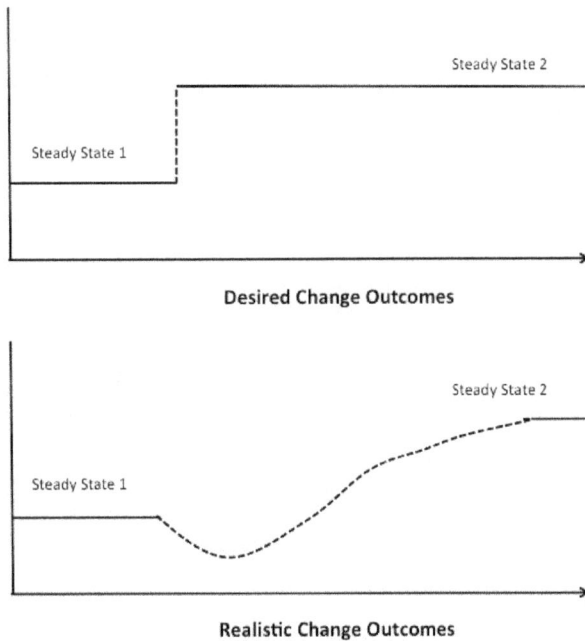

Desired Change Outcomes

Realistic Change Outcomes

Figure 6.4. Change from the Old to the New

When a change initiative is lead unsatisfactorily, or when its potential consequences are not clearly understood, its outcomes can cause instability in an entity, like the example shown in Figure 6.5.

Instability presents itself in many forms but the most common form of instability in human entities are what I call *run-away and whiplash instability*.

Run-away instability is when a change initiative causes an outcome that can escalate or spiral out of control. For example, when relationships are badly managed during major transformational changes, peoples' morale and engagement plummets. Or, when scope creep in a project is not managed well, the project can get into serious schedule and cost distress, and expenses will spiral out of control.

Whiplashing instability is illustrated in Figure 6.5. For example, this kind of unstable result may occur after a product design change is introduced into the market. Customer numbers and revenues whiplash up and down during repeated but ineffective corrective actions to regain customers' trust. When the harmful effects are not cancelled in time, the result can be total loss of market share.

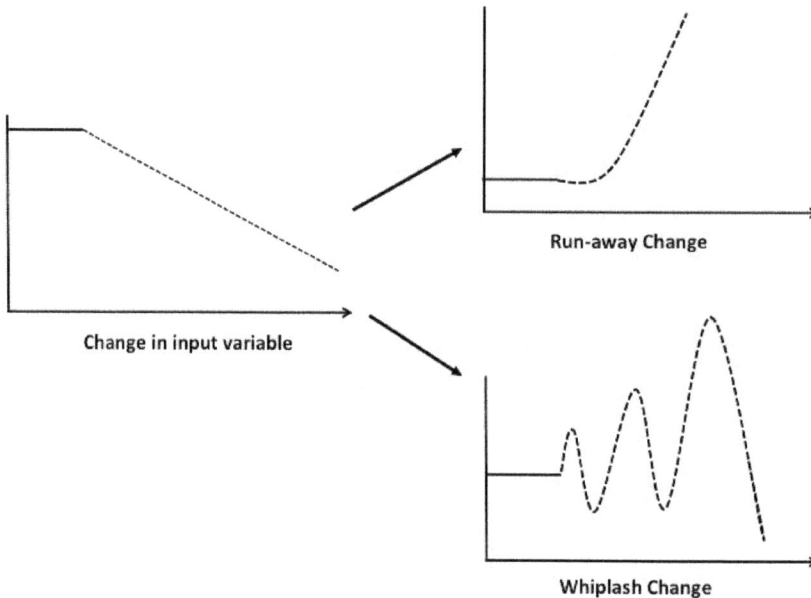

Run-away Change

Change in input variable

Whiplash Change

Figure 6.5. Change Instability

Interdependent complexity

Interdependent dynamic complexity as described by Senge is one of the main characteristics of change in entities that is highly visible, but not well understood[7]. Any entity, apart from perhaps small firms, is regarded as a complex system. How dynamic interdependent complexity works, can be explained by the four graphs in Figure 6.6.

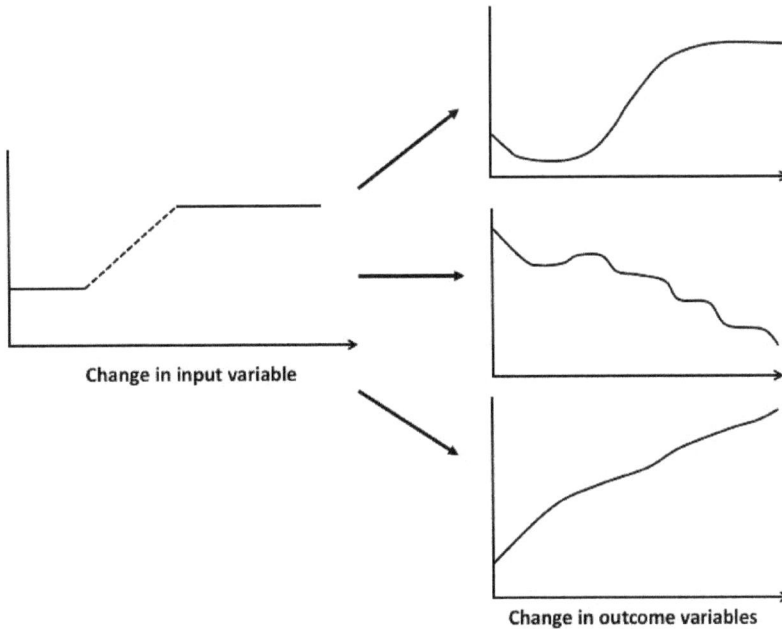

Change in input variable

Change in outcome variables

Figure 6.6. Interdependent Complexity

Interdependent complexity is associated with the interconnectedness of systems and subsystems. The more subsystems there are and the more linkages exist between subsystems, the higher the interdependency and dynamic complexity of the whole system. For example, let's say we make a change to an input variable, such as the quality of an input resource to reduce service costs. This is illustrated by the figure on the left-hand. The interdependent complexity characteristic of this change, causes 'unpredictable' changes to occur to other variables also. This is illustrated by the three figures on the right-hand of the figure. For example, because of the quality change in the input, the profit margin may rise markedly in the short term (as desired), but sales revenues and customer numbers start to drop in the longer term. In this example, the consequence of using lower quality inputs has worked its way through the system—customers are experiencing services with inferior reliability.

The entity's short-term gain produces a long-term problem with greater consequences.

Senge who first coined "Systems thinking", makes the point that we need to think of change in entities in a 'systems way'. We need to see the whole and the interconnecting parts of entities, and how they relate with the contextual environment. Senge, provides a framework or mental model to recognise such interrelationships—the dynamic patterns of change—rather than static snapshots of change. A mental model of systems thinking will prompt you to realise that changing the 'obvious thing' does not necessarily produce the obvious desired outcomes only. The change initiative may also cause other undesirable outcomes, that may show only months or years later than expected.

The essence of systems thinking is in considering the whole and the patterns of interrelationships, rather than thinking solely along linear cause-effect relationships. It acknowledges that change affects all interconnected processes that occur in entities, rather than regarding change as a once-off linear occurrence. Systems thinking enables you to understand how entities interrelate with the contextual environment.

The illustration in Figure 6.7 is a simple demonstration of how one may visualise an entity as a system of dynamic complex changes. In the illustration, the system has several interconnected sub-systems. The numbered subsystems are, for example, departments such as finance, engineering, purchasing, payroll, etc. In this example, a change is made to a variable at point A in the figure, with the objective to realise a desirable result in variable B, at the other end of the total system. Along the way, as the change at point A works through the entire system, a variety of other changes may also occur through interdependent subsystems. The little graphs above each connecting arrow, illustrate how the change that occurs at point A, could affect each of the other sub-systems. Some of the outcomes in subsystems may be desirable, while others may be unwanted. For example, a positive change at point A in the finance department, may lead to an unwanted whiplash effect in the production and marketing departments.

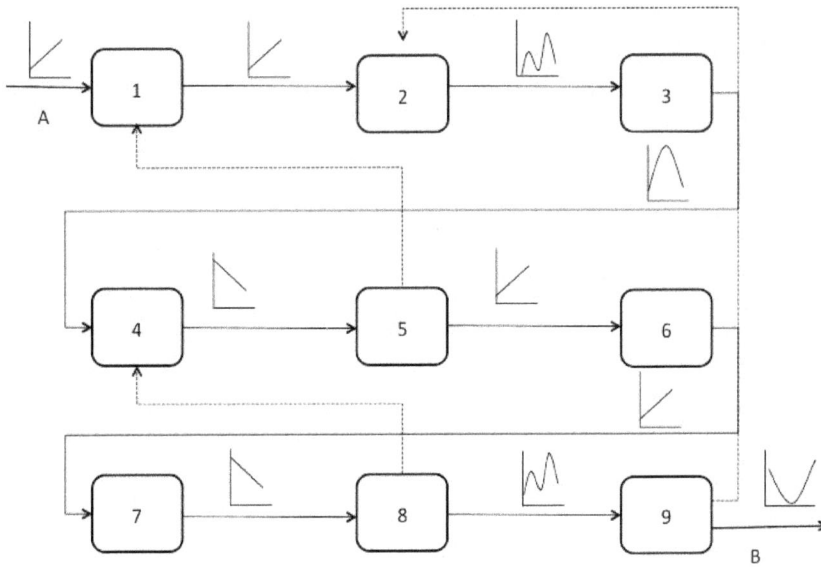

Figure 6.7. Dynamic Complex Systems

The characteristic of dynamic complexity illustrates the necessity to use performance measures and indicators throughout an entity and a proactive intelligence system that monitors the behaviours of subsystems too. This will enable your entity to quickly assess whether planned change initiatives cause desirable outcomes, and if not, why and where the unwanted consequences might occur.

Modes of Change

Change mode is a characteristic that is related to the intensity, complexity and quantity of change actions that are necessary to perform an initiative. Five easily distinguishable change modes occur commonly in entities. (See Figure 6.8)

- Continual improvements and development
- Incremental changes

- Step change or transitions
- Transformations
- Multiple, non-sequential, often non-related change
  initiatives—or any combination and number of the above.

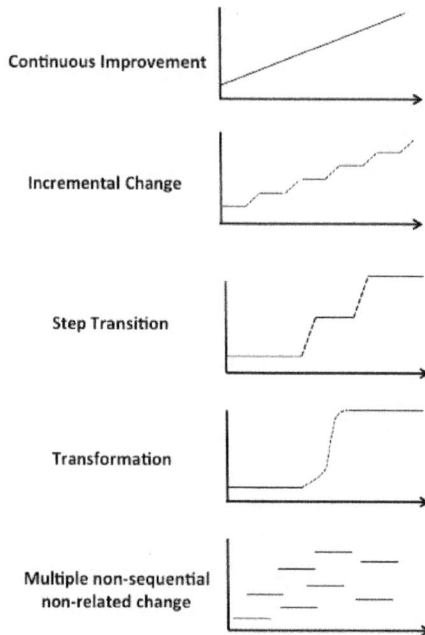

Continuous Improvement

Incremental Change

Step Transition

Transformation

Multiple non-sequential
non-related change

Figure 6.8. Change Modes

Continual improvement

Continual improvement and development is an entity's constant focus on actions to improve aspects or performance. Typical examples are: learning and acquiring new skills, training and improvement of products and services. Other subtler examples in this category are continual improvements in relationships, communication, conflict resolution, external relations, stakeholder relations, political savvy and improved intelligence.

Incremental change

Incremental changes are a series of small but deliberate frequent improvements in products, services, quality, processes, systems, customer relations and more. Innovative entities make incremental changes to their offerings on a routine basis. These are sometimes radical and disruptive and are pursued on a purposely-planned basis. Incremental change is characterised by small improvements, followed by short periods for problem solving, planning, piloting, experimenting, and testing, before the next improvement is implemented and the cycle repeated.

Step transitions

Step transitions and stepped growth can be either continual or intermittent transitions. Step transitions may vary from minor to major interventions. Growth or recovery advances through stepwise initiatives are often followed by periods of consolidation before another transition step is undertaken. Step transitions normally result in the substitution of what was, with something new or different, instead of simply adding continual improvements.

Proactive step transitions are based on S-curve or lifecycle renewals for growth, such as acquiring or organically developing new ventures, spinning-off non-core activities, revival of the lifecycle through innovations and process re-engineering exercises. Proactively identify the need for step transitions when you identify opportunities for growth or renewal ahead of time, that is, before the current S-curve runs out of steam, and before your competition gets ahead of you. Proactive step transitions require that you anticipate early warning signals. (Refer to Chapter 10: Anticipate stage in the Change Dimension)

Step transitions in proactive entities follow intentional patterns—are evident as continual successions of growth and performance transitions. Deliberate growth transitioning steps are reinforced by continual improvements and incremental change initiatives that smooth the way between initiatives.

Transformation

Transformational change initiatives are often highly reactionary change interventions aimed to realign entity, or to secure its survival. Transformation is characterised by drastic, widespread, and often highly disruptive change initiatives.

Often the extent of transformation is so large that it requires fundamental shifts in the leaders' and followers' behaviours and culture. Transformation might even require a revision of the entity's original purpose. In a sense, it means that a 'new entity' is created in entirety. The transformational changes required are often at the most fundamental level, such as the purpose, culture or vision. Some of the leaders and followers may therefore not see themselves belonging in the 'new entity'. This happens when the new entity does not represent their personal values or purpose anymore, or when the purpose of the new entity is radically changed.

Many entities do not survive extensive transformational initiatives. Transformational initiatives draw so much energy and resources from the entity, which may be already under stress, that the entity and its people eventually 'surrender'. In cases such as these, entities become ready targets for acquisition and take-over. Subsequently the new leaders would want to make further changes so that the entity would fit their purpose, culture, strategy, structure and leadership. So, the remainder of the original entity is yet again subject to further changes.

The need for transformational initiatives can be prevented if you consistently implement proactive continuous improvements, incremental changes, and step transitions to renew your entity's lifecycle—that is, when you keep your entity on the left-hand curve of its lifecycle. Change-oriented leadership, can protect your entity against the need for major reactive transformations later in its lifecycle and create change-fitness. When your entity is change-fit, it will perform well when a major transformation does indeed become unavoidable for reasons beyond your control.

Even the most farsighted entities can be caught unawares by external circumstances, and drastic measures such as divestments, downsizings, mergers, or take-overs may be necessary. Such large transformations are triggered by market or government collapses, or economic and natural disasters. Entities that have built robust reserves and capacities to render them agile and resilient, have survived the worst economic, market, political and natural disasters. It is your task to create a change-fit entity that would endure such circumstances.

Multiple non-sequential, non-related change initiatives

This mode describes a situation when any combination and any number of the above modes exist in an entity.

I haven't found any source that discusses the leadership of multiple, non-sequential, non-related change interventions as a change mode. Change management practitioners would preferably not discuss them—they are messy, complex, and they can cause immense instability. Multiple, non-sequential, non-related change initiatives are prevalent in many medium and large organisations. In the age of change it has become the norm rather than the exception.   The following is a real-life example of a string of major change interventions that occurred simultaneously in one entity. There were also many other smaller interventions running concurrently in this organisation. The initiatives were all at different stages of implementation.

- Vision and strategy revisions
- Organisational culture realignment
- Major restructuring at divisional level
- Process re-engineering in several divisions
- Major renovation of global HR and payroll systems
- Introduction of a new enterprise resource management system

(ERM) with accompanying changes to all IT platforms across the divisions.

However, the wisdom behind some of these simultaneous initiatives is questionable. Typically, the leadership team is not fully aware of all the change initiatives that were going on across their entity, and the communication and relationship patterns are insufficient to ensure that all interventions are coordinated and optimised. The result is without fail that employees develop change-fatigue, resources are under allocated and overstretched and the entity's resilience gets exhausted. Peoples' perplexity with change spreads due to the confusion of priorities.

Leaders who lack appropriate change-oriented behaviours will fall in many traps posed by multiple, non-sequential, non-related change initiatives. Only the most resilient and agile entities will be sufficiently change-fit to employ this mode of change interventions successfully and repeatedly. I have discussed the depressing success rates for single change initiatives in Chapter 1. Statistics on the success rate of multiple, non-sequential, non-related change interventions in entities are unavailable. This kind of intervention demands widespread focus on leading change. The only remedy is to create entities that are truly change-fit—as opposed to be change-ready for individual initiatives.

Uncertainty

Uncertainty is the change characteristic that describes the level or range of unpredictability inherent to, or caused by change. The range of uncertainty can stretch from change with almost no uncertainty, to the realm of wicked problems and chaos. The levels in uncertainty are:

- Little uncertainty
- Familiar uncertainty
- Definitive ranges of uncertainty
- Unknown uncertainty
- Chaos and wicked problems.

Change with little uncertainty

Change initiatives characterised by well-known activities that have clear objectives, scope, and schedules belong in this uncertainty level. The outcomes are clear, well defined, and predictable—there are minor unknowns, if any, to deal with. Usually the change initiative is well planned with minor risk exposure and follows contemporary project or change management techniques to deal with variations.

Typical examples of change with little uncertainty (high predictability) are:

- Minor innovations to existing product ranges
- Continuous improvements to service delivery
- Small turnkey projects based on proven technologies.

Change with familiar uncertainty

When the level of uncertainty moves up to the level of familiar, foreseen uncertainty, with predictable levels, the need for risk management becomes evident. You deal with known uncertainties, but they are predictable and quantifiable. Contingency plans and risk mitigation alternatives will ensure that the change initiative stays on track toward its intended outcome. Any familiar event that can increase uncertainty is swiftly dealt with through risk mitigation management.

Examples of initiatives with familiar uncertainties may include:

- Incremental and continual improvements
- Process re-engineering
- Quality improvements
- Product or service differentiation
- Technology development by extension from known platforms.

Change within a range of uncertainty

On the next level of uncertainty, change initiatives may be realised through a variety of different change options. Each of these change options may be clearly identifiable, but individual variables of each alternative may not be entirely quantifiable. The outcomes of each of the options are thus not easily predictable either. Change-oriented leaders will develop different scenarios that qualify and quantify how each distinct option could unfold. Useful methods are for example, scenario analyses, diverse mental models, strategic options, risk management methods and decision trees.

Examples of change initiatives with variables that stretch over ranges of uncertainty are:

- Deciding on new ventures through acquisitions, mergers or organic growth.
- Acquisition of natural resource exploration rights based on inadequate geological information
- Innovation of new products or services
- Extensions to major facilities
- Expanding technology development by branching off into new unrelated applications
- Strategy formulation
- Recovery of an entity after a major failure
- New business models
- Culture change initiatives
- Re-organisations and restructuring.

Change with unknown uncertainty

For change initiatives with unknown uncertainty the variables and outcomes of the initiative are either unknown or unforeseen. Many factors may cause a change initiative to be classified as having unknown and unforeseen uncertainty. The unforeseen uncertainty may in fact be an 'overlooked' issue. For example:

- Overzealous leaders exclusively drive change initiatives and any suggestions of outcomes that are not in agreement with their views are summarily dismissed. The change initiative is doggedly implemented. Due diligence, risk analysis and contingency planning are either done haphazardly or ignored.
- System interdependencies may be ignored
- Risk management is absent or done scantily
- Insufficient actionable intelligence of the market, industry, competitor or technology trends have been gathered
- Intelligence may have been available, but ignored or disregarded as inconsequential
- The change initiative is under-resourced.

Not all events can be anticipated, for example, an unexpected withdrawal of key stakeholders in a change initiative, a hostile take-over, or the sudden departure of the leader of the change initiative. Typical examples of initiatives that pose unknown uncertainties are:

- Organisational culture change initiatives
- Entrepreneurial growth ventures
- Turnarounds
- Mergers and acquisitions
- Take-overs and divestitures.

Chaotic and wicked change

Chaos may befall some change initiatives. Initiatives that seem to have credible objectives, solid foundations and clear cases often become stuck, unravel or fail to deliver their intended outcomes.

Often change initiatives fall victim to several uncertainties posed by change drivers, change variables and intended outcomes. The variables seem to be of a VUCA nature—that is they are *Volatile, Unpredictable, Uncertain and Ambiguous*[8].

Chaos before, during and after change projects can erupt when entities become entangled with change events that are called 'Wicked change problems'. Rittel and Melvin coined the term "wicked problems" to describe certain types of complex change situations[9]. They describe the nature of wicked problems as messy, circular and aggressive, in contrast with relatively easy problems of regular change initiatives.

Wicked problems have incomplete, contradictory and constantly changing requirements. Their solutions are difficult to identify because of complex interdependencies across many seemingly unrelated systems. While you are busy solving a wicked change problem, the solution of one of its parts may reveal or create another, sometimes even more complex problem[10].

Entities create uncertainty and complexity when they overdo the change mode called 'Multiple, non-sequential, non-related change', as discussed before. Only the most change-fit entities can manage this mode of change successfully for a prolonged period. However, there are no statistical results available to prove how successful entities are with Multiple, non-sequential, non-related change' over extended periods.

Examples of change initiatives in this category of 'Chaotic and wicked' uncertainty are:

- Initiatives that are poorly lead and executed.
- 'Multiple, non-sequential non-related change' mode, executed year after year, without a breather.
- Natural disasters.
- National and international economic disasters.
- Political turmoil and war.

Resistance and barriers to change

"We have met the enemy; and He is Us"

Pogo – by Walt Kelly

Resistance to change is a behaviour response of hesitancy, reluctance or confrontation. Resistance occurs as a response to perceived driving forces of change, or a response to oppose change initiatives. It is any behaviour that attempts to preserve a current state or status quo. Resistance to change is a characteristic that has many facets, forms and sources. It may cause delays, extra costs, added complexity and failed change initiatives.

Barriers to change include inanimate sources of resistance, existing within systems, structures and processes of an entity. Barriers are often the consequences of past actions that may pose restrictions to forward momentum and change initiatives. Barriers to change can for example be an entity's culture, clunky business systems, leaders' pet projects, sunk costs, and conformist habits.

Resistance and barriers to change may not always be undesirable or destructive as such. Barriers and resistance can have both positive and negative influences on change initiatives. How you lead change will determine whether and how you constructively use barriers and resistance to the advantage of the entity. When you lead with a change-oriented mindset, and follow the principles in the Change Dimension, you will be able to moderate and use resistance and barriers positively.

Sources of resistance and barriers

Resistance to change is often ascribed to a broad spectrum of negative employee attitudes and disruptive behaviours. Resistance is always perceived from the vantage point of the person or entity that wants to initiate change. Resistance is however a double-edged sword and highly subjective. The proposer of change, and the entity that must undergo the change, will demonstrate different forms of resistance.

Leaders predominantly play the role of proposers of change. Leaders tend to view change initiatives in terms of moving towards a new or better state. You therefore tend to have a bias towards positive aspects and the advantages of the changes you propose. Those who will undergo the changes, tend to view change initiatives from the perspective of losses and risks they might experience because of the proposed changes. These opposing vantage points pose the challenge you must effectively overcome and turn around into constructive acceptance and ownership. Resistance to change is a normal human response because almost all change involves effort, losses and gains. When the losses are perceived as more than the gains, it is normal for people to cling to the familiar, the safe and comfortable. Change may be beneficial, but it also poses risks, losses and discomfort for people involved—especially when they do not understand the full consequences.

Change-oriented leaders will anticipate the most likely resistance behaviours when they propose changes and would regard that as normal. Resistance can serve as a very useful resource. Use resistance to resolve constraints and achieve better solutions with better consequences. The people who resist change are often the best sources of essential knowledge and information. Including them and addressing their concerns, well ahead of the introduction of change, may sidestep serious risks on time. Through inclusion people who may oppose certain changes may propose viable suggestions and identify better opportunities that would otherwise be ignored.

In entities, there are four main sources of resistance and barriers to change:

- Leadership
- Organisational
- Groups
- Individuals.

Leadership resistance

Ironically, the first place to look for resistance and barriers to change initiatives is at the very top of the entity. Carefully watch leadership behaviours in an entity and you will identify some of the strongest resistance behaviours. Identifying resistance behaviours posed by leaders will enable you to identify some behaviours you may have exhibited yourself. If you are honest with yourself then the list below will assist you to discover some of your own resistance behaviours. The next step is to do something about that.

Typical resistance behaviours leaders may show are:

- Constrained visioning
- Driving too many of initiatives
- Procrastination
- Urgency and focus of attention
- Risk aversion.

▽ Constrained visioning

Leaders often become so convinced that their vision of the future is the right and only one. This is especially true when a leader has created his entity through sheer entrepreneurial exertion and his entity has been coursing well along its life cycle and reached a prime position on the plateau of the S-curve. That is the probably one of most perilous times in the life of an entity, when everything seems to be working perfectly—the entity is at its most vulnerable. You have reached the pinnacle of success!

When success is so dazzling, leaders may often ignore critical external and internal drivers for change. They can become so deeply committed to advance their vision that they lose sight of an emerging context. The greater the personal ego, the more likely it is to enforce exclusive self-determined change initiatives. A big ego can present itself as an overconfidence in his ability to make accurate assessments of the environmental contexts and opportunities. When an overruling ego takes over, the leader would push his vision even harder, and ultimately become constrained by his own vision. Any sound advice or opinions that may appear like an opposition to his vision—even from trustworthy sources—is instantly regarded as 'bad resistance to change'. Ironically, in such a case the leader impersonates the greatest source of resistance.

▽ Driving too many initiatives

Overzealous leaders, driven to transform and drive the entity to better performance, often fall in the trap of creating too many change initiatives. Proliferation of initiatives causes reduced resilience, dilution of efforts, wasted resources, confusion about priorities, implementation delays and stunted performance.

Employees develop change-fatigue and resources are spread too thin. A perplexity with change initiatives spreads due to confused priorities. Employees will start to resist further change initiatives. Over time a barrier of demoralised people is erected and the resulting exhaustion and disengagement can take years to undo.

▽ Procrastination

Leadership procrastination and indecision are major barriers to change and have caused the collapse of many entities. Leaders may often vacillate to make timely decisions about important change initiatives. Procrastination is especially obvious when lifecycles are on their late growth and plateau phases. The success entities enjoy during these phases tend to blindfold leaders to make proactive decisions about the optimal allocation of scarce resources.

Long before you could be absolutely certain about the right vision for a change initiative, there will be subtle change signals and change drivers, observable in the external context. Perceptive change-oriented leaders are not only able to pick up these signals—they are impatient to exploit them as innovators and entrepreneurs. The danger of delaying until an opportunity or the context is perfect, is that your entity may miss the initiative altogether. When you must play catch-up, you may find that you have lost the game.

▽ Urgency and focus

Your leadership behaviours may create impressions that certain change initiatives are not important—creating barriers and resistance during their implementation. When you don't provide strategic direction and governance about the importance of necessary change initiatives, your focus and attention on other seemingly more pressing operational concerns will erect barriers against change initiatives.

A leader's excessive focus on short-term results (for example, the quarterly reporting cycle to shareholders) can create a barrier that diverts your attention away from important change initiatives. Short-term operational issues, opportunities and results can become your pre-occupation when you leave long-term change drivers unattended. My discussion on the topics of 'The Spell of Execution' and 'Speed' in Chapter 13 on the Execution Dimension, sheds more light on this behaviour.

▽ Risk aversion

Leaders' unjustified risk aversion poses major barriers to change. The level of risk aversion can be linked to a leader's fear of failure and tendencies of perfectionism. Some leaders prefer alternative courses of action that requires the least amount of changes to an existing state. Other leaders may delay or avoid decisions to change, to reduce the possibility of failure. They are considerably more concerned about potential losses than about potential gains. As a result, risk averse leaders will play it safe by not pursuing seemingly riskier change initiatives.

Carmeli and Sheaffer have found that organisational decline and consequential downsizing of entities are related to leaders' degree of risk aversion[11]. Leaders with risk-averse decision-making styles may be beneficial to the smooth operational functioning of entities, but this style may eventually result in stagnation and decline of entities. Leaders with higher risk aversion tendencies tend to be more cautious, and even apprehensive to implement change initiatives. Leaders that demonstrate less risk-averse tendencies are more willing to pursue change initiatives, and they have more innovative decision-making styles.

Organisational barriers

Several organisational barriers may cause obstacles to effective change initiatives. The main causes are:

- Resource constraints
- Inflexible structures
- Bureaucracy
- Culture
- Sunk resources, vested interests and pet projects
- Agreements with counterparties and stakeholders.

▽ Resource constraints

When your entity is unable to acquire the necessary resources such as finance, technology and skills, it obstructs implementation of change initiatives. Often the inability to change is linked to the location within which an entity operates. For example, your entity may face limited natural resources, such as water, land or energy sources. It may not be able to substantially increase its market share due to the size or growth rate of the local population, or it may be unable to increase its production or service capacity due to a lack of physical space.

▽ Inflexible structures

Rigid execution structures and systems are dominant in slow moving entities with inflexible leaders. Inflexible entity structures cause barriers to change and produce slow adaptation to new contextual trends. Agile entities have flexible structures with fewer layers, which gives them the advantage to easily change courses of action during adversarial events, and to pursue positive opportunities proactively.

▽ Bureaucracy

Entities develop necessary coordinating mechanisms over time, comprising of rules, regulations, processes and procedures. It is essential to continually develop and refresh coordination mechanisms as your entity grows from, for example, an entrepreneurial stage into a large multinational business. These coordinating mechanisms are required to maintain balances between unbridled organic growth and operational control of the entity.

Coordinating mechanisms usually start from very informal systems during the entity's infancy stage, to more formal systems in the advanced growth and maturity stages of the entity. Coordinating mechanisms can often become excessively bureaucratic during an organisation's mature stages—throttling the growth momentum in a critical stage. Leaders must make concerted efforts to curb the growth of unnecessary bureaucracy. The rules, procedures and systems may become so complex and rigid that they stifle change initiatives and innovation. When left unnoticed, slow but intensifying creep of bureaucracy creates major barriers to change—it can cause excessive delays, and finally causes an entity's premature demise.

▽ Culture

Established entity cultures that demonstrate values and behaviours that do not continually align with contextual drivers for change, can pose substantial barriers. An entity culture that is suspicious of ideas from the outside will regard suggestions to change with caution and often with hostility, especially when a suggested change may pose a threat to the successful and comfortable stability of the entity. These are so-called rigid cultures. Rigid cultures are the cause of many failures of change initiatives.

Often the rules of conduct, the values and the principles that created the entity's original path to success, are so deeply entrenched into the leadership and culture of the entity. When the entity and its leaders perceive that it is performing at the crest of the lifecycle, they have no sense of urgency to make changes for renewal or growth. Proposals for change at such a point will be met with resistance, even hostility. Such proposals will be regarded as an implicit criticism (and even explicit criticism) of the leader's successful vision, which may have been extraordinary up to this point on the lifecycle.

▽ Sunk resources, vested interests and pet projects

Sunk resources are the time, financial, human, and other resources that have been spent on an initiative such as a new project, system or change. Once an entity has gained momentum and embarked on a route to develop a project, a venture, or change initiative, the people involved are resistant to change direction or even discontinue the effort. Sunk resources is often used as a valid reason to justify the continuation of a shaky initiative and clear evidence that it would be unsuccessful is understated or disregarded. The inclination is to continue investing more resources to prove that the project will ('must') work, instead of stopping it. Behind the push to continue are many vested interests. The proponents of the initiative think they have a lot to lose when the initiative is stopped, even if it is the right thing to do for the entity.

A close relative to sunk resources is so-called pet projects. Pet projects are usually initiatives that are pushed by one or more of the leaders. It can often be directly connected to a leader's exclusive vision. Any sound suggestions to change or discontinue a project are met with stern resistance, especially when the leadership style is egotistic, arrogant and exclusive. Employees will continue to endorse pet projects for fear of loss of favour with the leader and potential damage to their careers.

▽ Agreements with counter parties and stakeholders

A tangible barrier to change is the legal and contractual commitments made with counter parties and stakeholders. These commitments may range from simple commercial agreements with suppliers, technology licences, government and public authorities, to extensive agreements with labour unions and key stakeholders. The agreements, laws and regulations will pose legal barriers and obligations on your entity. Such barriers will constrain the range of possible change initiatives you could pursue. However, change-oriented leadership will enable you to achieve the optimum change within the legal boundaries of such barriers.

Group resistance

Formal and informal groups often develop a host of idiosyncratic behaviours. Groups act and think in certain ways because of their shared values, norms, beliefs and assumptions. Groups establish values and norms, which reward certain types of behaviour and punish others. These values, norms, beliefs, and assumptions form the culture of groups. Groups develop strong opinions of what information they regard as relevant and irrelevant to their work. Group members are often more loyal to their subculture and they will jointly and individually defend the group, its culture and behaviours against unwanted influences.

Idiosyncratic behaviours can become so strong that individual groups form sub-cultures within the larger entity's culture. Depending on the type of change initiative, and how much it is perceived to threaten a group's, values, norms, beliefs, and assumptions, a group may react in ways that obstructs change. The herd instinct of groups will push compliance to the behaviours and norms of the core group. The members of the group make decisions based on the group's mental frameworks that may be detached from the realities of contextual change drivers and what the entity's stakeholders may value. Once subcultures become so strong, groups can form power coalitions within the entity. The stronger their power and influence becomes, the more the group would attempt to accumulate power, defend its power base and resist changes that are not in their best interest.

When you advocate changes, you may not only propose that certain groups do things differently, you may also intentionally or unintentionally require some groups to change their behaviours and subcultures. The change proposals may also threaten the power bases of these groups and threaten to break existing coalitions. When that is the case, such change proposals could be perceived as sources of conflict and initiatives will be met with resistance.

A related subculture barrier to change is commonly referred to as 'silos'. Silos are predominant in functional structures and professional bureaucracies. People in silos may often value their functional or professional interests higher than the values of the entire entity. They do not wish to share information with others. Their group becomes a source of power and status. When silos become the behavioural norm, they are formed to safeguard the interests of functions or organisational units, causing a breakdown of communication, collaboration and the free flow of intelligence. Because communication between units is difficult across silo walls, change initiatives across the entity encounter internal barriers. Individual units or groups might not resist change initiatives, but because the silos exist, communication barriers make the implementation of change initiatives difficult. Silos have the additional effect of reinforcing subgroup cultures. Because collaboration with the rest of the entity is restrained, the opportunity for inclusion into the entity culture is also restrained.

Individual resistance

To lead change initiatives effectively, it is important that you understand the reasons individuals pose certain kinds of resistance. Leaders should be concerned about individual resistance when peoples' behaviours are disruptive and persistently negative, or when individuals become dysfunctional when performing their normal duties. Individual resistance to change is a normal human response and is caused by a variety of factors. Resistance can occur when an individual's own assessment of the outcomes of proposed change initiatives differs from the outcomes you or the entity may envisage.

Frequent causes of individual resistance to change are:

- Poor relationships and exclusion
- Misaligned purpose and values
- Confusion
- Perception of uncertainty
- Perceived gains and losses
- Individual circumstances

▽ Poor relationships and exclusion

Poor relationships are a major cause of resistance to change and are often the most obvious reason. Any change proposal will be met with some measure of resistance, if respectful, trustworthy and inclusive relationships between the proposer of change and the receivers of change are not yet established. Resistance may be unnoticeable at first, but it can show through behaviours such as blunt refusal, procrastination, political game playing, and superficial compliance with change proposals.

Perceptive leaders with advanced emotional intelligence skills, can observe behaviours that occur due to a lack of proper relationships. Engaging the necessary leadership behaviours to rebuild and strengthen trust and respectful relationships may take longer than anticipated. It means that change initiatives may have to be delayed until trustworthy relationships are in place. When this essential behavioural process—establishing trustworthy relationships—is disregarded and change initiatives are enforced, the initiatives may work in the short term. But, the lack of trust and inclusion will haunt the entity in the long term in the form of disengagement and performance losses.

Often resistance to change is due to a lack of inclusion in change initiatives. People feel excluded from change processes when only a select few people are involved, and when the same 'privileged' people are always involved in initiatives—under the guise of efficiency and speed. When you lead change with restricted inclusion, the process can create an atmosphere of exclusivity, suspicion and low trust. By building trustworthy relationships first, you will have favourable influence on your followers, in the short- and long-term. Your people will recognise that proposed change initiatives reflect the mutual purpose of the entity, and they will not resist them.

▽ Misaligned purpose and values

Individual resistance surfaces when there is misalignment between an individual's and the entity's purposes and values. When a case for change implies that the entity wants to adopt a different purpose, values, or vision, individuals will analyse how the new change aligns with their own purposes and values. When there are misalignments, you can expect significant resistance from some people—some may even leave the entity depending on the degree of misalignment.

▽ Confusion

Misunderstandings between leaders and followers often result from insufficient dialogue and lack of inclusion. The assumption that your people understand and would accept change initiatives is often wrong.
  On the other hand, followers' assumption that their leaders will appreciate how they feel and what concerns them about initiatives are often also inaccurate or incorrect. Confusion occurs when people do not understand the full implications of change initiatives. They could lack an understanding of the case for change, the benefits, rewards, risks and consequences. Unless misconceptions are uncovered, discussed and clarified, through dialogue, confusion will cause resistance.

▽ Perceptions of uncertainty

People will resist change initiatives when their perceptions of uncertainties involved differ from their leader's perception.

People may not appreciate the drivers for change in the same way as their leaders, especially when they have not been included in the Pre-Life-Cycle of initiatives. You may have gained actionable intelligence and formed a perception of the uncertainty of a range of factors. The remainder of the people in the entity will form their own views on how uncertain the variables, the success factors and the desired outcomes would be. If knowledge about how we came to our conclusions about planned change initiatives is not developed and shared inclusively, resistance to change will surface. In such a situation, an announcement of a change initiative would cause a shock or a surprise to your people. Unlike you or your leadership team, they were not privy to the actionable intelligence behind the change initiative. People might perceive the need for the change initiative as unnecessary and their risk of loss as substantial. They will perceive the consequences to be negative and therefore resist the change.

▽ Perceived personal gains and losses

People will resist change when they perceive that a change initiative might cause them to lose considerably more than they would gain. They fear the loss of something with personal value. A personal loss can be:

- Loss of relationships
- Loss of rewards and status
- Loss of personal power and authority
- Loss of competencies and fear of failure
- Loss of personal identity
- Personal circumstances

Loss of relationships: Peoples' sense of security is often based on their network of reliable relationships. Changes in an entity's structure, systems and processes may require people to form new relationships and disengage existing ones. Often organisational changes involve a transfer to new roles and physical relocation of individuals. Consequently, the undoing of relationships (that may have been longstanding) will cause resistance, especially when the people involved have developed familiar work connections and friendships. People will feel emotionally hurt and can even experience grief at the loss or change of longstanding work relationships.

Loss of rewards and status: When a proposed change initiative may cause a change in someone's title, reward or status, it will create reasons for substantial resistance, especially when the change means a reduction in value of these personal status symbols. Examples of real and perceived losses of status and rewards are, for example, a change of office location, change to a lesser title, reduction in perks, reduction in bonuses, and reduction in number of reporting staff.

Loss of personal power: When people focus on what they stand to lose personally instead of focusing on the gains or losses of the entity, such 'selfish' resistance is often caused by their sense of loss of personal power. Resistance from individuals will be strongest when the proposed changes involve a shift in their power base and level of authority. Corresponding with shifts in an individual's power and authority, there are often changes in relationships, status, prestige, reputation, coalitions, influence, and authority over resources. Leaders and individuals who may potentially lose power and authority due to a change initiative will resist such a proposal.

Loss of competencies and the fear of failure: For some people their range of skills and competencies form their identity and sense of personal pride. Any perceived threat to their skills and competencies is a perceived threat to their identify and self-esteem, and will be met with resistance. People fear the loss of skills and competencies caused by change for two reasons. They may fear that the change will cause their hard-earned skills and competencies to become redundant. They may also fear that they will be unable to acquire necessary new skills and competencies to cope with the requirements of the initiative.

Loss of personal identity: Where a job has become the 'identity' of a person, work related changes may be perceived as a loss of personal identity, especially during times when people are made redundant. They feel they must find a new identity. Job losses are severe intrusions in peoples' lives and often have traumatic psychological consequences. Changes that threaten the personal identity will be met with strong resistance, even hostile retaliation.

Personal circumstances: Personal circumstances of individuals and leaders alike, can pose substantial barriers to change. Circumstances that can cause resistance are both internal and external. For example, when any of the following concerns exist, you can expect resistance to new change initiatives:

- Lack of adequate training, skills or competencies to cope with planned changes
- Lack of resources to deal with current workloads
- Lack of resources to achieve new change initiatives *in addition to* current workloads
- People may have to change their commuting schedules and means of transport due to location changes of facilities, offices and personnel
- Consequences to their family; for example, additional health care or child care of family members may become necessary when work situations change.

Intensity of change initiatives

All the different characteristics of change I discussed above—stability, interdependent complexity, uncertainty and resistance become more intense—more pronounced, stronger and have broader impacts, as life cycles of entities, product and services, mature through their stages.

I define five categories of *'Change Intensity'* as illustrated in the *Change Continuum*, Figure 6.9. In each category is a list of typical change initiatives that could occur in that category. The intensity of change initiatives increases as one moves from the left to the right on the *Change Continuum*, across the five categories.

The change intensity categories coincide approximately with the stages of life cycles namely: *Infancy, Growth, Plateau, Decline, Death or Recovery* (refer to Figure 6.1).

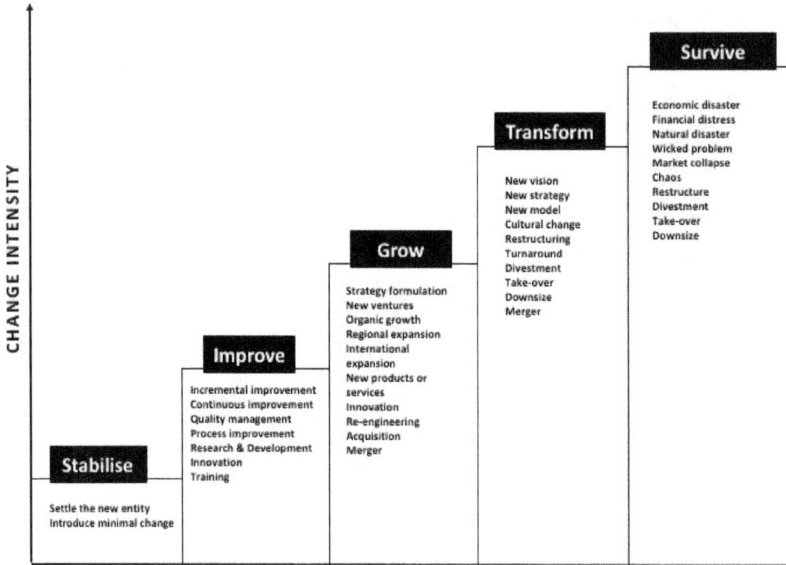

Figure 6.9. Change Continuum

Change intensity categories are:

- **Stabilise.** In the Stabilise category only a few change initiatives may be introduced. The entity first endeavours to stabilise the viability of the initiative, before it is ready for the next stage in its lifecycle.
- **Improve.** The Improve intensity category includes those initiatives that are intended to improve current performance. Initiatives in this category are for example, incremental improvements, continual improvements, process improvements, innovations and training.
- **Grow.** Grow includes the kinds of initiatives that are intended to take advantage of the intrinsic growth potential in a life cycle, and move it onto an accelerated growth path. Initiatives in this category are for example, strategy revisits, new

ventures, organic growth initiatives, re-engineering, acquisitions, mergers and expansions.

- **Transform.** Transform includes those initiatives that are intended to transform the life cycle to return declining performance to former levels of performance. Often the intent here is to improve performance, albeit sometimes too late. Initiatives in this category are, for example, a change of vision, a new strategy, a new business model, downsizing, restructuring and divesting.

- **Survive.** Survive includes those initiatives that can secure the survival of an entity after distressing change events. Changes that occur in this category are, for example, financial distress, market collapse and political upheavals. Drastic initiatives are necessary to revive the lifecycle, if feasible. Initiatives in this category are, for example, widespread downsizing, comprehensive restructuring and divestiture.

Figure 6.9 illustrates how all the different change characteristics intensify as one applies change initiatives that range from the 'Stabilise' category to the 'Survive' category. Change intensity is therefore dependent on the life cycle stage, and the type of initiative that is applied. The horizontal axis shows the five intensity categories—ranging from least intense, 'Stabilise', on the left, to most intense, 'Survive', on the right. In the figure, each category contains some familiar change initiatives or events that are typical for that category. The vertical axis shows how the intensity of change initiatives increases as we move across the categories from left to right on the horizontal scale. Furthermore, as change intensity increases, the need for your leadership direction, time, and attention, to ensure the success of change initiatives, increases concurrently.

The illustration of increasing intensity of change initiatives, emphasises the point that unremitting leadership attention to lead change initiatives is vital. It is a fundamental leadership task—it cannot be demoted to lower levels in the entity. In the early stages of life cycles, initiatives are vulnerable and highly susceptible to external changes in the contextual environment. Change drivers demand constant surveillance to ensure the viability of new initiatives. In later stages, when life cycles become mature, initiatives could become self-sustaining. However, due to the natural law of diminishing growth potential as a life cycle approaches the plateau of the S-curve, initiatives become vulnerable again. That occurs at a time when it is normally least expected.

Summary

You will lead change successfully when you and your followers understand the character of change, and take mutual ownership of change initiatives. Your leadership role is to inspire and equip your followers to understand the character of change and accept change as a natural phenomenon that can be used to mutual benefit.

People show numerous psychological, emotional and behavioural reactions to change initiatives. All change, regardless whether it is positive or negative, has an impact on people, teams and the entities involved. The psychological, emotional and behavioural impacts of change on people vary with its intensity. On the one end of the spectrum they may show pure joy, while on the other end of the spectrum, absolute despair. For leaders, their greatest concern is the loss of performance, engagement and productivity, and the waste of resources that occurs when their people show negative psychological reactions to change.

Many psychological and behavioural response models show that, from the individual's perspective, change is perceived as something external—something that is being done to them or something that happened to them. Individuals may perceive that they have little or no part in the creation of the changes that affect them. The psychological response models are applied successfully in their various disciplines. However, when we apply them to lead change in entities, they demonstrate significant shortcomings.

Similarly, the designs of many change management models have related shortcomings. Many of them, though with advanced methodologies, follow the traditional 'unfreeze, change, and refreeze' paradigm. The majority of change management models are designed to commence with change processes from the moment change initiatives are introduced, and proceed stage-wise to support their implementation. Traditional change management models do not start at the beginning of the Pre-Life-Cycle, which is the best commencement point.

In the age of continual change, you will have successful change initiatives, when you create a state of dynamic equilibrium between your entity and its context. Your entity should reach a continuous state of fitness for change—it must always be ready for the next initiative. We cannot unfreeze, change and refreeze entities anymore, and allow them to transition into periods of comfortable static equilibrium until the next initiative arrives.

The adoption of a leadership mindset that would generate a dynamic equilibrium in an entity starts with the introduction of Pre-Life-Cycle principles. The Pre-Life-Cycle is the subject of the Change Dimension, which is discussed in the next chapter. The Change Dimension integrates necessary behaviours leaders need to proactively deal with both positive and negative initiatives in the age of change. Initiatives can be incremental and continual improvements, new innovations, growth, acquisitions, mergers, as well as less positive initiatives, such as restructures and recoveries from disasters.

Notes

1. *The Global Risks 2014 report. The World Economic Forum. 9th Ed.*

2. *The Global Risks 2014 report. The World Economic Forum. 9th Ed.*

3. James Canton, J. 2006, *Extreme Future - The top ten trends that will reshape the world,* Penguin, New York.

4. See sources like the World Economic Forum, The Population Institute, The European

Union Institute of Security Studies, *The Trend Compendium 2030, by R Berger.*, and books such as the Extreme Future by James Canton.

5. Harbour, J. L. 2009, *The Performance Paradox.* CRC Press, New York.

6. Harbour, J. L. 2009, *The Performance Paradox.* CRC Press, New York.

7. Senge, P. M. 2004, *The Fifth Discipline – The Art and Practice of the Learning Organization*, Currency Doubleday, New York.

8. The concept called 'VUCA', emerged in the late 1990's from the military fraternity. They have noticed that more and more initiatives fall victim to several uncertainties posed by drivers and variables of change. The variables of change seem to become increasingly Volatile, Uncertain, Complex and Ambiguous. This phenomenon of change gave birth to a now widely used acronym called VUCA

9. Rittel, H. & Webber. M. 1973, 'Dilemmas in a General Theory of Planning', *Policy Sciences*, vol. 4, pp. 155–169.

10. Conklin, J., Basadur, M. & Van Patter, G.K. 2007. 'Rethinking Wicked Problems: Unpacking Paradigms, Bridging Universes', *Next Design Leadership Institute Journal*, vol. 10. pp. 1-30.

11. Carmeli, A. & Sheaffer, Z. 2009, 'How Leadership Characteristics Affect Organizational Decline and Downsizing', *Journal of Business Ethics*, vol. 86, no. 3, pp. 363-378

7. The Effects of Change on People

People don't dislike change, they dislike unpleasant surprises

Introduction

All changes, regardless whether positive or negative, have an impact on people, teams and entire entities. The psychological, emotional and behavioural impact of change on people varies with the intensity of change initiatives. In Chapter 6, I have discussed how the level of intensity can vary across a continuum from little intensity, such as during an initiative's early stabilisation stage, to severe levels of intensity such as during attempts to secure an entity's survival.

People show numerous psychological, emotional and behavioural reactions to change initiatives. On the one end of the spectrum they may show pure joy, while on the other end of the spectrum, absolute despair. For leaders, the greatest concern is the loss of performance, engagement, productivity, and the waste of resources that occurs when their people show negative psychological reactions to change. Is it possible to lead successful change initiatives without the consequential losses associated with peoples' natural psychological reactions to change?

By following the principles of the natural Pre-Life-Cycle, which I have built into the Change Dimension, you will reduce many of those losses. The Pre-Life-Cycle will help you to understand how peoples' psychological reactions occur—before, during and after change initiatives. You will be in a powerful position to lead change more successfully. An entity full of change-fit people who are agile, resilient, and engaged throughout change initiatives, will be on a route to success.

In the age of change, successful leaders and entities will be those that are continuously able to face new drivers for change in their contexts. They will anticipate, recognise, and quickly respond to short- and long-term signals, and will seize opportunities sooner than their competitors.

To lead entities successfully in the age of change, you need a thorough understanding of the Pre-Life-Cycle. It will be a significant new leadership skill. A second and equally important leadership skill in the age of change, is the ability to enable your people to pass smoothly through psychological transitions—to become change-fit.

Several key contributing factors determine how your people will react to and moderate their psychological and behavioural reactions to change initiatives. Three important factors are:

- The leader's success record of leading change initiatives with proper sensitivity to their peoples' psychological reactions to change.
- The entity's success record of implementing change initiatives and how peoples' behavioural reactions were managed during change initiatives.
- The level of readiness and level of fitness your entity has for specific initiatives, and to face contexts of continual change.

Psychological, emotional and behavioural transitions

Change management literature focuses mainly on the negative features of people's psychological, emotional and behavioural transition cycles during and after change. But, people may also show significant positive emotions and behaviours during transition cycles. 'Culture shock' transition models are a good example of the latter. Inclusive change-oriented behaviours create, enhance and build upon positive psychological responses to make change initiatives easier, more enjoyable and beneficial for the people and the entity. When you apply inclusive behaviours your change initiatives will become more successful and your entity will improve its performance.

There is no argument that changes such as lay-offs, downsizing, business collapse and natural disasters are negative and would trigger negative psychological responses. Change-fit entities—however—that are skilled in the principles of the Pre-Life-Cycle, would be pre-prepared for, and may even avoid, negative changes.

Sadly, in my experience, often people that are involved in 'positive changes' such as process improvement, innovation, new ventures, continual improvement, culture changes, growth expansions, mergers and acquisitions, also experience negative psychological responses. Such change initiatives should have been perceived and experienced as positive, or at least neutral. So where is the missing link?

In change management literature, you will find numerous well-known human psychological response models that describe how individuals pass through several psychological, emotional and behavioural states when they experience significant changes in their lives or work. I encourage you to study some of the models referenced in Table 7.1.

Understanding how humans experience psychological transitions *after* the introduction of change initiatives is an essential leadership competency. A good understanding of your own psychological and emotional reactions to change will also help you to understand and cope with your own transitions.

Table 7.1 Psychological and Emotional responses to Change – Theories and Models

Five Stages of Grief, On Death and Dying, Kübler-Ross (1969)

Transitions Model, Expanded Kübler-Ross model, Adams, et al (1976)

Emotional Cycle of Change, Kelley & Conner (1979)

Family Therapy model, Family Therapy and Beyond, Satir (1991)

Managing Transitions, Making the most of Change, William Bridges (1991)

Transition Cycle, Human responses to change, Williams (1999)

Four Stages in Response to Change, Harvard Business School, Luecke (2003)[1]

Culture Shock, Obeng (1960), Sargent (1970), Berry (1980), Marx (1999)

Transtheoretical model of behaviour change, Behaviour in health and education, Prochaska, et al (2008)

The human psychological and behavioural response models listed in Table 7.1 were founded in a variety of disciplines, for example:

- Family therapy (Satir[2]),
- Bereavement counselling and counselling the terminally ill (Kübler-Ross[3], Adams et al[4])
- Work and life transitions (Williams[5], Bridges[6], Kelly & Conner[7])
- Anthropology[8] (Culture shock models, i.e. Obeng, Sargent, Marx)
- Health and education behavioural change (Prochaska)[9]

The scientists and practitioners who founded these models make distinctions between the concepts of '*change*' *and* '*transition*'. *Change* in their vocabulary is a consequence of change drivers—it is a new state, such as a new corporate culture, new strategy, new product line, new role, new manager or a new team. In these models, from the individual's perspective, *change* is perceived as something external—something that has been done to the individual or something that happened to him. The individual had no (or very little) part in the creation of the change. *Transition is* the internal psychological process an individual undergoes to adapt to his new state of *change;* psychologically, emotionally and mentally.

Although these models have been specifically developed for application in other disciplines, such as family therapy, bereavement, health and addictive habit therapy, they are extensively applied to manage change in all kinds of entities. Human psychological and behavioural response models are mainly used *after* change initiatives have been introduced, and occasionally during change implementation. They offer several coping and remedial measures for each stage of transition.

When change events are perceived to be 'negative surprises', the people involved will consequently experience negative psychological and behavioural transitions. They need assistance to cope and transition from their previous psychological state to a new state of equilibrium. The psychological and behavioural response models are predominantly used for these circumstances—situations when people experience negative and often traumatic transitions. Very often these transitions are a consequence of planned or unplanned reactive change initiatives that occurred unexpectedly, such as restructuring, retrenchment or demotions.

Most psychological and behavioural response models have three or four main transition stages. Refer to Table 7.2 for four examples. Some of the models have more detailed intermediate stages within each main stage.

I divide the behaviour response models into two categories:

- Models that begin with negative change.
- Models that begin with positive change.

Table 7.2 Psychological and behavioural response model – Transition Stages			
Models that begin with negative changes		*Models that begin with positive changes*	
Adams et al	**Bridges**	**Williams**	**Obeng**
Shock	Ending	Positive events	Honeymoon
Transition	Neutral Zone	Transition	Culture Shock
Adaptation	New Beginnings	Adaptation	Recovery
			Adjustment

Models beginning with negative change

For example, the models of Satir, Kübler-Ross, Williams, and Adams, have three stages such as shock, transition and adaptation, in the case of Adam's model. They start with an undesirable surprise, usually something perceived as negative, or an unexpected ending of a current state. Transitions that start negatively begin with unexpected 'shocks' (Kübler-Ross), unpleasant surprises or foreign elements (Satir), uninformed optimism (Conner), major losses, betrayal, loss of trust, or damaged relationships. These events can have an impact on the individuals, their teams and consequently their entities. The models of Kübler-Ross, Satir, and Adams are examples of this category.

Models beginning with positive change

Psychology and behavioural response models that start with positive changes, such as the culture shock models, are significantly different.

They commence with a 'positive surprise' in a person's life and have four stages (Obeng, Marx)[10]:

- An initial 'honeymoon' phase
- Onset of 'culture shock'
- Reality checks and recovery from the shock
- Adjustment and adaptation, or accommodation to the new culture.

Transitions that commence positively begin with events such as new business ideas, innovations, new corporate cultures, new strategies, entrepreneurial ventures, new job opportunities, promotions, etc. Models that start positively, commence with what is commonly referred to as the 'honeymoon' phase. The models of Marx and Obeng describe psychological and emotional transitions that commence with positive changes.

Figure 7.1 illustrates how positive and negative transition cycles would look normally. The top curve illustrates negative transitions, while the bottom curve illustrates positive transitions.

The horizontal axes in Figure 7.1 show the time it would take an individual or group to transition from the moment a change initiative is introduced, to the point where they have fully transitioned into new states. The time to complete transitions differs from individual to individual and is dependent on the intensity of the change event in a person's life.

The vertical axes in Figure 7.1 illustrate how psychological, emotional, and behavioural characteristics of individuals or groups, can oscillate during transitions. Such oscillations cause fluctuations in peoples' performance and productivity. The amplitude of the oscillations also differs from individual to individual and depends on the intensity of the change event, the amount of pre-warning, and the level of support individuals get before and during transitions.

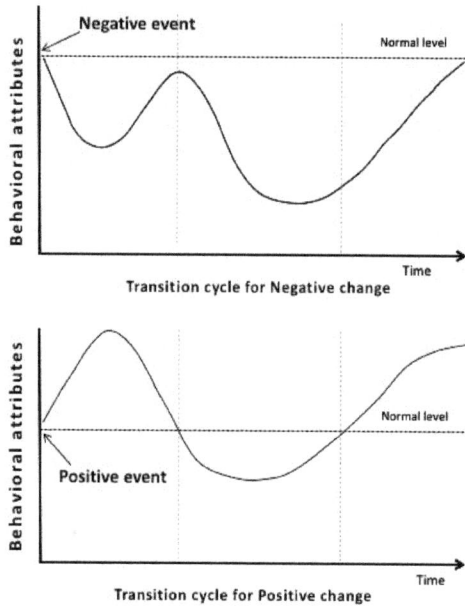

Figure 7.1. Psychological Response Curves for Positive and Negative Change Events

Psychological, emotional, and behavioural characteristics that are particularly relevant to individuals, their performance, and consequently the performance of the entity, correlate to factors such as:

- Engagement
- Productivity
- Energy levels
- Efficiency
- Confidence
- Competency
- Perceived well-being
- Morale
- Self-esteem

The curves in Figure 7.1 show how such personal and group behavioural characteristics oscillate over time as people transition from their previous states into new states. When change initiatives in entities are perceived to be significantly negative, transitions usually take at least nine to twelve months, and often much longer. For example, individual role changes that need substantial adjustments of self-perception, is an example of a significant negative change.

Change transitions are experienced differently by different groups of people involved in change. For example, the initiators of change (normally the leaders) are generally highly exited and positive about the changes they endorse. They do not experience the same negative transition cycles that the intended adopters or unintended recipients of these change initiatives would. Change initiators generally experience positive transition cycles like the bottom curve in Figure 7.1. When we do not involve intended adopters and unintended recipients of change initiatives during the development of initiatives, the introduction of change initiatives could be perceived as 'unpleasant surprises' or 'distress'. In such cases, the transition cycles of intended adopters and unintended recipients follow negative patterns as illustrated in the top curve of Figure 7.1.

Shortcomings of the psychological response models

The psychological response models are applied successfully in their various disciplines. However, when we apply them to lead change in entities, they show significant shortcomings, most notably:

- Before any change initiative is introduced or implemented, there is a period during which an initiative is anticipated, studied, incubated, launched and implemented. This period before a change is introduced represents the 'Pre-Life-Cycle' (see Chapter 6). None of the psychological response models incorporate this crucial period, that is, before change happens. In fact, quite correctly these models were never intended to include any stages *before* change happens.

- The psychological response models are normally applied from, or after the moment a change event happened, when it is a 'surprise' to the recipient—either positive or negative. The models are designed to assist people to cope with transitions *after* the event. There are no *before* stages—because the change event that occurred has been anticipated. Treatment to cope with transition starts at, or after the crucial moment of change happened, and continues until the patient recovers to a former equilibrium state, or a potentially better state. Often these models are applied long after a change event happened, such as when an entity finally realises that their people are in serious need of assistance to effectively complete the necessary transitions.

- Because we have relied so long on these models that have an approach of 'treatment *after* the change event', we have become accustomed to an unchallenged assumption that change is something that happens 'to' us, by something or someone outside our sphere of influence. We have unknowingly accepted that we are generally excluded from the Pre-Life-Cycle.

Leaders' unrealised expectations

When leaders introduce changes in old-fashioned ways they expect that their exclusive and well-conceived initiatives will improve performance, productivity or other variables, soon after their initiatives have been announced and implemented.

However, what often occurs instead is a fall in performance, productivity, engagement, trust, etc. People that were not included in the Pre-Life-Cycle, before the initiative went live, experience a sense of shock or unpleasant surprise, with predictable negative psychological response patterns. A significant gap in expectations develops. This gap is usually ascribed to 'resistance to change' and a 'lack of buy-in'.

Figure 7.2 is an illustration of the gap between expectations—the actual performance of individuals, groups or the entity—and the performance expectation of the leader.

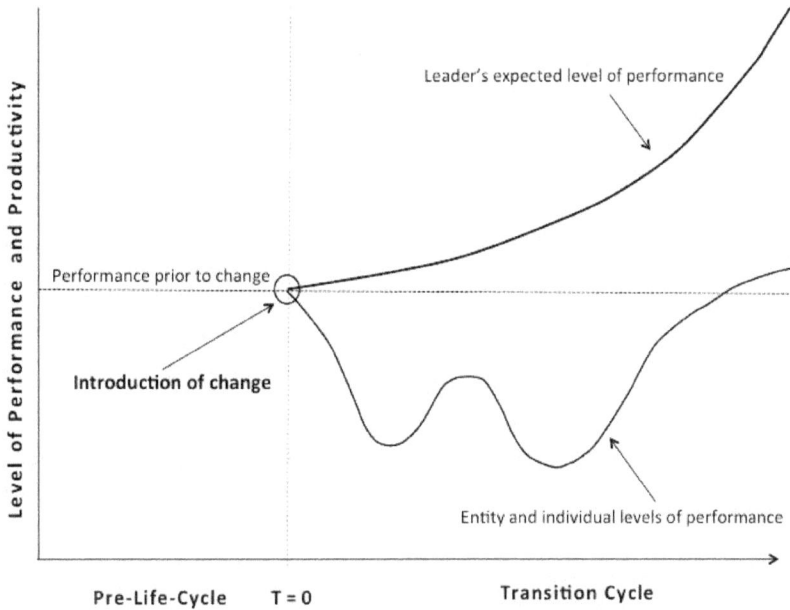

Figure 7.2. Gap between Expected and Actual Performance

In an attempt to overcome this gap in expectations, change management models (such as those listed in Table 7.3) are employed to sell the initiative, so that the entity buys-in to the initiative. The psychological response models, discussed before, are often used as aids in change management models to manage peoples' negative responses to the introduction of change initiatives. Refer to Table 7.3 for examples of some well-known models. Change consultants apply psychological transition models to assist entities and their people to cope with individual and group transition processes.

Table 7.3 Examples of Change Process Models[11]
Lewin Change Management Model Lewin (1952)[12]
Nadler & Tushman Congruence model Nadler (1977)[13]
Organizational Transitions Model Beckhart & Harris (1987)[14]
Schein's expanded Lewin Model Schein (1992)[15]
Kotter 8-Step Change Model Kotter (1996)[16]
Nine-Phase Change Process Model Anderson & Anderson (2010) [17]
Harvard 7-Step Change Process Model Luecke (2003)[18]
Booz & Co 8-Step Change Management Model Aguirre, et al (2007)[19]

Unfortunately, the same shortcomings of the psychological response models discussed before, have spilled over into the designs of many change management models. The same implicit principle of starting therapy, counselling, or coaching, on, or after a change initiative is introduced, is built into change management models. Change management models are designed to commence with a change process from the moment change initiatives are introduced, and continue stage-wise to support the implementation of initiatives. Change process models do not commence from the beginning of the Pre-Life-Cycle.

The ignorance about the effect on peoples' psychological transitions after the introduction and during change initiatives is a major contributor to the poor success rate of change initiatives. I discussed the failure rate of change initiatives in Chapter 1. Old school leaders' typical knee-jerk reaction to the expectations gap in Figure 7.2, and delayed performance improvement, is to put additional pressure on the entity to deliver the change initiative on the expected performance level, and within shortened timeframes. Such leadership behaviour can show positive short-term results, but it normally has the opposite effect, resulting in loss of trust and engagement, delayed outcomes and poor performance in the long run. The disappointment that follows unrealised and delayed performance is a direct outcome of the fact that these leaders do not allow for the necessary psychological transitions to occur in their people, teams and entities.

Change-oriented leaders, on the other hand, will include their people in the Pre-Life-Cycle of initiatives, from inception, and work mutually toward successful change initiatives.

Continuous dynamic equilibrium

In the early 1950's, Lewin[20] developed the renowned force-field model for change. He demonstrated how the tensions between the driving forces for change on the one hand, and psychological responses on the other, could explain why people may show resistance against change. Figure 7.3 illustrates Lewin's force field model.

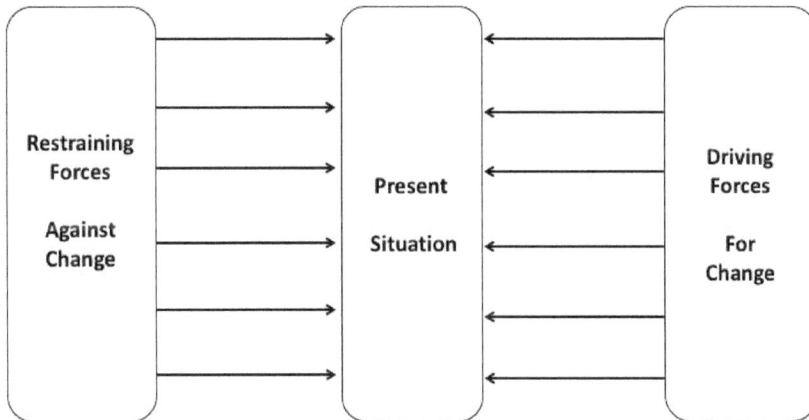

Restraining Forces

Against Change

Present

Situation

Driving Forces

For Change

Figure 7.3. Lewin's Force Field of Change

Lewin's force-field model is based on the idea that changes in entities are caused by driving forces (internal and external), on the right-hand side of the force field. On the left-hand side of the force-field are opposing, restraining forces (resistance and barriers). The magnitude, direction, and number of factors that encourage change (right-hand), or discourage change (left-hand), work to push the change initiative one way or the other. Lewin's model suggests that opposing forces will work against each other, moving the point of equilibrium either to the left or the right until a new state of equilibrium is reached.

During the leadership era in the 1950s, when there were only occasional organisational changes, Lewin concluded that for change to happen, there are three basic steps in the process of overcoming tensions between driving forces for change and resistance to change.

Lewin's three steps for change are:

"Unfreeze — Change — Refreeze"

In Lewin's change process model, stability and equilibrium in the entity occurs when the driving and restraining forces return to a new balance or new static equilibrium. A basic premise of his model is that an entity will always endeavour to recover its equilibrium after a change has successfully occurred. The new equilibrium is that new state an entity is comfortable with, after a change initiative has been implemented.

The principle of the Lewin three-step model is one that suggests a stepwise linear process. Since the early Lewin model, the same mindset has prevailed for many decades in the design of almost every change process model available today. Table 7.3 provides some examples. The number of steps and the detail in each step have increased in sophistication but the essence of the models is still the same as the Lewin's three-step process.

Like psychological response models, we find the same implicit and unchallenged notion that change is outside the sphere of influence of the people in the entity, and that they may be excluded from the Pre-Life-Cycle. Contemporary change process models normally commence after change initiatives are announced and follow stage-wise processes to support change implementation. Some more advanced change management models start at pre-planning stages of initiatives, but none starts at the beginning of the Pre-Life-Cycle.

Change management models are designed to deliver large-scale transformation initiatives, with project management precision and thoroughness—swiftly and with minimal potential resistance. At least that is the intension. The design and application of change management models are not well suited to foster cultures that favour change agility and resilience, or to develop change-oriented leadership behaviours. Most of the well-known change management models were designed during leadership eras when change initiatives were planned in an exclusive fashion, commonly in a top-down leadership style. Change management models deliver good results when change initiatives are well planned and the people involved are psychologically aligned to the cause and the purpose of the initiative.

The new dynamic model for the age of change

People don't dislike change, they dislike unpleasant surprises

Any change initiative begins long before its introduction—from the point when it is barely a weak signal or a vague idea and advancing through its natural Pre-Life-Cycle. To lead change inclusively you must integrate the natural Pre-Life-Cycle into your usual leadership behaviour and into the mindset of your entity. This principle was introduced in Chapter 6 and forms the framework for the Change Dimension, as discussed in the following chapters.

In the age of change, change is a continually dynamic process. Linear process models that regard change as discrete, predictable and static events, will not serve entities any longer. We are leading in a world where the drivers for change and the restraining forces against change are continually in flux.

In the age of change, we cannot unfreeze, change, and refreeze the entity, and it cannot transition into a period of comfortable static equilibrium. It must be in a continuous state of 'bubbling'—ready and fit for the next initiative. In the age of continuous change, you will only be successful if you lead your entity unto an ascending dynamic equilibrium within its context of continually changing forces and restraints. This continuous dynamic pattern of change is illustrated in Figure 7.4.

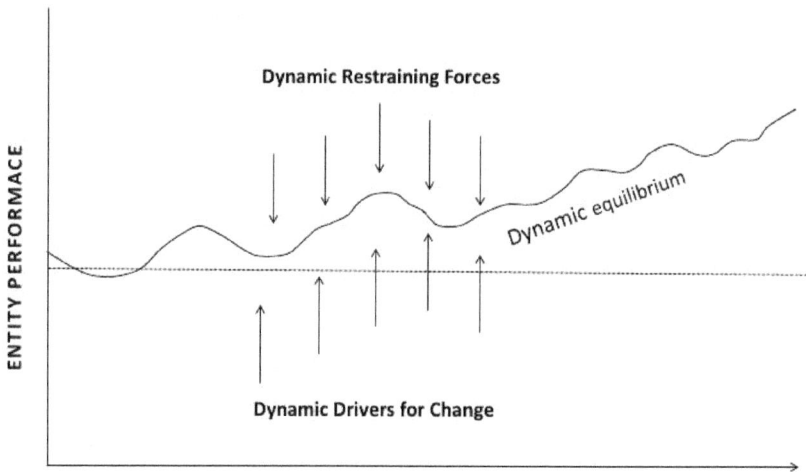

Figure 7.4. Continuous Dynamic Equilibrium

Instead of considering change as something that we—especially the leaders—can exclusively discover and plan, we must realise that change is an ongoing inclusive process. We aim change towards achieving the mutual purposes of our entity. We adopt a dynamic systems perspective and we appreciate how the interdependent parts of our entity and the external context affect each other. We lead change as something that occurs continually, by adopting change-oriented behaviours. We include our people in the Pre-Life-Cycle so that our entity can adapt proactively to expected and unexpected changing contexts.

Consequently, the performance gap that is obvious in Figure 7.2, will narrow significantly when we lead change inclusively and apply the Pre-Life-Cycle to change initiatives. Everyone will be on the same page, every step of the change initiative. The moment change initiatives are announced, there will be fewer unpleasant surprises and unexpected shocks. My assertion is that even when you have to occasionally lead negative change initiatives, the resulting psychological impacts and transitions people may suffer will be moderated. The normal psychological and emotional peaks and valleys, as illustrated in Figure 7.1, will be smoother, and the time it would take to make the individual transitions will be shorter. The entity's expected performance levels will be more sensible and transition periods will be shorter, adding substantial value to the change initiative and the entity.

How to create a leadership mindset that incorporates the Pre-Life-Cycle is the subject of the Change Dimension which is discussed next. The Change Dimension integrates the necessary behaviours you need to proactively deal with positive and negative initiatives in the age of change, such as incremental and continual improvements, innovations, growth, acquisitions, mergers, restructuring and recovery from disasters.

Summary

People show numerous psychological, emotional and behavioural reactions to change initiatives. All change, regardless whether it is positive or negative, has an impact on people, teams and the entities involved. The psychological, emotional and behavioural impacts of change on people vary with its intensity. On the one end of the spectrum they may show pure joy, while on the other end of the spectrum, absolute despair. For leaders, their greatest concern is the loss of performance, engagement and productivity, and the waste of resources that occurs when their people show negative psychological reactions to change.

Many psychological and behavioural response models show that, from the individual's perspective, change is perceived as something external—something that is being done to them or something that happened to them. Individuals may perceive that they have little or no part in the creation of the changes that affect them. The psychological response models are applied successfully in their various disciplines. However, when we apply them to lead change in entities, they demonstrate significant shortcomings.

Similarly, the designs of many change management models have related shortcomings. Many of them, though with advanced methodologies, follow the traditional 'unfreeze, change, and refreeze' paradigm. The majority of change management models are designed to commence with change processes from the moment change initiatives are introduced, and proceed stage-wise to support their implementation. Traditional change management models do not start at the beginning of the Pre-Life-Cycle, which is the best commencement point.

In the age of continual change, you will have successful change initiatives, when you create a state of dynamic equilibrium between your entity and its context. Your entity should reach a continuous state of fitness for change—it must always be ready for the next initiative. We cannot unfreeze, change and refreeze entities anymore, and allow them to transition into periods of comfortable static equilibrium until the next initiative arrives.

The adoption of a leadership mindset that would generate a dynamic equilibrium in an entity starts with the introduction of Pre-Life-Cycle principles. The Pre-Life-Cycle is the subject of the Change Dimension, which is discussed in the next chapter. The Change Dimension integrates necessary behaviours leaders need to proactively deal with both positive and negative initiatives in the age of change. Initiatives can be incremental and continual improvements, new innovations, growth, acquisitions, mergers, as well as less positive initiatives, such as restructures and recoveries from disasters.

Notes

1. For a comprehensive list and descriptions of change models refer to Holman, P & Devane, T. 1999, *The Change Handbook*, Berrett-Koehler, San Francisco

2. Satir, V., Banmen. J., Gerber. J, & Gomori. M. 1991, *The Satir Model: Family Therapy and Beyond*, Science and Behavior Books.

3. Kübler-Ross, E (1969) On Death and Dying, Macmillan, New York

4. Adams, J., Hayes, J. & Hopson, B. 1976, *Transitions: Understanding and managing personal change*, Martin Robertson, London.

5. Williams, D. 1999, 'Human Responses to Change', *Futures*, vol. 31, pp. 609 – 616.

6. Bridges, W., & Bridges, S. 2009, *Managing Transitions*, DeCapo Press, Philadelphia.

7. Kelley, D. & Conner, D. 1979, 'The Emotional Cycle of Change', in *The Annual Handbook for Group Facilitators*, eds. J. Jones, J. & J. Pfeiffer, University Associates, San Diego.

8. See Sargent, C. 1970, *Psychological Aspects of Environmental Adjustment*, Unpublished manuscript. See Marx, E. 1999, *Breaking Through Culture Shock*. Nicholas Brealey Publishing London. See Obeng, K. 1960, 'Culture Shock: Adjustment to new cultural environments', *Practical Anthropology*, vol. 7, pp. 177 – 82. See Berry, J. W., "Acculturation as Varieties of Adaptation," in Padilla, A. (ed.), Acculturation: Theory, Model, and Some New Findings (Washington, D.C.: AAAS, 1980).

9. Prochaska, J.O., Redding, C. A. & Evers, K.E. 2008, 'The Transtheoretical Model and Stages of Change', in *Health Behavior and Health Education*. 4th ed., eds. K. Glanz, B.K. Rimer, & K. Viswanath, Jossey-Bass, San Francisco.

10. Marx, E. 1999, *Breaking Through Culture Shock*. Nicholas Brealey Publishing London. See Obeng, K. 1960, 'Culture Shock: Adjustment to new cultural environments', *Practical Anthropology*, vol. 7, pp. 177 – 82.

11. For a comprehensive list and descriptions of change models refer to Holman, P & Devane, T. 1999, *The Change Handbook*, Berrett-Koehler, San Francisco.

12. Lewin, K. 1952, *Field Theory in Social Science*, Harper and Row, New York.

13. Nadler, D.A. & Tushman, M.L. 1977, 'A diagnostic model for organizational behaviour', in *Perspectives on behaviour in organisations*, eds. J. R. Hackman, E. E. Lawler & L. W. Porter, McGraw-Hill, New York.

14. Beckhard, R. F. & Harris, R. T. 1987, *Organizational Transitions: Managing complex change*, Addison-Wesley, Reading, Massachusetts.

15. Schein, E (1992) Organizational Culture and Leadership, 2nd edn, Jossey-Bass, San Francisco, CA .

16. Kotter, J. P. 1996, *Leading Change*, Harvard Business School Press, Boston.

17. Anderson, D. & Anderson, L. A., 2010, *Beyond Change Management, 2nd edn*, Pfeifer, San Francisco.

18. Luecke, R. 2003, *Managing Change and Transition.* Harvard Business School Press, Boston.

19. Aguirre, D., Finn, L. & Harsak, A. 2007, Ready Willing and Engaged, Booz & Co, Chicago.

20. Lewin, K. 1952, *Field Theory in Social Science*, Harper and Row, New York.

8. **The Change Dimension - Stage 1**

ENABLE

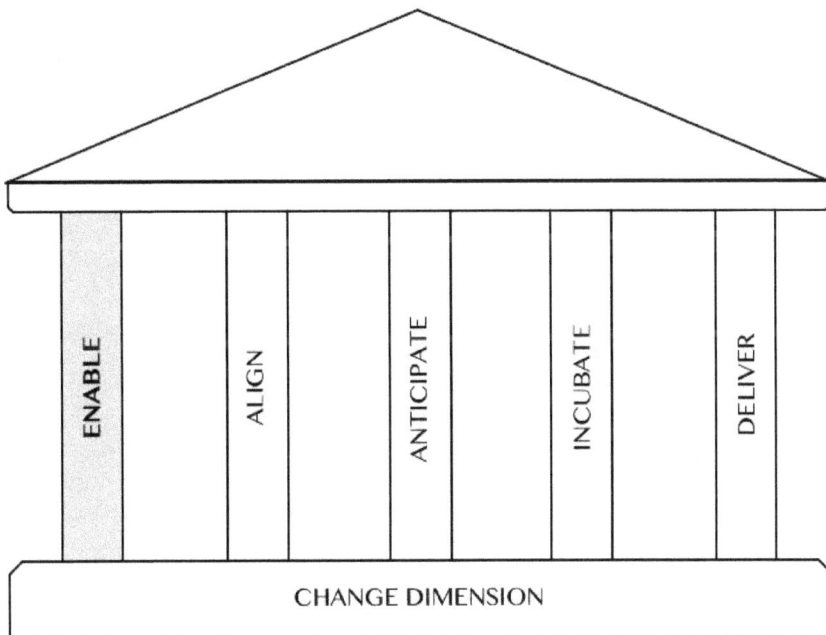

Enable is the first of the Change Dimension's five stages. It represents the change-enabling behaviours you need to cultivate in your entity.

Change-enabling behaviours equip your entity to meet any change and uncertain circumstances with confidence and positive resolve.

By mastering the principles in this chapter, you will personally demonstrate change-enabling behaviours and continually develop a culture that is conducive to change. I grouped the change-enabling behaviours into three sets (Figure 8.1), notably:

Change-oriented culture

Change the culture and sub-cultures in your entity so that your people become change-fit, and your entity become agile and resilient to face continual change. Create a culture that fosters creativity and innovation; that shows an appropriate tolerance to risks.

Inclusion

Lead inclusively, by consciously and actively engaging people in change initiatives through all stages of the Change Dimension. Inclusion assists people to have less anxiety with psychological and emotional transitions. They will show higher levels of engagement and feel aligned to the entity's mutual purpose.

New mental models

Change your own mental models and those of your people and develop new thinking habits. Your entity can then accurately perceive and timeously exploit change drivers in diverse and advantageous ways.

Create a change-oriented culture

The actions and behaviours leaders exhibit and endorse set powerful examples. Your behaviours create and develop a specific culture in your entity. If you want to enable a change-oriented culture, there are several behaviours you need to consistently develop.

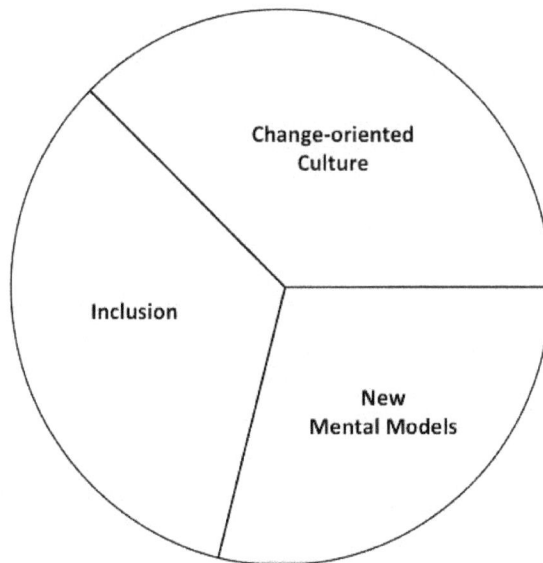

Figure 8.1. Enabling Behaviours for the Change-fit Entity

In the age of change, it is critical that leaders foster cultures that are open to change, experimentation, innovation, and growth. Without change-oriented cultures entities will slide down their S-curves into ultimate demise, sooner rather than later. That is, if competition did not get the better of them long before the downward slide began.

The creation of a change-oriented culture is something that is carefully developed and it must be sustained over time. It does not happen spontaneously. Entities often fall into a slumber land of comfort and change-resistance after successful change initiatives, or during a long successful ride up the S-curve.

The prevailing culture in an entity is often the major source of resistance to change. The leaders in such entities preserve engrained, change-opposing cultures. Before you can attempt to initiate and implement change initiatives successfully on a continuous basis, you will have to change the culture first. This is not a minor endeavour—it must be led sensibly. Especially, when the leadership team is the main source of resistance.

Your leadership behaviours are critical to the success of change initiatives, through all stages of the Change Dimension. Creation of a culture is a real test of your leadership values, principles and trust. People will observe how well your behaviour is aligned with what you say, what you do, and the purpose of the entity.

You play the pivotal role in changing everyone's behaviours. You must diligently model, pursue, observe and align the necessary behaviours during change initiatives. Failing that, those old legacy and unwanted behaviours will creep back into your entity, and stifle your initiatives' progress. Since your entity's culture provides the driving force behind your peoples' behaviours, it is common-sense that all necessary behaviour changes must become part of your entity's culture.

Behaviours can range from simple task related behaviours on the one end of the spectrum, to longstanding ingrained values, beliefs and mental models on the other end of the spectrum. Any change initiative will require behavioural changes to some degree. For example, the range of behaviours that needs to alter can stretch from something as simple as changing how tasks are done, to as complex as changing the entire organisational culture. That may involve changing the entity's purpose, values, principles and mental models.

Your entity's culture is its collective expression of consistent behaviours that have been established over a period. Its culture is formed over time through a continual cycle that establishes and reinforces behaviours that are considered appropriate for the entity. I have designed the 'Culture Reinforcement Cycle' to illustrate how this reinforcement cycle works—see Figure 8.2.

An entity's culture can be described as a combination of the mutual values, people's beliefs of what is right and wrong, common mental models and common 'undisputable' assumptions. These characteristics of culture form a continually reinforcing cycle that determines how

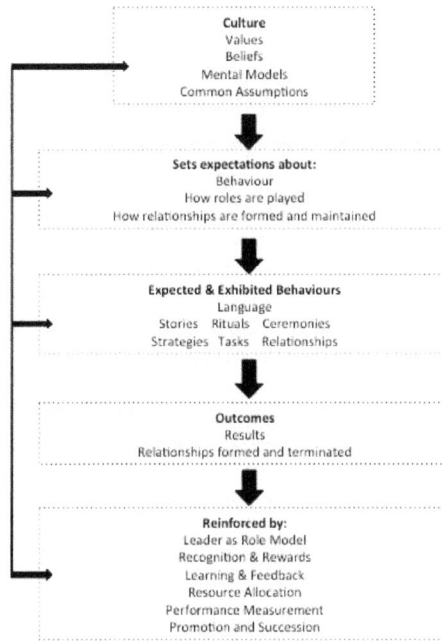

Figure 8.2 depicts a flowchart with the following boxes connected by downward arrows, with a feedback loop returning to the top:

Culture
Values
Beliefs
Mental Models
Common Assumptions

Sets expectations about:
Behaviour
How roles are played
How relationships are formed and maintained

Expected & Exhibited Behaviours
Language
Stories   Rituals   Ceremonies
Strategies   Tasks   Relationships

Outcomes
Results
Relationships formed and terminated

Reinforced by:
Leader as Role Model
Recognition & Rewards
Learning & Feedback
Resource Allocation
Performance Measurement
Promotion and Succession

Figure 8.2 Culture Reinforcement Cycle

behaviours are supposed to be exhibited by everyone in the entity. It concerns behaviours related to how roles are played, how work is done, and how relationships are formed internally and externally. Expected behaviours are established and are discernible through how leaders and people talk, the stories they tell, rituals they perform, strategies they formulate, and the relationships they form.

The expression of culture is also clearly visible in the tangible outcomes and the types of relationships that are formed, such as how services and products are presented to customers, or how the entity relates to its customers and stakeholders.

The founding leader of an entity initially creates the culture of the entity. However, as the leadership may change over time, so does the culture change too. A leader's behaviours are the key origins of an entity's culture and how the culture evolves. Your behaviours are continually observed and mimicked by your people. Through your behaviours, people will clearly detect if your heart is really in a change initiative or not.

As the leader, you are in the best position to change and reinforce the culture in your entity, by using several behavioural reinforcement mechanisms. Edgar Schein[1], the famous authority on organisational culture, lists several primary mechanisms leaders can use to change and align their entities' behaviours and cultures.

I have built Schein's behavioural reinforcement mechanisms into the 'Culture Reinforcement Cycle'—see the box at the bottom of Figure 8.2. Schein's reinforcement mechanisms are highly visible behaviours you can use to create and reform entity cultures, for example:

- The issues you care about, measure, and control
- Your behavioural reactions during important events
- How and where you allocate resources
- How you model your role—how you give feedback and how you share knowledge
- How you reward and recognise people for their contributions
- Who you recruit and promote, and who you include and exclude from important decisions.

Leaders perform these actions daily, whether they are conscious about them or not. The importance of these mechanisms is that you can consciously and intentionally use them to successfully change your entity's culture and influence the course of change initiative. Use the mechanisms authentically to embed the desired behaviours in your entity.

Cultivate inclusion

When you act inclusively you are acknowledging that everyone has a stake in the entity—everyone belongs and has ownership of the mutual purpose, and everyone wants to contribute to the achievement of the mutual purpose.

Coupled with a change-oriented culture, inclusion is a group of leadership behaviours that promotes change-fitness. I have discussed inclusion in detail in Chapter 4. Inclusion is one of the cornerstones in the Relationship Dimension. It is essential for fostering change-oriented cultures that enable successful change initiatives.

To emphasise the importance of inclusion to enable change, I designed a two by two matrix that shows the degree of inclusion on the vertical axis, and the degree of leaders' change-orientation, on the horizontal axis. The matrix in Figure 8.3 has four quadrants, each one illustrates a different type of change-orientation.

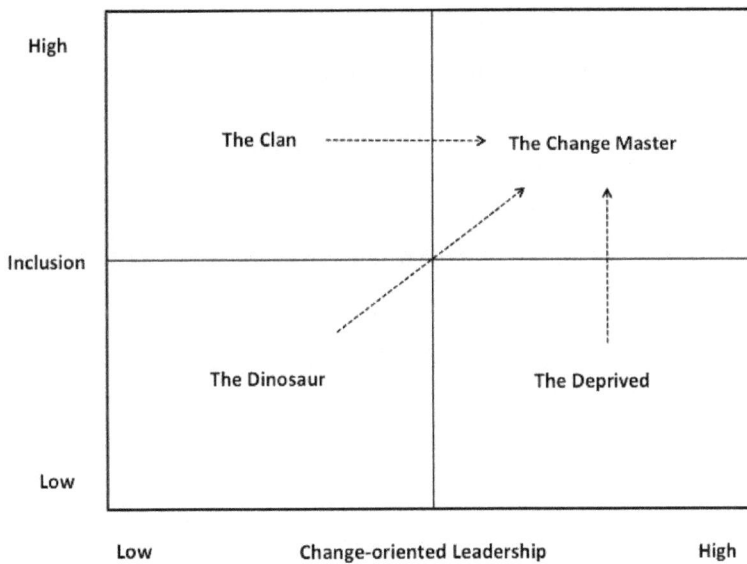

Figure 8.3 Inclusion vs. Change-oriented Leadership

Change Masters

Leaders of entities who are 'Change Masters' practice complete inclusion and high levels of change-orientation.

'Change Masters' show the following characteristics and behaviours:

- Leaders walk and talk change-oriented behaviours, in combination with appropriate levels of Relationship and Execution behaviours.
- Leaders correctly spread their resources and attention between business-as-usual (BAU) operations and change initiatives.
- Adequate resources, systems and processes are provided for change initiatives: human, financial, time and intelligence.
- Discriminatory budgets, measures and metrics are applied, to allow for differences between change initiatives and BAU.
- The culture is conducive to change
- Levels of inclusion are high—empowerment, collaboration, and engagement are evident.
- People have ownership and are accountable for change initiatives—there are clear lines-of-sight.
- People are engaged with change initiatives and able, willing and eager to take change initiatives head-on.
- There is a balanced approach to risk taking.
- They continue to be agile and resilient—they are capable to launch new opportunities as well as withstand negative and unexpected events.

The Deprived

'The Deprived' are entities that implement change initiatives frequently, however with suboptimal success. Their success with change initiatives follow the usual disappointing pattern of change deficits, as described in Chapter 1. Such entities have attempted many change initiatives, i.e. innovations, acquisitions, commercialisation, or growth, but are performing below potential.

The characteristics of 'The Deprived' and their leaders are made obvious through their behaviours, for example:

- Change initiatives are planned and driven from the top, but lack inclusion of the people.
- Leadership dictates why, when and how change initiatives happen, with limited buy-in or acceptance from the workforce.
- Visions for change initiatives are incongruent, and misaligned with the mutual purpose of the entity, due to a lack of inclusion.
- Little leadership support for the psychological transitions of people. (Chapter 7)
- People are change-fatigued and disengaged.
- Resources are spread thinly across too many change initiatives

'The Deprived' may show change-orientated behaviours and employ change management process models. However, for 'The Deprived' to become 'Change Masters' they need to become more inclusive. They need to include their people in change initiatives, right from the first stage of the Change Dimension and thereby significantly improve their performance.

The Clan

The 'Clan' is an entity who has an inclusive culture, but dwell too long in the comfort of mature life cycles. The 'Clan' leaders are oblivious to clear signals of change and signs of demise. They have a culture that is averse to change and slack on innovation.

The 'Clan' can be diagnosed when the following behaviour symptoms exist. Note that only a few of these symptoms need to be present to have the nature of a Clan.

- People are engaged (at first), eager to add value and make positive changes—and they want to be included.
- The people may realise the need for change and strive to make changes, and would try to push the leaders to advance change initiatives.
- Leaders respond with small, sporadic or non-strategic incremental changes (that may often be cancelled).
- Leaders gravitate back to a narrow, stagnant, business as usual mindset.
- A lack of direction from leaders presents itself, with low tolerance for risks and innovative initiatives.
- Learning occurs sporadically and mistakes are not tolerated—and often harshly penalised.

If leaders of a Clan do not change their behaviours, to foster a change-oriented culture, the situation cannot be rescued and the entity will spiral into the 'Dinosaur' quadrant. Continued absence of change-oriented leadership will eventually lead to diminishing inclusion as well. As positive change initiatives fail to get traction, frustration emerges within the ranks. Collaboration drops, silos form and a lack of trust sets in. They become disillusioned and eventually disengage.

If you follow the Change Dimension consistently you may rescue an entity that is sliding from 'Clan' to 'Dinosaur". A new leader who is fortunate enough to inherit an entity that were originally inclusive, engaged and eager to make proactive changes, may be able to move the entity across to become 'Change Masters'. The main condition is that the leader and the entity must become more change-oriented.

The Dinosaur

The 'Dinosaur' quadrant illustrates cultures with both a low orientation to change and low inclusivity. 'Dinosaur' leaders and entities are often caught unexpectedly, they become 'Dinosaurs' by the changes that happen 'to' them. However, these changes are seldom surprises to onlookers.

Characteristics and behaviours of 'Dinosaur' entities are:

- Employee engagement is poor
- The entity is rife with politics
- Command and control is the predominant leadership style
- Leaders seem oblivious or detached to change drivers in the contextual environment and the need to adapt
- A strong anti-change and risk-averse culture exists
- Decision-making is exclusive—behind closed doors, involving a small number of confidants
- Due to lack of collaboration, engagement, learning and leadership support, little if any innovation occurs
- Change initiatives that occur are mainly of a reactive nature—they are about coping and survival. (Chapter 6)
- If these change initiatives occur, it is decided unilaterally and pushed through within a culture that is noticeably resistant. Unilateral behaviour reinforces disengagement and performance drops further.

'Dinosaur' entities typically undergo what Gary Hamel[2] calls a "*Process of Surrender*". The process starts with leaders and entities that are myopic, overconfident, or unable to see the changes on the horizon. Leaders in 'Dinosaur' entities underestimate the strategic intent, the extraordinary resourcefulness and the unconventional tactics of competitors. Usually, when it is obviously too late, the entity goes into a state of shock or surprise. It tries to recover lost ground from competition. The competition's innovating lifecycles have surpassed theirs. Because the entity is now locked in a defensive mode, it spends extraordinary resources to regain lost territory, it loses the agility and resilience it may have had, becomes too lean, until it is spent. The inevitable eventually dawns on the leaders and the final episode of the entity is its departure from the scene.

When an entity is in a 'Dinosaur' state of affairs, there may be still an opportunity to rescue it. The remedy is to completely refresh the leadership ranks, start with inclusion, and implement the *Change Dimension*.

Develop new mental models

"Thinking is the hardest work there is, which is the probable reason why so few engage in it"

Henry Ford

Senge[3] describes mental models as our deeply ingrained assumptions, generalisations, pictures and images that influence how we understand the world and how we act.

Very often, we are not consciously aware of our mental models, or the effects they have on our behaviour. The mental models we use are generally good enough for routine execution tasks. When it concerns change-oriented leadership in entities though, our mental models are lacking.

The mental models we apply to initiate and lead change determines how successful we will enable change-oriented cultures. Also, your mental models will define how successful your change initiatives will be.

The predominant mental model in Western leadership is one of analytical and stepwise logical thinking. However, change and change drivers do not normally behave in linear fashion. Linear analytical logic has been developed into an extraordinary science since the early Greek philosophers. Analytical thinking is a powerful skill that is useful to break complex phenomena into smaller and easier understandable parts. However, change drivers behave in complex, non-linear, ambiguous, chaotic and uncertain ways. Therefore, we need different mental models to discern and understand change and change drivers.

Integrated change-oriented mental models comprise of combinations of several linear and non-linear thinking skills. These thinking skills are used interactively and iteratively until one reaches acceptable views about the object of one's thoughts. Change-oriented mental models should include as many as possible of the thinking skills illustrated in Figure 8.4.

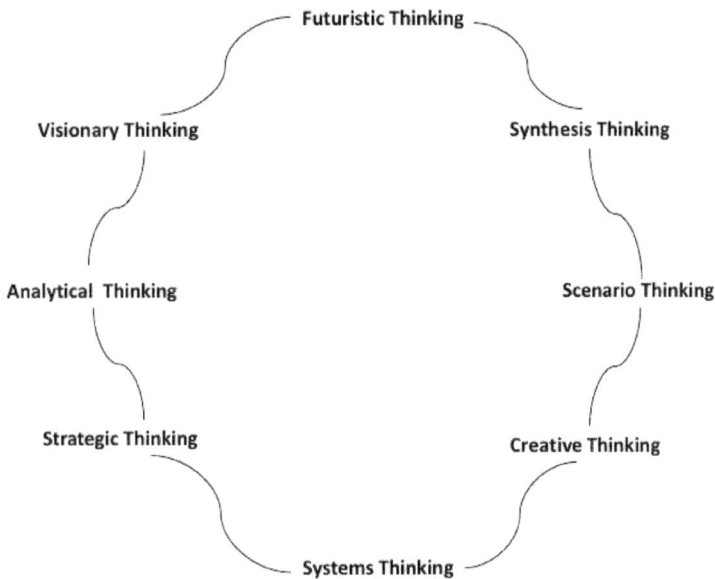

Figure 8.4. Thinking skills for integrated change-oriented mental models

The change-enabling mental model in Figure 8.4 shows that different thinking skills are used in combination, iteratively and interchangeably. Rather than using any one mental model exclusively, they should be used in combination to build upon each other. Note that apart from linear analytical thinking, the rest of the skills in the mental model are predominantly non-linear, creative and integrative.

Very few people will have an equal or abundant ability in all the thinking skills. You may not yet have these skills, but the good news is that you can acquire and develop them through study, experimentation and practice. What is important is to be unprejudiced about thinking skills that may seem foreign.

Some people may be exceptionally good at one or two of the thinking skills. Others will have a specific talent or preference for another thinking skill. This is one of the main reasons why inclusion and collaboration is so essential. By including people with diverse thinking skills, you can build an entity with enormous multifaceted mental capacity that can handle changes of any kind.

Thinking without action leads to nothing.

Action without thinking can lead to disaster.

Analytical thinking

Analytical thinking is a very important skill and it has a central place in the Execution Dimension (Chapter 13). It is also an essential skill in the Anticipation stage of the Change Dimension.

Analytical thinking is the skill that is most developed in western educated leaders. Leaders acquire analytical thinking skills from early ages in preschool and through their education, for example, the sciences, commerce and law.

Unfortunately, analytical thinking is often used exclusively, especially during the early stages of change, when complexity and uncertainty about change drivers are at their highest. Counterintuitively more non-linear and creative mental models should be applied during the early stages of change initiatives. Analytical thinking skills, which are pre-occupied with logic, often lack the creative genius that emerges when people apply non-linear thinking skills. Consequently, I emphasise that leaders embrace mental models that will better enable change—those thinking skills that lean towards non-linear and creative thinking.

Scenario thinking

The Royal Dutch Shell Corporation is famous for the introduction of scenario thinking. Shell developed and used scenario-thinking methodology for decades and has had vast success with strategic planning and driving change initiatives because of that. Kees van der Heijden and Pierre Wack[4] are the most influential authors on this topic.

Scenario thinking involves constructing a set of plausible futures that could exist in the contextual environment. Each plausible future is called a scenario. Scenarios are not forecasts or predictions of the future, but provide a look at the future through different lenses. It is about plausibility within the uncertainty of the future. Different scenarios are often mutually exclusive.

I have illustrated scenario thinking in Figure 8.5. A 'future space' is like a time cone, starting from where you are today. The context is well defined in the near term and less defined in the long term. There are driving forces for change in the here and now. As the number of change drivers in your current context increases, the time cone will flare out wider in the future state. Conversely, the number of plausible scenarios to be considered for your future space is lower when you have a few change drivers in your current context.

Scenarios are the different plausible 'stories' that could play out within the time cone, e.g. S1 to S4 in Figure 8.5. The set of plausible scenarios should provide sufficient definition to adequately describe the whole future space.

Simple examples of future scenarios could be:

- S1: A high number of competitors enter your market within a socio-politically unstable context.
- S2: Disruptive technologies significantly change your market context, within stable local and global economies.

The set of scenarios do not have to describe every possible future—only

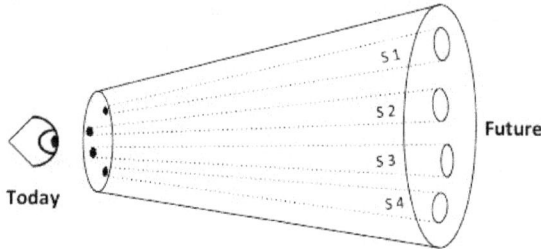

Figure 8.5. Possible 'Futures Space' with Plausible Scenarios

the plausible ones that can have significant impact on your future entity. Four to five wide-ranged scenarios are typically an adequate number for a scenario-thinking exercise. They are often represented in a two by two matrix, where the extremes of two significant variables are considered. In this example S1 to S4 could be combinations of high/low disruptors and high/low socio-economic stability. It is useful to give scenarios easy to remember names, such as 'Utopia', 'Doldrums' or 'Vultures'.

The methodology is based on several and often extreme scenarios; it therefore offers alternative viewpoints on the nature and future direction of change drivers. Scenario thinking focuses the mind on the main high impact uncertainties and systemic interrelationships. It does not resolve uncertainties, but significantly reduces complexity to make strategy formulation a lot easier.

Scenario thinking also helps to identify missing information that might be essential to accurately anticipate how a change initiative should be formulated. It can assist to generate viable options and directions that position change initiatives for success. Often change drivers are due to events that have already happened and the outcome is inevitable. Shell refers to certain change drivers as "predetermined outcomes" and use the saying: "It has rained in the mountains, so it will flood in the plains".

Scenario-thinking processes are inclusive by nature, because it encourages the inclusion of wide-ranging views. It also encourages participants to follow non-linear synthesis of diverse intelligence. It creates an ability in entities and leaders to overcome barriers and sources of resistance. The process encourages people to focus on contexts, challenges and plausible outcomes, rather than what is solely in their individual interest.

When scenario thinking is done inclusively it will reduce resistance behaviours like the following:

- Disagreements between leaders causing inconsistent, wasteful and disorganised change initiatives.
- Prejudiced, self-centred, and inflexible leadership behaviours, leading to misaligned change initiatives.
- Constrained, prevailing visions of the future and group-think
- Proliferation of change initiatives that can cause dilution of effort, waste of resources, disengagement and delays.
- Indecisiveness and procrastination.
- Risk aversion to initiate and implement change initiatives.
- Vested interests of leaders, teams and individuals.

Benefits when using scenario thinking, are:

- Uncovering important change drivers.
- Improved recognition of uncertainties, complexities and interrelated variables involved in your contextual future space.
- Having open and inclusive strategic dialogues—essential to make change initiatives succeed.

- Increasing engagement and alignment to the purposes of change initiatives.
- Enhancing organisational learning about your entity's future, vision and challenges.
- Positioning your entity to become more agile and resilient to manage future challenges.

Futuristic thinking

Futuristic thinking is an ability to have a sharply focused, almost telescopic, progressive view that recognises and defines how the future might evolve, in a clear and concise manner. Futuristic leaders look further than the current state and see what can be.

Since leading change is about leading an entity from its current known state to a new (future) state, leading change is inseparable from the future, whether the future is tomorrow, or fifty years ahead. It is therefore essential that leaders can demonstrate sound futuristic thinking—thinking that creates the future for their entities and people. Futuristic thinking not only forewarns entities of potential threatening events ahead of time, but also advances better futures by exploiting positive trends, and creating opportunities.

Futuristic thinking requires the use of mental models that are unconstrained by your entity's past, asking creative questions about possible futures, and 'unknown-unknowns'. Past performance and trends must be thoroughly studied with the aid of analytical thinking skills, but futuristic thinking requires your entity's creative imagination.

Visionary-, systems-, creative- and scenario thinking skills complement futuristic thinking. Their use enriches futuristic thinking by developing ideas that could be advanced into real change initiatives—changes that will align with the mutual purposes of your entity.

Your role is to look beyond the immediate and obvious—to recognise several futures that are possible and viable, and to mutually develop the 'future space' for change. Unless you and your entity have a common understanding of your likely future space, you cannot lead with clear direction.

Your success with futuristic thinking depends on your ability to include and engage your people. I have yet to meet a leader that unilaterally has all the futuristic wisdom to create a clear, all-encompassing vision of the future. The true futuristic leader is an inclusive one. The task of futuristic thinking is profound, requiring wisdom and discernment.

Leaders must challenge assumptions, constraints and resistance that exist within themselves and their teams, and question common wisdom that prevails in their entities. A leader must also be open to be challenged about his assumptions, biases and blind spots. When you rid yourself and your entity from constraints erected by habitual mental models, it unlocks your ability to think futuristically.

Systems thinking

I discuss 'Systems thinking' (coined by Senge[5]) in Chapter 6. It relates to a specific characteristic of change, namely interdependent complexity.

The mental model of systems thinking considers the interrelationships and patterns of change drivers, rather than isolated, static 'snapshots' of change. The essence of systems thinking is the ability to consider the whole and the interrelationships of subsystems, internally and externally, rather than thinking exclusively in terms of linear cause-and-effect relationships.

Systems thinking assist leaders to recognise that changing the 'obvious' does not necessarily produce the 'obvious' desired outcomes. A seemingly positive change, that also has systemic effects, may cause undesirable outcomes within your system (entity). These undesirable outcomes may sometimes show up months or years later than you would have expected.

Senge makes the point that we need to think of change in a systems way so we can perceive the whole and the interconnecting parts in entities. Refer to Chapter 6, Figure 6.5 for an illustration of systems of dynamic and complex changes.

At a higher level, systems thinking enables you to form a mental picture of the interconnections your entity has at an industry, national or international level. A systems mental model supports thinking about the systemic dynamics in your entity's contextual environments. For example, a specific change driver may initiate changes in the demographics of your national markets. Initially only weak trends may be noticeable in other industries. However, because of dynamic interconnectedness those demographic changes may spill over into your industry and have major effects on your entity.

In combination with other non-linear thinking skills, systems thinking will enable you to anticipate:

- How to deconstruct flawed mental models of your entity or its sub-systems, and with the help of synthesis thinking, reconstruct new mental models that are aligned with preferred 'future spaces'.
- How your entity interrelates with its contextual environment.
- How causes and effects work their way through systems.
- Underlying behaviours in systems that may cause system problems or opportunities.
- Patterns of change that are continual, cyclical, periodical, run-away, or whiplash that can cause performance issues.
- How changes will affect performance stability.
- Interdependent complexity and how changes affect interdependencies.
- Where barriers and resistance against change may occur.
- Where and when to create beneficial changes in a system.

Creative and innovative thinking

Creative thinking produces novel ideas for change initiatives, solving problems, or developing something new. The main characteristic of the creative mental skill is that it is unbiased and unconstrained by any preconceived mental models. Creative thinking incorporates whole brain thinking, the so-called left-brain (logical and analytical) and the right-brain (artistic and creative).

Creativity can be learned, enhanced and increased. We often hear that only certain people are creative. More accurately however, some of us may be more creative than others are. Some of our creative works may be more visible or tangible than others' works. The fact is that everybody has creative potential. To be creative your specific creative potential must first be identified and then exercised in a favourable context that allows you to be creative. Like any other cognitive effort, creativity may not come easy and may not show spontaneously. It must be developed and exercised thoroughly.

Creative thinking uses the other thinking skills as inputs and outputs. It is an integrative mental process that creates new ideas, solutions, artefacts and changes to existing situations. It is mostly non-linear, inclusive and intuitive. However creative thinking can also use structured processes like linear analytical thought processes as sources for creative ideas and to logically order creative ideas after the creative process is complete.

Innovative thinking advances creative thinking into a skill that converts creative ideas into viable, useful, valuable change initiatives, solutions or artefacts. It transports the creative into the tangible. The integrative skills of creative and innovative thinking are iterative and recursive. When ideas cannot be converted into valuable innovations they are changed or discarded. Old ideas are revisited, or new ones created. The innovative mental process continues iteratively until viable change initiatives, solutions or artefacts are created.

Synthesis thinking

Synthesis thinking is the imaginative reconstruction or re-combination of thoughts, ideas, information and knowledge to create something that may not have existed before.

The process of synthesis thinking is non-linear. The product of synthesis thinking is *greater* than the parts of which it is built from. Something of greater value, ability, or positive effect than the original parts, or the sum of the parts, is created.

To apply synthesis thinking effectively, you would need a diversity of thought processes to construct or reconstruct new wholes. Synthesis thinking gets its building material for a new whole through the inclusive integration of other thinking skills, such as analytical, scenario, systems and creative thinking. The outcomes of synthesis thinking could be new systems, visions, strategies, future directions or new innovative concepts. There are no rules in its application, for example, thought material from visionary, strategic and creative thinking can be synthesised to construct new systems or new change initiatives.

Strategic thinking

Strategic thinking is an inclusive and iterative mental model that uses a combination of skills and diverse intellectual inputs from many people to create viable directions for the future. Strategic thinking is the glue between your entity's current state of affairs and its vision for the future.

Strategic thinking is an essential leadership skill. Without it change initiatives cannot be effectively led, nor initiated. It is an ability that synergistically integrates many different thinking skills in such a way that creative and mutually attractive strategies are formulated—strategies that will realise your entity's vision and purpose, that are implementable, and that will deliver proactive change initiatives.

Three strategy gurus describe strategic thinking as follows:

Minzberg[6] states that strategic thinking is a synthesis process. It involves intuition and creativity. The outcome of strategic thinking is an integrated perspective of the entity within its contextual environment. *Strategic planning*, on the other hand, he says is primarily about analytical study. It is about breaking down strategic objectives into smaller steps, and formalising the steps so that they can be implemented.

Hamel[7] sees strategy formulation as a revolutionary act. He says that strategy formulation must follow ten principles for strategy to be truly revolutionary (not anarchic or chaotic). By following his revolutionary principles, he says leaders will increase the chances of discovering progressive strategies. His first principle says that *'strategic planning' is not strategic* (like Mintzberg). He says a critical problem in entities is the failure to distinguish between strategic planning (which is a linear analytical process) and strategic thinking, an integrative mental model that synthesises revolutionary thinking.

Ohmae[8] sees strategic thinking as the synthesis or reconstruction of past and future events in the real world in the most advantageous way. Strategic thinking does not always follow linear analytical logic. It contrasts sharply with conventional analytical approaches that are based on linear thinking. Strategic thinking also contrasts to thinking that is based solely on intuition, which is reaching strategic conclusions without any analytical thought. Breakthroughs in strategic change initiatives he says will come when you apply a combination of rational linear analytical thinking, and creative non-linear integration (synthesis thinking) of different change drivers into new advantageous configurations.

Visionary thinking

Visionary thinking enables the leader to identify specific game changing future directions for his entity, and specific initiatives, from amongst several viable options in a 'futures space'. Change-oriented visionary thinking is at the very core of leadership. Refer again to the definition of leadership (Chapter 2):

Leadership is a trust relationship among leaders and followers who execute actions and perform change initiatives aimed at achieving mutual purposes.

Visionary thinking is the creation of mental pictures of change initiatives that reflect the mutual purposes. It is creative and it shapes the future. Visionary thinking builds upon futuristic thinking. Futuristic thinking envisions what the future might look like—whereas visionary thinking comes up with creative initiatives that fits that future and may change the direction of an entity. Visionary thinking is an integrative cognitive skill that interprets past, present and future intelligence and forms a clear view of the future direction. It also uses synthesis and strategic thinking to shape and define viable and compelling new initiatives and directions.

Every change initiative, however small or large, must have a vision for success. Every initiative's vision for success should fit into the realistic future space. If the vision for success for a change initiative does not fit into a viable future space—the change initiative will not succeed.

Change-oriented leaders also include and engage their people and stakeholders to co-create the visions and change initiatives. The outcomes of visions that were defined in an inclusive manner are change initiatives that are viable, compelling, and aligned to the purpose.

Summary

Enable is the first stage of the Change Dimension. To Enable a change-oriented mindset in your entity you need to cultivate three sets of behaviours:

- Leading a change-oriented culture that is open to change, continuous improvement, experimentation, innovation, risk taking and growth.
- Practising and modelling inclusion by consciously and actively engaging people in change initiatives through all stages of the Change Dimension. To create inclusion, leaders of an entity

must acknowledge that everyone has a stake in the entity—everyone belongs and has ownership of the entity's mutual purpose, and everyone wants to contribute to the achievement of the mutual purpose.

- Actively combining and applying a variety of different mental models. Mental models such as analytical, scenario, strategic, systems and futuristic thinking need to be used in an integrated way. Other mental models leaders should introduce as part of the Enable mindset are: synthesis, creative, innovative and visionary thinking.

Notes

1. Schein, E. H. 1992, Organizational Culture and Leadership, 2nd edn, Jossey-Bass, San Francisco.

2. Hamel, G. 1996, 'Strategy as Revolution', *Harvard Business Review*, July-August, pp. 69-82

3. Senge, P. M. 2004, *The Fifth Discipline – The Art and Practice of the Learning Organization*, Currency Doubleday, New York.

4. Van Der Heijden, K. 2005, *Scenarios - The Art of Strategic Conversation*, John Wiley, West Sussex, England. See Wack, P. 1985, 'Scenarios: Uncharted Waters Ahead', *Harvard Business Review*. September-October.

5. Senge, P. M. 2004, *The Fifth Discipline – The Art and Practice of the Learning Organization*, Currency Doubleday, New York.

6. Mintzberg, H, 1989, *Mintzberg on Management – Inside our strange world of organizations*, Collier Macmillan, New York.

7. Hamel, G. & Prahalad, C.K., 1989, Strategic Intent, *Harvard Business Review*, July-August, pp. 148- 161.

8. Ohmae, K, 1983, *The Mind of the Strategist*, McGraw-Hill, New York.

9. **The Change Dimension - Stage 2**

ALIGN

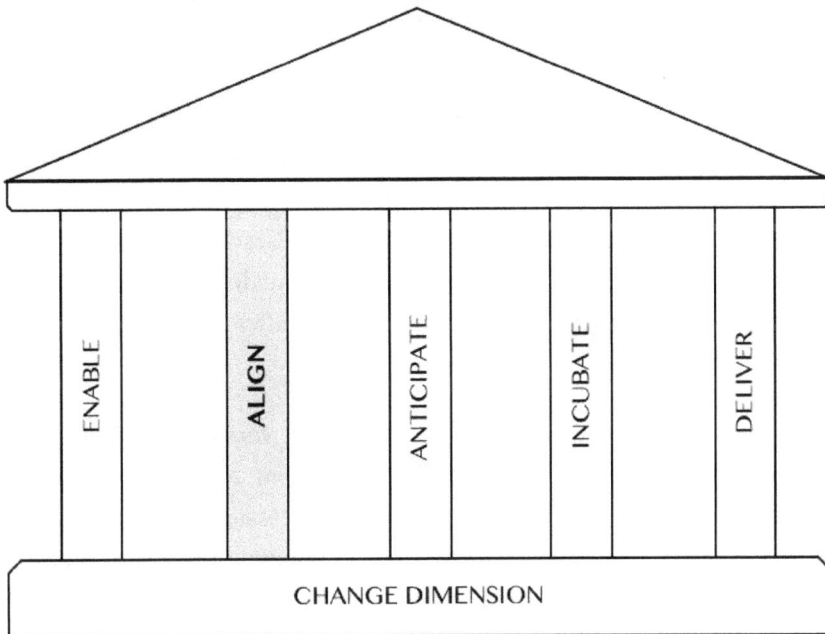

The Align stage covers those leadership actions and behaviours that will ensure your change initiatives are fully aligned with your entity's mutual purpose. In the Align stage I discuss the proactive actions you can take to prepare your entity to be agile and resilient so that it will respond timeously to change in your contexts from an advantageous position.

In the previous chapter, we covered the Enable stage. The focus of the Enable stage was to permanently create an environment that is conducive to change. Align is the second stage of the Change Dimension. In this stage, the focus is turned toward the entity, its systems, processes and resources. To lead change initiatives that will be successful the entity must be continually enabled and aligned.

By nature, change causes misalignment when it is not led correctly. The old replaces the new. When your entity is aligned for change, you will have a major competitive advantage.

Change and stability are opposite poles on a continuum, yet they are interdependent counterparts. Relentless change without some stability will eventually lead to exhaustion and demise. Permanent stability on the other end of the continuum breeds complacency and because of 'unforeseen change', leads to surprise, followed by instability and eventually, by chaos. The *Change Continuum* I have illustrated in Figure 6.9, Chapter 6, is an illustration of how the paradoxical forces of change and stability play out. On the *Change Continuum*, stability is on the far-left end, and chaos on the far-right end. Paradoxes are opposites, yet they co-exist to some degree. One cannot realistically have one or the other—either change or stability. There is always a degree of both present.

Closely associated to the paradox of change versus stability, is the paradox of resilience versus agility. They seem to be opposites but they are complementary forces. Agility is a necessary characteristic for entities to lead change successfully, especially now in the age of change. Yet an entity that focuses on becoming increasingly agile and lacks an unyielding resilient backbone, could impair its ability to change and may eventually cease to exist. Entities that focus single-mindedly on agility, run the risk that the resilience they have gets eroded to such a point where they would need serious reactive and invasive change initiatives to halt the damage and turn the entity around. A typical example is entities that drive leanness (with the supposed aim to become increasingly agile) to the point that they cannot withstand major adverse impacts—they simply lost their resilient backbone in the process.

A key leadership skill to lead the paradoxical forces of change is your ability to align the opposing tensions of change and stability. The paradoxes of change versus stability, and resilience versus agility, illustrate why it is essential to maintain an aligned entity. It is like sailing a boat. You must constantly trim the boat's sails to balance the forces of the boat against the forces of the wind, for the boat to stay on course toward your destination.

When you constantly lead in a change-oriented way your entity will become agile. However, you should also ensure that your entity sustains a reliable and robust backbone. Your entity needs the fall-back of sufficient capacity, capability and other resources to depend on when it must deal with substantial changes. Agile entities and people can tackle change and turn it positively. But, they need a haven of resilience that empowers them to confront continual change. Resilience offers such necessary stability and backup support to lead change in an agile fashion—an entity that is pre-prepared and change-fit. Resilient entities are resolutely aligned about how they would lead change. When your entity has adequate resilience, your people can spontaneously and boldly act to confront change, knowing they can rely on the necessary capacity, systems and resources.

The principle of alignment

The general principle of alignment for change is to purposely commit leadership time, entity capacity, capability and other resources to proactively govern change initiatives.

The leader must ensure the following elements are aligned with the entity's mutual purpose and change initiatives:

- Change governance: the mandate to govern change initiatives, the change team, and a suitable governance structure.
- Resource allocation: financial, capacity, and capability and other resources required for change initiatives.
- Systems and processes: performance measurement, reward and recognition, accounting, recruitment, technical support systems and processes necessary to support change initiatives.

Figure 9.1 illustrates the principle of continual alignment. The practice of always being aligned is essential for your entity to be agile, to deal with continual change and be change-fit.

Figure 9.1 Continual Alignment for the Change-fit Entity

If a flexible, yet robust 'spine' as illustrated in Figure 9.1, is absent in your entity, it will cause change barriers, which in turn will lead to resistance from people and groups. Typical change barriers you would expect are:

- Inconsistent governance of change initiatives

- Change initiatives that are misaligned to the entity's mutual purposes and strategy.
- A lack, and misallocation of necessary resources to deliver change initiatives (time, people, finance, skills, capabilities, and capacity)
- Shortages and obstacles to allocate the necessary capabilities and capacities to adequately deliver and integrate change initiatives
- Existing systems and processes are obsolescent and work against change initiatives. For example, performance management and reward systems are not aligned to the objectives and new behaviours required for change initiatives. This puts the survival of the new initiative at risk.

Change barriers are a major source of human resistance to change. Consequently, if we proactively resolve and remove entity barriers to change, many causes for human resistance will also dissolve. Entity barriers are often overlooked as a major cause of failure of change initiatives. Leaders regularly take it for granted that the entity either has the requisite resources or assume that the initiative will somehow easily fit into the entity once it has been implemented. Neither assumption is correct. Your entity should be prealigned for change, for initiatives to be successful. Generally, entities are aligned to support regular operations to deliver their offerings (Chapter 13 – Execution Dimension). However, alignment for change and alignment for regular operations are different, and often compete head-to-head for resources. When change initiatives are considered, evaluated, incubated and implemented, entities often struggle to successfully deliver them when these barriers have not been removed.

In the age of change, we need leaders that will effectively lead daily operational execution, *and* simultaneously align the entity for change initiatives.

Change Governance

The governance of change initiatives is the first area to consider. The primary objective of change governance is to direct effective implementation of the Change Dimension in your entity. Change governance should be a permanent, yet highly flexible co-ordination mechanism. Change governance can be led by a team or committee that has the necessary mandate, systems and procedures to ensure change initiatives are lead according to mutually recognised guidelines. The change team can be a group of senior leaders and key people in your entity. The membership in the governance team should be rotated at least once a year, to refresh collective mental models of the team. Also invite other (e.g. non-senior) staff members, to make up half of the team. These 'general' staff members are also rotated regularly. The principle of rotating members ensures that viewpoints stay fresh and current, and it reinforces a culture of inclusion. The death knell for change-governance is to have a separate function or silo that manages change in the entity. The principles of change leadership must become a pervasive and inclusive culture throughout the entity—everyone must own change.

The change governance team must have the necessary authority and accountability, separate from operations and business functions, to prevent preferential or biased agendas from slipping into change decisions. It has a well-defined and delegated mandate and charter that clarifies its authority, objectives, roles, rules and membership. The governance charter is also revisited on a regular basis.

Your change governance team has the following objectives. It must ensure:

- Clear leadership and direction for all change initiatives.
- Change initiatives are aligned with the mutual purposes, strategy, and culture.
- All change initiatives (financial and non-financial) are managed in one portfolio of initiatives.

- Everyone shares a common understanding of the contextual changes that affects the entity.
- Change initiatives are aligned with the needs of your clients, customers and stakeholders.
- Change initiatives are transparent across the entire entity and where appropriate, with external stakeholders.
- The entity functions as a dynamically aligned system so it can seamlessly implement and integrate change initiatives.
- Clear understanding of existing capabilities, capacities and infrastructure that are available or can be acquired, to ensure effective implementation and integration of initiatives.
- Appropriate structures, systems and processes are implemented and acquired to ensure change initiatives can deliver as promised.
- Consistent change management processes and methodologies are applied to implement change initiatives.
- Prioritisation and resource allocation mechanisms are in place, including a clear set of predetermined parameters and rules. (See Incubation in chapter 13)
- The entity's change initiative portfolio is regularly assessed, initiatives are prioritised and if necessary, removed to free up capacity.
- Unnecessary delays in decision-making are identified and removed.

Normally, large change initiatives (or projects) have dedicated governance procedures and mechanisms, but their governance should conform to the entity's general change governing rules. This will ensure that alignment and consistency occur across all change initiatives.

Resources

Three broad resource categories that are necessary to implement and integrate change in entities: financial, capacity and capability resources. To achieve alignment to change, a sensible allocation and reallocation of these resources are extremely important. Proper reallocation of resources allows you to deal proactively with change—it builds capacity and capability and avoids wastage.

It is essential that you proactively assess the availability of resources for initiative *implementation*, as well as resources for initiative *integration*. So often entities assume that because they have sufficient resources for *implementation*, the necessary resources to *integrate* the initiative into the entity's business-as-usual operational system (BAU) will also be available. This is a flawed assumption and it often leads to many failed change initiatives.

There are clear differences between resources necessary for *implementation* and resources necessary for *integration* of change initiatives.

- Resources necessary for change *implementation* are vital in the Deliver stage of the Change Dimension (Chapter 12). Some resources may be available in your entity while others have to be sourced in, acquired or developed methodically.

- Resources necessary for *integration* of change initiatives are required *after* the initiative has been implemented, signed off and has gone live as a viable initiative. These resources are necessary for continual assimilation of the initiative within your operational and functional systems. They ensure that changes intended by the new initiative truly turn into business-as-usual.

Aligning financial resources

Consider the following principles to align financial resources for change initiatives:

▽ Create clear line-of-sight in the change initiative portfolio

Put all change initiatives in a managed portfolio, like conventional capital project portfolios. Often non-capital change initiatives do not get the same scrutiny as capital investment decisions do. Yet change initiatives consume substantial resources that have large financial implications.

In combination with a portfolio approach, you could also allocate financial resources in a stage-wise manner. Don't commit the full funding at the start of an entire change initiative. It gives the change governance team the opportunity to measure progress and add value to change initiatives as they mature through several stages. Only when intermediate milestones and performance targets are satisfactorily met, is further funding allocated. Stage-wise allocation focuses and prompts regular scrutiny of resource utilisation. It helps to ensure change initiatives that don't meet intermediate milestones are exited in time. This discipline will free up resources to be reallocated more productively elsewhere.

▽ Do planning for implementation earlier

By doing the planning process for implementation earlier– now, during the align stage–you could allocate financial and other resources in advance. This discipline will speed up the decision-making process because affected parties would have to budget and pre-allocate resources at earlier stages. The planned resources are however not irrevocably committed, but they are earmarked in plans for the future. This leaves less room for surprises and supports the entity's resilience.

▽ Separate allocated budgets for change

Separate budgets are allocated for change initiatives, on unit and entity level. When budgets for change initiatives are absorbed within operational budgets (BAU), it is difficult and often almost impossible to isolate and track the performance of individual initiatives.

Allocating earmarked budgets—for improvements, growth, innovation, acquisition, restructure, or any other change initiative—means that change initiatives do not have to compete on an unequal basis with established operations. Change initiatives should not compete with usual operations (BAU) unless they are specifically intended to improve an existing element in an execution system (Execution Dimension, Chapter 13). Every change initiative is budgeted and assessed on its own merit. Following the principles of the Incubate stage will ensure that your change initiatives are properly evaluated, yet separated from established operational units. This discipline is especially useful when an intended change initiative will impact on a large portion of an entity.

▽ Create discretionary budgets for change

In addition to dedicated budgets for specific change initiatives, there is another useful practice to further enhance agility and resilience. Pre-emptively allocate a discretionary change budget, in anticipation of pending, though unknown, change initiatives. Discretionary change budgets can range between five and twenty percent of change initiative portfolios. Discretionary budgets are particularly useful for entities in fast changing industries that continually produce emerging and disruptive innovations. Resources need to be readily available and apportioned swiftly.

Entities that do not have this kind of agility would customarily cut into other committed resources or be too sluggish to address the pending change need in time. The entity then becomes too lean and eventually loses resilience. It may not be able to face a major disruption or crisis—leading to its demise.

An entity who follows this practice knows it can afford to put some of its resources at risk, with the added reward of being agile. When the entity doesn't have discretionary resources, its resilience is at risk. Moreover, when you do have to confront a major reactive change—such as a natural disaster event, or sudden dips in your markets, the discretionary budget might just pull you out of the crisis.

▽ Don't trim the change initiative budget

Trimming budgets for change initiatives after they have been committed, to 'improve' earnings in the short term, is a clear indication of misalignment of objectives. When you want to foster a culture of change and innovation you must ensure that funding for change initiatives is done consistently in a disciplined way. There must be a compelling case to reduce the budget for mutually agreed proactive change initiatives once it has passed all the stages of the Change Dimension.

Aligning capacity resources

Capacity resources are discussed in detail in Chapter 13 about the Execution Dimension. Capacity is a *quantitative or volumetric term* associated with many kinds of resources. It applies to both tangible and intangible resources. Capacity resources have limits and boundaries. Examples are the size of an office building, the output capacity of a service team, the production capacity of a factory, or the limits of a production process.

Aligning your entity's capacity resources is about regular assessment, reprioritisation, and reallocation of capacity resources. Well aligned capacity resources for new change initiatives reduce the need to acquire additional capacity, thus saving expenditures.

Attempting to initiate and implement additional change initiatives when your entity's capacity is tightly stretched or fully utilised will cause resistance to other initiatives. Your peoples' engagement will drop and failure of change initiatives is almost certain. This seems like a motherhood statement, yet I have often seen initiative overload occur for this reason.

When a change initiative goes live after implementation, and some capacity misalignment exists, the initiative will display lacklustre performance. The level of success of the change initiative will be below your expectations. Similarly, throwing good resources after bad will not resolve the consequences of prior poor decision making. It will however rob the rest of the entity of its valuable capacity resources.

Carefully consider your entity's capacity to enable change. Pick the right winners upfront and assign adequate capacity to allow them to succeed. This disciplined habit of optimised capacity utilisation helps to preserve the entity's agility and resilience. Your entity will always be proactively prepared to seize new initiatives when they present themselves because you can make necessary capacity readily available.

Aligning capability resources

Capability resources are discussed in detail in Chapter 13 about the Execution Dimension. A capability is *the ability and competency* to transform lower value resources into higher value resources.

Aligning capabilities for change is first about creating an accurate representation or inventory of your entity's current capabilities, and secondly about matching the inventory with the required capabilities for future change initiatives. Regularly assess, rank and validate your entity's capabilities against internal and external benchmarks.

Entities often overestimate their capability to *implement* and *integrate* change initiatives, only to realise too late that there are gaps to fill. Overestimation of capabilities leads to delays, expensive inefficiencies, and often failure of initiatives.

Equally, entities often underestimate certain strengths within their capability profiles and then miss out on opportunities that could have been pursued.

Key benefits of an accurate and regularly updated capability inventory, are:

- It informs you about your entity's fitness for change.
- Gaps such as capabilities that are dated, in surplus, or in short supply can be dealt with in advance. The inventory can identify serious capability vulnerabilities and an overreliance on for example, key specialists, or technologies.
- An inventory that references capability requirements for future change initiatives will enable you to acquire, redeploy and develop necessary capabilities on time through training, acquisition, or partnering.

Alignment of capability and capacity resources for change initiatives should be done in parallel since they are often interdependent. For example, when you reallocate capacity resources in your initiative portfolio (e.g. process plant capacity), some capability resources (e.g. engineering and technology specialists), might also be released for redeployment elsewhere.

Entities underestimate the time and resources required to develop or acquire necessary capabilities. The return on investment is however well worth it. When you proactively follow this discipline the need for expensive restructurings and layoffs is less.

Systems and Processes

To implement change initiatives successfully you would usually need improved or new systems and processes. At the entity level, some key systems and processes must be aligned to support a change-fit entity. Two vital ones are:

- Performance measurement system.
- Reward and recognition system.

▽ Aligning performance measurement

Design your intelligence system to circulate performance information of change initiatives to the rest of the entity to trigger proactive responses from people, enhance learning and reinforce inclusion.

Consider the following aspects of your performance measurement system regarding change initiatives:

- Design a performance measurement system and process that links the objectives of change initiatives to the strategic goals and mutual purpose of your entity.

- Ensure every individual's objectives, accountabilities and key performance indicators that relate to change initiatives are tracked and linked to the success and performance of change initiatives.

- Remove redundant and unnecessary measures that inhibit change-orientated behaviours.

- Ensure that it clearly identifies and quantifies the returns on resources invested in change initiatives.

- The performance measurement system must make clear distinctions between performance measures for change initiatives and performance measures for operational initiatives, particularly at the unit and individual initiative level. Change initiatives, which are in a development and maturing phase, should not be measured with the same yardsticks as stable, steady state ongoing operations. You would not measure a young child who is learning to walk in the same way you would measure an adult, for whom walking is a normal activity.

- Key objectives of performance measurement systems are primarily to drive better performance and inform proactive course corrections and secondly, to accurately record past performance. I often observe the opposite order of objectives. When the key objective is primarily about recording, and reporting historical performance, performance measurement systems discourage adoption of change-oriented behaviours.

- Most performance measurement systems are heavily skewed towards financial and lagging (historical) indicators. Lagging indicators are of limited value when you must implement and integrate change initiatives. When your performance measurement system is heavily biased towards financial measures, managers in your entity will focus mainly on actions that will drive the short-term bottom line. Other important change drivers such as innovation, collaboration and inclusion, which are essential to embed change-oriented cultures and are vital to the success of change initiatives, will get lip service and no real action.

- While some lagging indicators are relevant to change initiatives, predictive (leading) measures that are forward looking are more useful. Instantaneous leading indicators are invaluable to determine if a change initiative is on a success path or whether it needs course corrections. Leading indicators show when proactive reallocation of resources is necessary.

- Align performance indicators for post-implementation–for the initiative embarking on its life cycle. Design leading indicators to predict and identify inflexion points on life cycles (S-curves of initiatives). This will serve as flags for immediate scrutiny. Sudden rises, plateaus or decreases in performance of a mature initiative could signify important changes in the life cycle of a product, business or service.

- Ensure that your performance measurement system allows for staged change implementation. Change implementation stages are reviewed at predetermined milestones (review gates). Measures are revisited and may be changed from stage to stage. Criteria for milestones and reviews at each stage must be clear and unambiguous.

- Regularly review the suitability of measures to track change initiatives. Focus on using leading indicators. Use both input and output measures to track the success of changes in your entity. Examples of inputs are employee time or funding, and outputs can be the quality of a changed service or new product.

▽ Aligning rewards and recognition

For change initiatives, the outcomes and performance of initiatives are less certain than for established operational initiatives. Consequently, to encourage a culture of innovation, trial-and-error, experimentation and risk tolerance, your reward and recognition system needs to encourage the right behaviours.

- Ensure that your reward and recognition system makes clear distinctions between rewards and recognition for change initiatives, and rewards and recognition for current operational activities.
- Use your reward and recognition system to reinforce a change-oriented culture and inclusive behaviours. It should encourage your people to pursue and achieve successful change and to be a change-fit entity.

Summary

The second stage of the Change Dimension—Align—are those leadership behaviours and actions that will ensure that your entity's intended change initiatives are fully aligned with its mutual purpose.

Change and stability are opposite poles on a continuum, yet they are interdependent counterparts. Closely associated to the paradox of change versus stability, is the paradox of resilience versus agility. An important leadership skill in the Change Dimension is the ability to align the entity so that opposing tensions and paradoxical forces are effectively managed.

As the leader, ensure that the following elements in your entity are closely aligned, to enable successful change initiatives:

- The entity's mutual purpose sets the true north on the compass for any intended change initiative. Initiatives that are not aligned to the mutual purpose need serious reassessment.
- Change governance: this provides the mandate to govern change initiatives, change teams, and a suitable governance structure for your entity. Change governance is a permanent, yet highly flexible instrument for leading change.
- Resource allocation: financial, capacity, capability and other resources required for change initiatives must be proactively determined and assigned to initiatives.
- Systems and processes: performance measurement, reward and recognition, accounting, recruitment, technical support systems and processes—all the necessary systems, must be aligned with the above to support intended and future change initiatives.

Align behaviours and practices. This is essential to create an entity that is agile, yet resilient, and to become change-fit to deal with continual change. Once we have an entity that is Enabled and Aligned for change, we can effectively Anticipate necessary change initiatives. Anticipation is the topic of the next chapter.

10. The Change Dimension - Stage 3

ANTICIPATE

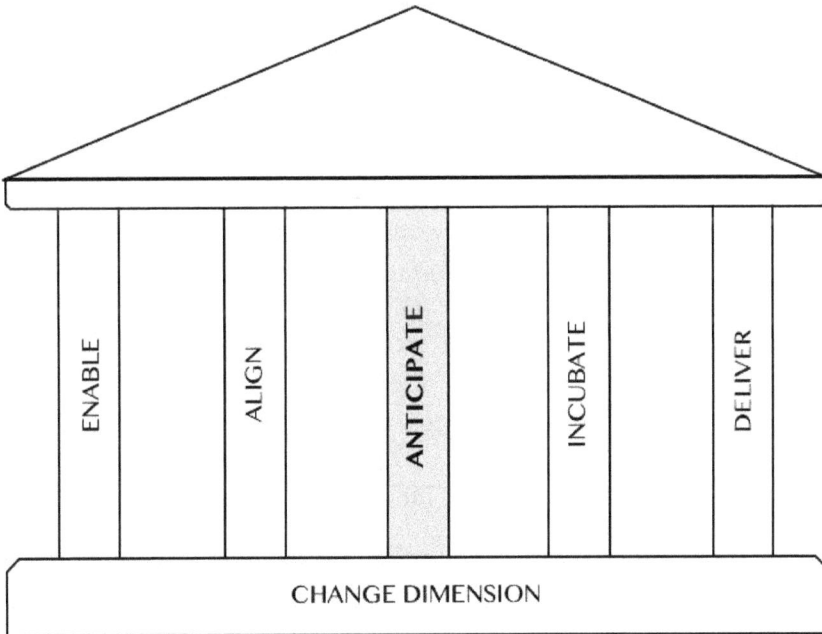

What is routine today was once born from change.
Every change was once born from a faint signal, an idea, or an event.

Anticipation – Introduction

In the previous two chapters, we discussed the Enable and Align stages of the Change Dimension. Anticipate is the third of the Change Dimension's five stages. We have to proactively anticipate changes and the long-term consequences. Change that takes place under stress or because of a crisis is seldom achieved constructively.

Anticipation focuses on what is plausible and possible for the future. It also considers possible future consequences of change initiatives.

The future seems to arrive faster than we think, especially in the age of change. We are now on the rising leg of the Mega-S-Curve. We are well and truly in a VUCA world.

We cannot deal with this uncertain future by relying solely on annually updated plans or on a linear cause-and-effect mindset. We have to continually pay attention to and anticipate a multitude of change drivers.

Proactive change requires strong anticipation behaviour. Anticipation needs to be both inclusive and future-oriented. Anticipation of change cannot be done effectively while we assume that one person or an exclusive group has all the answers, which must be accepted by a less informed entity. Inclusion involves people to explore different change alternatives and develop viable options.

When you introduce the change discipline of anticipation, your entity will move smoothly from one that merely has the potential to lead change, to an entity that proactively leads change.

Change drivers are seldom random. Change drivers follow patterns—however random the patterns may seem to the uninformed. Sharpened anticipation skills and understanding of how future patterns emerge, will help your entity to lead change. You need to cast your pre-emptive mental net wider and apply different mental models across a broad range of sources to uncover the drivers of change in your context.

The progressive leader spends dedicated time and resources to anticipate change. The payoff is huge. Anticipating change is not like predicting the future—it is not possible to discern every detail in uncertain futures in the VUCA world. The future does not unfold as a random presentation of events. It is possible to anticipate probable futures and scenarios with rigorous methods that identify and evaluate signals, sequences, and patterns.

Anticipating change drivers ahead of your competitors creates distinct strategic advantages. It opens the potential for new innovations, new entities, new visions and new directions well before rivals do. You also gain an ability to timely identify risks and threats—and to proactively evade adverse consequences. Anticipation significantly empowers you to create springboards for change initiatives and it helps to avoid perceptions that change 'happens to you'. You can better focus your time and resources to act proactively and avoid sliding down lifecycles that plateau or decline.

The Anticipate stage of the Change Dimension will help you to diligently develop anticipation skills to gain timely foresight of emerging changes and future change drivers. This chapter contains the detailed steps on how you can gather and interpret existing intelligence that will assist timely anticipation. By moving through the different steps, you can employ several of the mental models discussed before, to generate better feasible change options.

Many change drivers may often seem outside our control, but with disciplined anticipation you can brace your entity against adverse impacts. Illustrations of emerging changes are for example, the recent financial crises that originated from distant continents, disruptive technologies that originate from unrelated industries, or new government regulations. We can't anticipate everything but we can surely anticipate many change drivers to become change-fit.

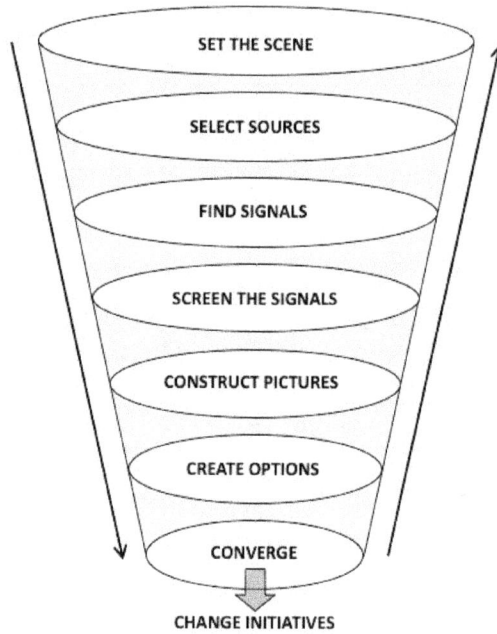

Figure 10.1. Anticipate Change Funnel

The 'Anticipate Change Funnel'

In Figure 10.1, I illustrate the process of anticipating change by way of a funnel. The *Anticipate Change Funnel* is designed to deal with all kinds of data, information and knowledge. It systematically extracts from, and adds value to a broad information base. Through a rigorous reduction, creative and synthesis process, a small number of viable change options are identified.

The funnel is unique in its kind, because it not only systematically extracts and reduces information, but with the aid of non-linear mental models it also adds value to information, and it does that in a recursive process. Most information funnels follow a once-through and linear analytical process: a large amount of information is reduced to a small number of options in a once-through process. In the *Anticipate Change Funnel* the process can cycle back in the funnel to any previous step when intermediate results are unsatisfactory. Also, the funnel is continually updated with new data, information and intelligence.

Step 1 – Set the Scene

In the first step of the *Anticipate Change Funnel* we set the scene for gathering and creating intelligence. The intelligence is necessary to identify change drivers and the correct change initiatives. We set the scene by asking strategic questions and using dialogue to kick-start and feed the change anticipation process. The questions are essentially non-operational by nature and must be broad and forward-looking.

There are signals that can enlighten us on possible future changes. We therefore should ask ourselves: What do we already know? What *should* we know? Consider the strategic intent of your entity, its business-as-usaul operational environment and the context it operates in. Reflect on the signals already known to you, but importantly, consider that there are many signals not yet known to you or the entity.

- Specific questions: What is the current context of your entity? How might the future contextual environment unfold? Which intelligence items do you need to shape your understanding of pending change? What are the change drivers that may influence the maturity of S-curves in our entity? Intelligence that signals earlier than expected plateauing or decline is vital to initiate proactive change strategies.

- Broad but important questions: Are there hidden and unnoticed drivers of change? What non-obvious strategic intelligence do you need to be continually ahead of the curve? Questioning like this will ensure that your entity does not become myopic and ignorant of change drivers that may seem irrelevant to the uniformed.

Step 2 – Select the Sources

Signals of pending future change can be extracted from a variety of sources. In this step, we identify possible sources and select the right ones to use. Following the strategic questioning in step one, we find and select sources that will provide us with change signals. Rather have many sources that can potentially inform you on potential change signals, than being overly selective. At this point in the anticipation funnel, more is better. Remember, the funnel works like a filter in steps to come.

Sources of change signals can be categorised into three main groups, that is, internal, external and interested and affected parties. It is important to obtain about equal amounts of change intelligence from all three groups of sources.

▽ Internal sources

Internal sources of signals for change are often neglected or ignored. Yet it is one of the most fertile areas you must pay attention to and develop inclusively. Negligence of internal sources leads to overdue, reactionary change initiatives that could have been avoided.

Internal sources are the people involved in change, that is, the change initiators, change adopters, internal stakeholders and unintended internal change recipients—therefore almost everyone! The internal sources will differ between change initiatives and contexts.

Internal sources are important for a number of reasons:

- Your own people are excellent sources of opportunities, knowledge and intelligence. A highly inclusive culture will exponentially increase the value this source can add.
- They provide signals on threats and opportunities to the entity's competitive capabilities, resource capacities, flexibility and resilience.

- Internal sources are useful barometers of many different barriers to change that may exist or are likely to develop.

▽ Interested and affected parties

Interested and affected parties are related to your entity in one form or another, yet they are not part of your entity. Sources like:

- Your customers, clients and users
- Suppliers
- Formal and informal networks
- Collaborative partnerships
- Competitors
- Industry groups
- Community groups
- Stakeholders
- Regulators

▽ External sources

External sources are essential to help identify signals and trends that indicate increasing turbulence, uncertainty, and volatility—well before the momentum of change drivers picks up.

- Social media
- Financial markets
- Third party intelligence and knowledge providers
- Consultants
- Other industries
- Legislators
- Political groups

Step 3 – Find the Signals

Scrutinise the sources and note all the signals of pending change, including those outside your industry. Look at the trends, patterns and relationships. Be aware that signals and trends are interconnected and future changes outside your current context can have a significant influence on your entity.

Signals can be any form of data or information about potential internal and external change drivers relevant to your contexts. Signals of many different kinds will vary in quality. The point in this step is not to decide on the significance of any signal solely based on its quality, or the volume of signals. It is simply an unfiltered gathering process that must be effective and capable of capturing all signals that may be relevant to your change context.

It is important to look for probable spill-overs and dynamic effects that could follow the signals. Signals from other unfamiliar contexts can spill-over into your contextual environment and cause a viral effect upon your entity.

Signals have various forms and qualities. They are, for example:

- Internally detected, gathered, and monitored information. Your entity must have an internal intelligence system in place that regularly provides and updates signals on:
  - Threats and opportunities
  - Innovative ideas for change
  - Risk profiles
  - Barriers to change
  - Internal complacency
  - Positions on S-curves.
- Noise (or apparent noise). Noises can seem like insignificant information. Only disturbances at first. Noise often has short durations and fades off quickly. Noise is always prevalent in emerging trends. Noise is the embryo of weak signals. Noise often dampens important signals. It is highly sensitive to the

context. We need to 'listen to' the faint signals within noise, or we may miss the sounds of warning or opportunity.

- Weak signals are early warning signals that point to potential opportunity or harm. When noise becomes louder and more consistent, it can be considered as a weak signal and it may be important to your entity.

- Emerging trends are trends that start strong, die-off, and may re-appear later, or originate from another source. Emerging trends need scrutiny—they may unexpectedly develop into strong change drivers.

- Strong trends are trends that either powerfully advance, or powerfully disrupt driving forces for change. They adjust the speed and momentum of a driving force, and indicate imminent significant changes.

- Events. One or many seemingly unconnected events may cause the emergence of new trends. Events that cause global driving forces for change are often, but may not necessarily be connected to your specific local context (See Chapter 6). Such global change events may not necessarily occur near your entity, but may cause strong change signals that can spill-over into your context.

- Ideas. Be on the lookout for new ideas—especially those nonconformist ideas from left field. Scratch around in contexts seemingly distant from yours and in industries seemingly unrelated to yours.

- Look out for 'old or dead' ideas—they can often come alive again—depending on the context, and who applies creativity and innovation to them.

- Failures. Other's and your entity's failures can be useful signals for change. Purposely identify and qualify failures that occur in your fields of endeavour, and within adjacent fields.

'Failures' are potential gold mines of new innovations, new opportunities, and warnings of threats that can be avoided.

Step 4 – Screen the Signals

Which signals reflect a pending change that will have a significant impact on the strategic intent of the entity, the operational environment, or the context the entity operates in?

Screening is the fourth step in the anticipation funnel. In this step, we screen and select relevant subsets of signals. Signals are sorted and filtered to identify patterns, interdependencies, opportunities, anomalies, threats, and change initiatives. Screening is the first essential step toward making sense of a vast number of diverse signals.

The objectives of Screening signals are to:

- Determine clear change patterns from the signals.
- Discover change characteristics hidden in the signals—such as: Is the signal suggesting for example, process improvements, innovation, competitive directional changes, restructuring, or a pending disaster?
- Discover systemic interdependencies between different signals. Would these interdependencies develop and grow in strength and lead to stronger change drivers and larger impacts on the entity?
- What are the interdependencies between observed signals and the usual operations of the entity?
- Which signals are spilling over from other contexts?
- The speed and momentum of approach of the signals.
- What are the dynamic impacts of the signals that could, for example, require modifications to the entity's execution systems?
- Are there internal barriers, sources of resistance, fears, or

comfort zones, that will inhibit anticipated change initiatives? Where in the entity do these barriers and resistance exist?

Today entities have a vast choice of mathematical and analytical tools to filter, sort and pattern large amounts of data and signals (so-called Big data and Analytics). The increasing power and storage capacities of computer hardware make screening increasingly easier. Data-mining software that use mathematical and statistical algorithms, called business analytics, are widely available to filter and model vast quantities of real time consumer and retail data. Furthermore, some of these software algorithms have artificial intelligence characteristics—they can be programmed to learn from the patterns they have detected and analysed, and therefore improve upon subsequent rounds of signal analyses.

Herein lies the significant challenge to effectively lead the process of anticipation. The correct selection of screening and patterning criteria and methodologies are critical to obtain accurate indications of potential change drivers. The simple act of screening means that certain amounts of knowledge content will be discarded or lost. The question is: Is it critical; and which parts of the content are unnecessary? This fact—selecting the correct parts of knowledge content—is the key reason why the anticipation process must be a recursive process. The sources of signals, the methodologies and outcomes of screening signals, must be challenged frequently. Screening and selection methods, and filtering criteria must be revisited and regularly improved to ensure the anticipation process is always fresh and the intelligence produced is perceived from multiple viewpoints.

Step 5 – Construct Pictures and Pathways

In this fifth step, we start to create intelligence that will lead to change initiatives. We take the screened and selected subsets of signals and apply other non-linear mental models to construct plausible future pictures and pathways. We derive meaning from the selected signals through an inclusive process. We consider the interrelationships of the selected set of signals and create pictures of how the combined effect of the signals will shape the future. This very important step goes beyond the linear cause-and-effect of individual trends and signals. We employ the principles explored in the Enable stage (Chapter 8) to reframe signals into plausible future pictures and pathways. These plausible pictures and pathways may become your entity's potential change drivers in later steps.

Screened signals are interpreted, reframed and synthesised to determine the significance, speed, momentum, direction and magnitude of potential change drivers. They are shaped in ways that ensure the new change directions would make sense from a variety of vantage points.

Pictures and pathways comprise of:

- Potential change-drivers
- Estimated magnitudes of impact of change-drivers on the entity
- Risks and threats to the entity that need to be avoided or mitigated
- Opportunities worth pursuing
- Positions on the S-curves of your entity and its offerings
- Potential timing of change initiatives
- Alternative options for change initiatives

Anticipation and timing to respond to change goes hand in glove. Timing is a critical success factor for any change initiative. Timeous anticipation directs correct timing of change implementation.

Figure 10.2 illustrates an example of what could happen to an entity if the construction of pictures and pathways was not done regularly and rigorously. It shows a typical lifecycle of a change signal as it matures from a weak signal to a full-blown opportunity, threat or crisis. On the vertical axis, it shows the time remaining to act on the signal.

In Figure 10.2 the illustration starts with a weak emerging signal that suggests the arrival of a potential new disruptive technology (or potential threat). At this early instant in time the entity may decide it is not worth the effort to spend resources to investigate this weak signal—they believe there is still plenty of time left to watch its development.

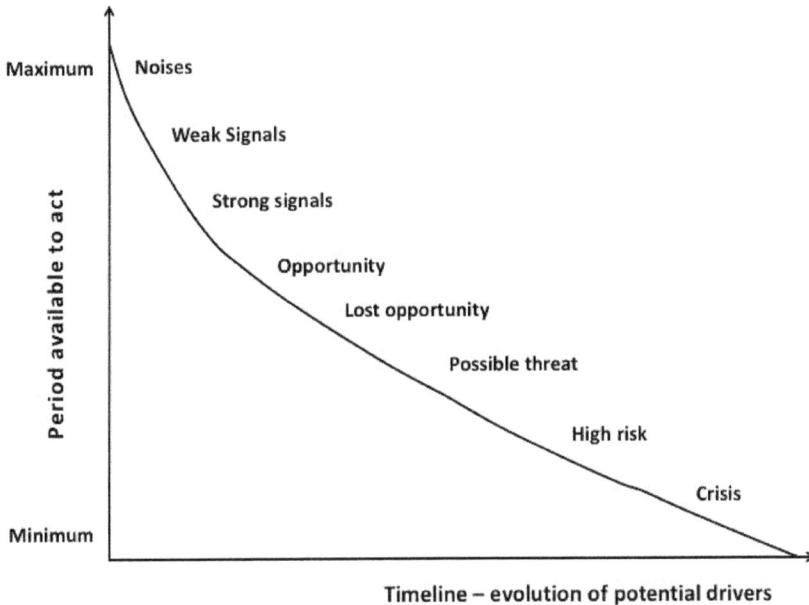

Figure 10.2. Evolution of a Change Signal over Time and Time Remaining to Act

After a few months, information about this innovation (or disruptive threat) becomes more definite and it turns out to be a trend that may have positive advantages for the entity if they pursue it. However, the leaders did not gather enough essential intelligence on this signal, at this instance, and decide to wait a bit longer. They believe there is ample time left and they are confident the entity will catch-up if they must.

Yet more time passes and new information indicates that several small competitors have embarked on this new disruptive technology. Initial market statistics show that the innovation is gaining momentum in its particular market. Clearly the leaders are now in a position where they must decide—an expensive decision at this stage. Do they pursue this innovative technology by developing their own version from scratch—that could take many years—or, do they purchase a costly license from rivals to enter the market with the new innovation?

Undoubtedly in this example, at this juncture the leaders have long lost the initiative. As it so often happens, the next stage could be that the competitive situation deteriorates further. The new disruptive innovation does not only pose a market threat, it creates a crisis by destroying the current technology's market. The entity may have to exit the market. The rival has beaten the entity in the market by performing diligent anticipation of change.

Obviously, the course of the weak signal in this example could have taken other directions. The point is that constructing different pictures and pathways from several sets of signals is a crucial part of anticipation because it guides better timing of change initiatives. Anticipation must be done continually to keep you updated on the latest change intelligence. If not, you could slide down a curve such as the one in Figure 10.2. You could be too late to take advantage of opportunities or take proactive actions against threats.

Step 6 – Create options

From the pictures and pathways, identify a set of potentially viable change initiatives for each of the plausible future pictures and pathways. Employ the principles explored in the Enable stage of the Change Dimension, and elaborate on potential initiatives. You now develop 'straw men' on how you could act in your selected pictures or pathways—your draft change initiatives are taking shape. No detailed scoping is done at this stage.

In step 6, the pictures and pathways from step 5 have matured into your entity's change drivers, since you resolved to act on them.

The following methods can be used to increase the quality and scope of options into better and more feasible change initiatives:

- Create and explore initiatives with scenario thinking. Envisage alternative futures, especially those that do not necessarily follow current trends.

- Syntheses of future focused directions, change strategies and potential responses. Use systems and innovative thinking to synthesise different new options by combining distinctive individual pieces of intelligence in new ways.
- Test and experiment on initiatives first, by performing further research, innovation, pilots and prototypes.
- Form and use third parties, specialists and collaborative partnerships to test and experiment potential change initiatives. Collaborative partnerships can improve costs, resources, quality and timing of potential change initiatives.
- Share created options with non-related entities and third parties to test your hypotheses, exchange lessons learned, and generate innovative solutions for similar challenges.

Step 7 – Converge

Converge is the final step in the *'Anticipate Change Funnel'*. Converge narrows the set of potential viable initiatives to a prioritised short-list that could address your change drivers. Revisit your questions in the first step—Set the Scene. What needs to be different, what are the change signals, which change initiatives should we consider, what actions should we consider, how and when do you need to act?

Depending on how many change initiatives have been generated and shortlisted, it may be necessary to prioritise— especially when your entity needs to conserve its resources and maintain resilience. The final prioritised short list of change initiatives will be considered for further development in the next phase of the Change Dimension—the Incubation stage.

The short-list of change options should cover the following, in broad terms:

- The change context within which the solution is required
- Estimated resource requirements
- Level of maturity of the change initiative—how long will it take to become a viable option?
- Do we need extraordinary procedures to implement the change initiative?
- Gaps in the entity's capability and capacity that need to be addressed, or that may develop because of the initiative
- Impact on the entity's resilience and agility when the option is implemented
- What are the other alternative solutions (options) to the change initiative
- The people who will be involved in, and impacted by, the initiative
- Expected behavioural and psychological responses by people involved
- Timing and risk parameters.
- The urgency, speed, impact, and consequences of the change initiative
- Is the initiative part of a series or sequence of other change initiatives?
- What are the systemic interdependencies between the change initiative and sub-systems

The list is not meant to be exhaustive and should be adapted depending on your contextual environment. Options for change initiatives generated by the **'Anticipate Change Funnel'** are not defined in detail yet. Detailed definition will occur in the Incubation and Delivery stages of the Change Dimension.

Continually challenge the Anticipation Process

Revisit, question, and refresh the inputs, outputs and methods used in every step to prevent biases from settling in. Biases inhibit the entity to pick up signals—often signals that are critical change drivers. Because the anticipation process can be cognitively demanding and mentally intimidating, it is natural for people involved to prematurely get set on ideas, trends, methods and opinions. Bias is a natural way to cope with vast amounts of information and complexity.

As leaders, we should continually challenge the way we anticipate change:

- Be conscious that your people may have fears or concerns that prevent them from detecting and exposing change drivers and signals. When you spot such fears or behaviours, your entity may not yet be fully inclusive.
- Create opportunities for open debate about pictures, pathways and options and do not suppress conflicting and competing opinions. Safe environments that encourage expression of fears, doubts and concerns lead to identification of biases, resistance, problems, solutions and better change opportunities.
- Use diverse groups to discuss and challenge assumptions behind change initiatives that flow through the funnel. Groups can consist of people from diverse levels, backgrounds, skill sets, and functions, ensuing a diversity of perspectives. Revitalise groups by changing the membership on a regular basis.
- Use groups who can champion and clarify change initiatives to a broader employee base, gather feedback for the rest of the entity, and act as continual points of contact for monitoring the progress of change initiatives.
- Challenge participants in the anticipation process to spend

time with customers and actual users. Often the party who purchase and the party who use a product or service are not the same—and their preferences, behaviours and habits may differ a lot. Ignoring such differences may lead to false assumptions.

- Depending on the internal culture, the anticipation process can become bogged down in excessive detail analyses or consume more time and resources than necessary. This is especially true when there is a high aversion to risk in your entity's culture or its leaders' behaviour. Check for an acceptable balance between the amount of detail work and the value added to the change intelligence that is generated. When you are in doubt, rather err on the conservative side.

- Premature intervention in the anticipation process often leads to hasty decisions that could lead to the failure of initiatives.

- Frequently review the sources of intelligence, tools and methods employed in the process. Intelligence generated is only as good as the inputs and the methods used. Challenge the process to come up with new sources, new signals, and new methods.

- Ensure that feedback loops between the anticipation process and other systems in your entity are seamless. If your entity is not up-to-date about several potential change drivers it faces, the intelligence system needs to be redesigned so that inclusive organisational learning can occur. Since not every person in your entity can feasibly take part in the anticipation process, the entity must rely on active engagement and knowledge management systems to include everyone.

Final thoughts about Anticipation

Anticipation of change can be done by entities of any size, ranging from a one-person business to very large global corporations. One person can use it as a disciplined thought process. On the other end of the scale, the process can be implemented as a rigorous disciplined change intelligence system. The process can be applied with the level of complexity warranted for the size and skill level of the company. How to best use it is a matter of degree.

Once you have a change anticipation process in operation and your people have mastered good anticipation discipline, it will save time and ensure that few opportunities are missed. Besides, it will ensure that the right opportunities and threats are addressed timeously. The intent is that it should be done with a manageable and reasonable time commitment.

Many leaders are astute anticipators. They can perform the full anticipation process, almost intuitively, on a given change driver in their minds within seconds—from the moment they observe a signal or trend, to the moment when they determine potential changes necessary in their entity. However, herein lies the significant trap of exclusion. When anticipation is done unilaterally by the leader, it is an exclusive process and the rest of the entity is left behind. They must have the opportunity to participate and get on board. Failing this leads to disengagement with the Pre-Life-Cycle and resistance. An anticipation process that is done inclusively can take a while longer and a larger number of people to work through data sources, information and intelligence. However, the return on investment by being inclusive throughout the anticipation process, is that you can identify initiatives that are less reactionary, meet less resistance and have higher chances of success.

Summary

Anticipate is the third of the Change Dimension's five stages. Leaders should encourage proactive behaviours to anticipate changes and their long-term consequences. Change that takes place under stress, duress or because of a crisis is seldom achieved successfully. Anticipation focuses on what is plausible and possible for the future. It also considers many possible consequences. Anticipation must be done inclusively to obtain the full spectrum of potential change options.

The *Anticipate Change Funnel* is designed to encourage proactive anticipation behaviours in entities. The funnel deals with all kinds of data, information and knowledge. It systematically extracts from, and adds value to a broad information base. Through rigorous reduction, creative and synthesis processes, a small number of viable change options are identified. The *Anticipate Change Funnel* is unique—it systematically extracts and reduces information, and with the support of non-linear mental models, it also adds value to produced intelligence, and it does so in a recursive manner.

The *Anticipate Change Funnel* follows seven steps:

- Set the Scene
- Select the Sources
- Find the Signals
- Screen the Signals
- Construct Pictures and Pathways
- Create Options
- Converge to viable initiatives.

It is important to regularly revisit, challenge and refresh the inputs, methods and outputs of every step of the funnel, to prevent biases settling into the entity's mental models.

———

11. The Change Dimension - Stage 4

INCUBATE

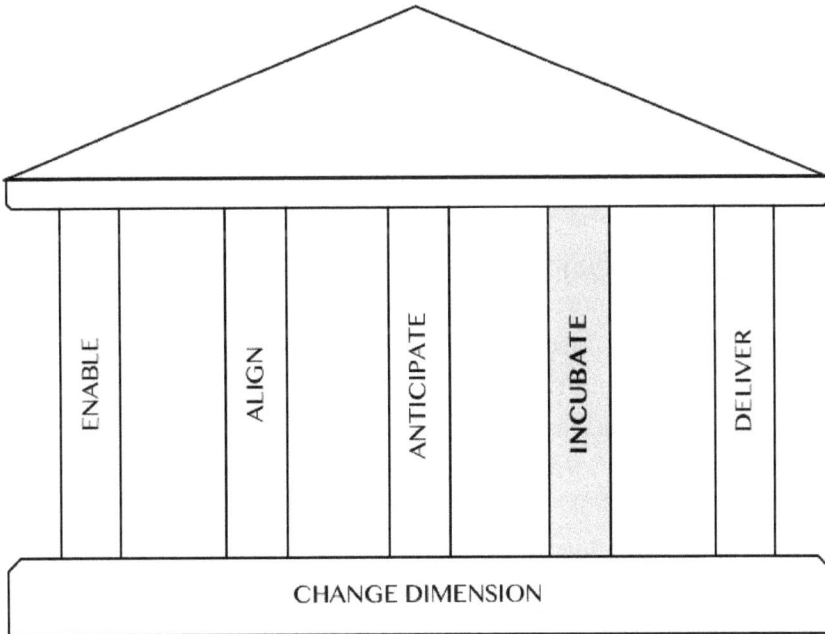

Change will occur successfully when conditions are suitable.

In the Incubate stage we foster dedicated, suitable conditions to support successful selection, implementation and integration of change initiatives

The outcome of the Incubate stage is the assurance that viable change initiatives are ready for the next Delivery stage.

The prioritised shortlist of change initiatives that were generated in the Anticipate stage are further nurtured and developed in the Incubate stage. We add significant improvements and value—we identify areas that will save time and expenses. The Incubate stage enhances alignment, readies change initiatives for delivery, and shortens implementation schedules.

In the Incubate stage we determine how many resources will be allocated. It is a crucial step in the Change Dimension. In the subsequent Deliver stage, you will spend substantial resources to develop and deliver the initiative in its intended location. That is why it is critical that the Incubate stage is done with great care—to ensure that you invest the right kinds and amount of resources in the best initiatives.

When entities follow the usual approach to develop change initiatives—that is, without appreciation of the Pre-Life-Cycle—they do little work, if any, during the early stages of the Change Dimension. Sadly, I have seen too many cases where leaders omit the discipline that is similar to the principles in the Incubate stage. The common approach is to announce change initiatives and start right away with implementation. In these cases, change initiatives would transition from idea to implementation—almost instantaneously. These leaders announce and passionately sell their exclusive visionary change initiatives without the kind of proper proactive development I advocate in the Change Dimension. The success rates of such change initiatives are as poor as suggested by the statistics quoted in Chapter 1.

Objectives of the Incubate stage

The main objective of the Incubate stage is to ensure the right conditions are established for viable change initiatives that are ready to launch in the Deliver stage. During the previous stage—Anticipate—a prioritised short list of change initiatives is identified. In the Incubate stage, these initiatives are considered for further development and your task is to ensure that suitable, nurturing conditions are created for them. Your entity therefore aims to do the following:

- Determine if proposed cases for change are the right change initiatives for your entity at any point in time.
- Evaluate the proposed options for change initiatives in detail.
- Prioritise change proposals in the initiative portfolio. An excess of change initiatives will result in overload, disengagement, loss of focus and weakening of your entity's agility and resilience.
- Rigorously evaluate your entity's capability and capacity to implement and integrate change initiatives.
- Test and achieve complete alignment with the entity and stakeholders.
- Review if superior value and returns on resources on change initiatives will be realised.
- Identify parties that might resist initiatives and determine the reasons for resistance.
- Determine the next steps to progress the initiative into the Delivery stage.

Ready to enter the Delivery stage

A well Incubated initiative will be set for a successful launch during the next stage called Deliver—when the following aspects are complete:

- The case for change is complete and ready to be implemented.
- The people who are impacted by, and involved in the initiative are fit for change.

- The entity (systems, capacity, capability, resources) is equipped, aligned and ready to implement and integrate the change initiative.

If any of these aspects lack in readiness or alignment, continuing with the initiative could be highly risky. Delays, preventable resistance, cost overruns, stunted implementation and inevitable lacklustre success are the unwanted outcomes one could encounter.

I suggest the following approach for successful Incubation:

- Prepare the case for change.
- Diagnose readiness and alignment with a preliminary change-fitness assessment. When this change-fitness diagnosis fails; stop, hold or cycle the initiative back to previous stages in the Change Dimension.
- Complete the Incubation development work as identified in the case for change. Finalise Incubation with a comprehensive readiness review.

Develop the Case for Change

Incubation processes vary a lot. For example, the incubation process for an acquisition is a lot different in comparison to incubation processes for innovative technologies, or organisation restructures.

Preparation and development of a case for change includes detailed development work, dedicated processes and comprehensive reports that require earmarked capability, capacity and resource commitments.

To build the case for change you would rely heavily on the intelligence gathered during the Anticipate and Align stages. Often considerable additional development work should be done first, such as, experimentation, piloting, prototyping and testing to complete a case for change. The final case for change will recommend how the initiative should be progressed in the Delivery stage.

A case for change must show conclusively how the proposed initiative will address the change drivers that were identified in the Anticipate stage, how it is aligned with the entity, and to what extent the people involved are ready and fit for the initiative.

The Change Governance process (Chapter 9) relies heavily on a fully incubated case for change to accurately steer and prioritise initiatives in your change initiative portfolio. A comprehensive case for change is essential to accurately manage resources, capacity and capability allocations.

Each initiative has its own unique emphasis—therefore, the design of each case will differ. For example, consider the differences between capital expenditure projects, continuous improvement exercises and culture change initiatives. All of them involve substantial changes to an entity.

The Change Dimension provides you with the rigor and discipline to avoid a sense of complacency with change, even if you do particular change initiatives on a regular basis. As I have illustrated by the *Change Continuum* (Chapter 6), change initiatives vary considerably in the challenges they pose. For some entities change initiatives such as introducing new services, making acquisitions, or producing innovations, might be their regular occupation. Those entities may not regard such initiatives as change initiatives, but as their regular continuous business. However, we should be careful in our assessment of what is regarded as a change initiative or not. Consider the different kinds of challenges for every initiative, for example, consider the intensity, complexity, and systemic impacts, before you proceed (Chapter 6). What could seem like yet another routine initiative may pose serious consequences to your entity.

Commonly cases for change cover a conventional list of topics and actions as listed below. The content and extent of work will vary from initiative to initiative and is highly context dependent. Conventional cases for change normally cover:

- Strategic objectives of the initiative
- Governance and mandate
- Value propositions to be delivered
- Key supporting assumptions
- Key success factors
- Fatal flaws that could terminate the initiative
- Alternative options considered
- Development stage and development actions completed, i.e. experiments, pilots, prototypes and tests
- Next development steps
- Competitive analyses
- Market analyses
- Financial feasibility
- Resource, capacity and capability requirements and constraints
- Management and staff requirements
- Funds required
- Partners needed and selected
- Monitoring and reporting
- Organisational structure (to integrate the initiative)
- Technology and technical feasibility
- Operational requirements
- Manufacturing requirements
- Product quality standards
- Intellectual property
- Environmental assessments
- Health and safety assessments
- Community relations
- Legal and legislative issues
- Regulatory impacts and requirements

- Probabilistic risk analysis
- Change management execution plan.

In the age of continuous change new mindsets and proactive work are required to incubate change initiatives. Conventional cases for change generally regard initiatives as static, or stand-alone events. Little attention is given to the dynamic and systemic influences created by change drivers, the necessary relationships, and how people and stakeholders are affected by initiatives.

The following list is a guide for leaders to consider during Incubation—the items serve as prompts for preparing change-fit cases for change.

- What are the contextual concerns? (Chapter 3, see for example, the level, complexity, timeframe and location of contextual concerns.)
- Change sources and drivers identified in the Anticipate stage that triggered the initiative
- Different mental models considered and applied to generate incubation options for this case
- Impact of initiative on entity resilience
- Impact of initiative on entity agility
- Potential and imminent disruptors (market, technology, legislation, etc.) that may threaten this initiative
- Speed and momentum of potential disruptions
- Timeframe in which appropriate actions are necessary
- Impacts on customers
- Learning and feedback incorporated from previous initiatives
- Collaborative relationships that must to be developed
- Options considered and assessment criteria used to assess different options

- Opportunity costs of pursuing this initiative as compared to opportunity costs of other options that were rejected
- The people that will be impacted, i.e. adopters, recipients and stakeholders
- Transition support provided to people, before, during, and after change initiative
- Employee capacity and development requirements needed
- Cultural alignment, for example, during mergers and acquisitions
- Entity barriers that could choke the initiative
- Dynamic complexities and systemic impacts that the change initiative would generate in the entity
- Exclusions—those specific aspects that are not considered, covered or intended by the initiative
- How performance management of the initiative will be led, such as:
  - Key milestones
  - Trigger events
  - Exit triggers
  - Performance measures
  - Performance targets.

Diagnose preliminary fitness for change

Simultaneously, during the development of the case for change, the entity and your people must be diagnosed for their fitness to undertake the change initiative. In the Incubate stage you would be assessing a small number of potentially viable change initiatives. The main objectives of diagnosing preliminary fitness, is to test the alignment with the entity of the shortlisted change initiatives, and the fitness of your people for the initiatives.

I suggest a preliminary diagnosis of change-fitness for the change initiative shortly after it has been suggested or presented for Incubation. An initial high-level diagnosis before embarking on a full Incubation process will save time and resources and it will eliminate misguided and overzealous change initiatives—sooner rather than later.

A preliminary fitness diagnosis will call attention to several areas that may need further development, before the change initiative is ready for the Implementation stage. The diagnosis will indicate if and where there is residual behavioural resistance to deal with first. Unresolved resource allocation problems or cultural issues that are unfavourable to a change-oriented environment are examples of residual issues.

To assess entity and people fitness for a change initiative, ask the following questions:

- Do we really have to implement this change initiative?
- Are the leaders and the entity in alignment with the suggested change initiative?
- What are the remaining behavioural resistance issues?
- What are the remaining barriers the entity pose to the change initiative?

Answers to those key questions will provide you with important indicators on how fit your entity is for an initiative. A preliminary diagnosis will identify:

- Likelihood of success of the change initiative
- Residual change desirability mismatches
- Indicative capacity and capability misalignments, shortcomings and barriers in the entity
- Residual behavioural resistance.

Beckhard & Harris[1] were first to develop a useful diagnostic formula for preliminary change-fitness. Beer[2] subsequently adapted the formula.

For the Incubate stage, I have modernised the Beckhard & Harris formula to be more relevant to the age of change.

The change-fitness diagnostic formula reads as follows:

R < D x P x A = Effective Change Initiative

R = *Resistance* and barriers in the entity

D = The *Desirability* of a change initiative

P = A clear *Purpose* for the change

A = The entity's *Alignment* for the change

The three factors **D, P, and A**, must be positively present. If any of the factors are absent or insufficient, effective change won't happen. First fix those areas that lack before you continue with an initiative.

The formula states that the product of the three factors D, P, and A must be greater than R, the residual behavioural resistance that are against a change initiative. D, P, and A must also align and the product of D, P, and A must be greater than the combination of entity barriers and behavioural resistance. When R is greater than the product of D, P, and A, the chances of a successful change initiative are slim.

Figure 11.1 summarises the preliminary change-fitness diagnostic.

'**D**' tests whether a change initiative is at the right level of *'Desirability'*. When there is no clear case, desire or need to implement a change initiative, then why indeed should you change? When the entity or the leadership are divided about the desirability of specific change initiatives, there clearly is a demand to be more inclusive to resolve issues around desirability. Such a situation would suggest that you revisit the Enable, and Anticipate stages for the proposed initiative.

'**P**' determines if the *'Purpose'* of the change initiative is mutual and whether the change initiative is aligned with the vision and strategic

Resistance < Desirability x Purpose x Alignment ➜ Successful Change

D	P	A		Change Outcome
✓	✓	✓	➜	Successful change initiative
X	✓	✓	➜	Why do we need this change ?
✓	X	✓	➜	No clear direction, anxiety, frustration, delays
✓	✓	X	➜	Failure is a high probability

D - Desirability of the change initiative
P - Purpose for change is clear and aligned with entity's purpose & strategic direction
A - Alignment of change with entity structure, systems, capability & resource capacity

Figure 11.1. Diagnosing Change Fitness

objectives of the entity. For example, a growth initiative may be highly desirable, but not in alignment with the mutual purposes or the strategic direction of the entity. When you push ahead with such an initiative, it leads to anxiety, frustration, loss of direction, and loss of engagement. The initiative may stagger ahead, with delays, cost overruns, mixed results and failure.

'A' checks the entity's *'Alignment'* with the intended change initiative. Does the entity have the necessary capacity and capability to effectively perform this initiative? Does it have the appropriate systems, processes, structures, skills, and so on, to deliver the initiative successfully without compromising agility and resilience? Any misalignment will present as resistance and barriers that must be addressed in the Incubate stage.

Change initiatives may be highly desirable and aligned with the mutual purposes of the entity, but the entity could be unable to effectively perform the initiative, due to constraints in its capacity and capabilities.

When Desirability and Purposes are in place, but Alignment is lacking, it indicates that additional capacity and capability should be created, acquired or reallocated, *before* the change initiative can be implemented effectively. Pushing ahead with change initiatives without addressing misalignments properly will result in stunted change. It will restrain usual operations, and reduce agility and resilience. Any residual misalignment in capacity or capability will result in sub-optimal success.

'**R**' designates residual or emerging *'Resistance'* that have been unattended to in previous stages of the Change Dimension. When your diagnosis indicates that resistance (R), is greater than the combination of desirability (D), purpose (P) and alignment (A), then do not continue with the change initiative until you have dealt properly with the factors causing the resistance.

The starting point to identify and resolve resistance is to understand the origins and underlying causes. Your initial reaction to perceived resistance might be incorrect. Leaders mistakenly tend to believe that they have logical answers to make changes, and that the entity must follow their well-meaning direction because it is in its best interest. You should consider the full spectrum of peoples' behaviours—not only what they say, but also what they do and think about change initiatives.

Healthy resistance provides excellent fuel for innovation, debate and questioning of assumptions behind proposed change initiatives. In an inclusive change-oriented culture, you would encounter constructive resistance against change initiatives. That resistance should be used 'optimally' for constructive resolutions. Many sources of resistance are usually related to entity barriers, which can be resolved as discussed in Chapter 9 on alignment.

If you detect only minor resistance, it could be a sign of blind compliance, or hidden resistance—which can be exceptionally unhealthy for the success of a change initiative. You should dig deeper. When submissive or passive resistance is discovered too late in the change process, it will cause considerable damage and delays to change initiatives.

On the contrary, when you discover major resistance, it is a clear sign that the change initiative is not ready—not even to proceed with the Incubate stage. Insist that the initiative is moved back to earlier stages of the Change Dimension. Find out where in the process the initiative is stuck. You may have to do more work on the initial stages of the Change Dimension, for example, the Enable, Alignment or Anticipate stages.

Comprehensive Incubation Review

Review philosophy

A comprehensive Incubation review is necessary after the completion of the Incubation development work as identified in the case for change.

The main objective of the review process is to identify how ready we are to continue to the Delivery stage with the change initiative. If there are misalignments, or areas that are not yet ready—the case for change will need further incubation work, or the course of the initiative may have to be corrected.

Most change initiatives are multi-staged. Consequently, I recommend that one does a readiness review before a new stage commences. This kind of rigorous discipline is used extensively by entities experienced in large capital projects, innovation, and new product development initiatives.

Review team

Reviews of change initiatives pose excellent opportunities to create and establish an inclusive culture. Several review team members should be invited from areas that are not associated with the initiative. That will create impartiality and less bias towards the subject of the change initiative.

The incubation review team may consist of:

- You as the leader, who would act as the role model for the initiative, demonstrating the behaviours and principles you want to engrain in a change-oriented culture.
- The change governance team (Chapter 9). They are responsible for assembling review teams when cases for change are proposed for review.
- Peers from other groups, departments, or divisions that are impartial to the initiative.
- Representation from people and groups affected by the change initiative.
- Representatives of major stakeholders (when and where possible, and if applicable).

Review process

The change governance team (Chapter 9) follows your entity's change initiative charter and uses Incubation reviews to fulfil part of their accountability.

During Incubation reviews these points are addressed:

- The level of priority of the case for change in the entity's initiative portfolio.
- Validity of underlying assumptions and supporting evidence used to develop the case for change.
- Quality and reliability of the assumptions, processes and methods used to develop the case.
- Process and procedures by which the case for change topics have been developed.
- Learning and feedback from previous initiatives within the entity and elsewhere.
- Significant risks we could be exposed to, should the change initiative be delivered and integrated.

- Suitability of triggers for course corrections and timeous termination.
- Resources: Capacity and capabilities that are necessary, available, and reallocations that are required.
- Potential capacity and capability overloads that could be caused by the initiative.
- How delivery and integration will occur within the entity.
- Systemic interdependencies with existing systems, and potential risks caused by complex dependencies.
- Relationships that are necessary to advance the initiative.
- Psychological and emotional support necessary for various people or groups to help them with personal transitions.
- Talent and employee capacity development needs, for example, mentoring, coaching, training and job rotations.
- Stakeholder actions and reactions considered and contingency plans to address their concerns.

Outcomes and results of Incubation reviews

Not all eggs in the incubator will hatch, and that is fine...

The last step of an Incubation review is to consolidate recommendations made by the teams that proposed and reviewed the initiative. Several consecutive reviews may be necessary depending on the kind of change initiative. Recommendations of reviews are not simply 'Go' or 'No-Go' decisions, but must add value. Decisions of the review team may sit somewhere on a continuum between Go and No-Go. For example, the review team could propose one of the following actions for an Incubated change initiative:

- Go ahead with delivery—the case for change is ready and aligned with the entity and people.

- First run the initiative as a pilot program in one or more locations or contexts, before rolling it out in the whole entity.
- Break the initiative down into stages or smaller parts, to allow additional decision and trigger points and address areas of substantial risk exposure.
- Delay delivery, to better align the entity or people with the proposed change initiative.
- Do further development work on certain aspects of the case for change.
- Go ahead, but with specific contingency plans that must be in place before the Delivery stage commences.
- First develop necessary capacity or capabilities, before embarking on the proposed change initiative.
- Develop trade-offs or collaborative relationships with stakeholders or third parties prior to Delivery, to ensure successful integration of the initiative.
- No-Go. Stop the initiative. It may neither be in alignment, nor be ready for a variety of reasons. For example, it may not be aligned with the entity's mutual purpose or strategy, or the initiative will not deliver on its intended value proposition.

Outcomes of successful Incubation

When you have properly completed the Incubate stage, you will achieve superior outcomes for change initiatives. For example, your entity will:

- Reach change decisions sooner and cheaper
- Achieve faster growth
- Achieve better returns on resources committed to change initiatives
- Reduce implementation and integration schedules
- Save on costs and scarce resources through the stages

- Build an extensive initiative portfolio, while purging low priority initiatives
- Reduce the risks which change initiatives may transfer to the entity
- Achieve higher certainty about outcomes of change initiatives at a lower cost

Incubation saves costs

The graph in Figure 11.2 shows that during classic implementation the most significant cost inflexion point occurs when a change initiative is launched for implementation. Usually this is the point when the bulk of expenditures on the change initiative commences.

When you lead Incubation correctly, the costs of developing a change initiative up to and including the Incubate stage, are between 3% to 6% of the total resource expenditure needed to complete the initiative[3]. More than 90% of expenditures on initiatives are incurred *after* the launch, yet the most value is secured *before* the launch.

Expenditures on proper development through the early stages of the Change Dimension, including the Incubate stage, is a small premium to pay to ensure better success and better returns on your committed resources. That equally applies to change initiatives that have been abandoned. Which situation is better for the entity? A loss of 3% on a cancelled project, for the right reasons, or spending 150% on an unsuccessful project that should not have been implemented? The Change Dimension is designed to avoid these serious mistakes.

It is vital that your change initiatives are carefully developed, reviewed for readiness, and checked for alignment with the entity and the people involved, *before* it is launched. It is also critical that your change initiatives are reviewed at several checkpoints during Delivery—in the next stage. These review gates, checkpoints or key milestones serve as pre-agreed triggers. Checkpoints and milestones are discussed in more detail in the next chapter.

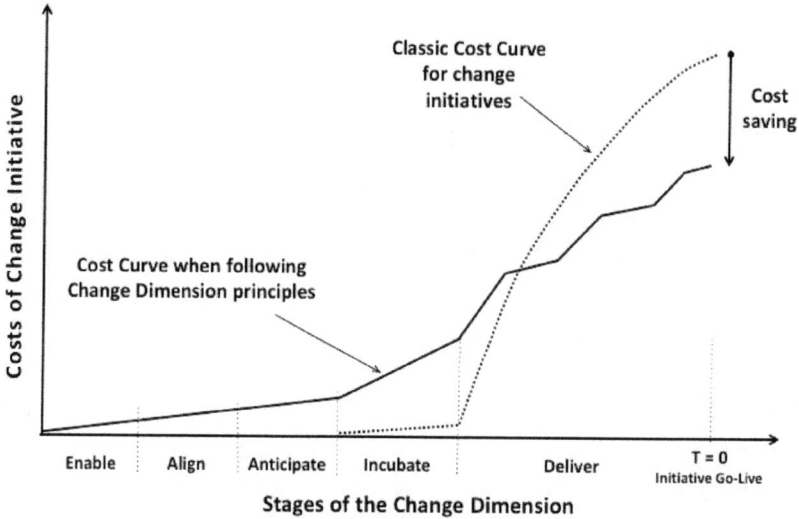

Figure 11.2. Costs of Developing an Initiative during its Pre-Life-Cycle

Customarily expenditures on change initiatives follow a curve as illustrated by the dotted line in Figure 11.2. Leaders who follow this traditional approach boast the rationale that 'time-is-money' and 'we just get on with it'. They spend as little resources as possible on the perceived fuzzy front end of the Pre-Life-Cycle. Yet there is undisputable evidence available about all kinds of change initiatives in various industries, that suggests following a focused and disciplined development of initiatives during their pre-life stages has significant benefits. It improves the probability of success, shortens implementation schedules and increases returns on applied resources[4].

Change initiatives that are prepared with solid front-end groundwork show success rates that are more than double that of initiatives that lack the disciplined front-end development methods I advocate in the Change Dimension[5].

Incubation saves time and increases speed

The key for leaders is to know when to step on the accelerator and when to step on the brakes

When clarity and certainty are low – slow down!

When clarity and certainty are high – Fast track

Conscientious front-end preparation of change initiatives avoids lengthy and costly delays that usually occur much later during the Delivery stage. These delays erode your anticipated competitive advantages, add extra development costs, and can eventually cause your entity to fail.

Using the rigor of proper Incubation can cut between 15% and 25% from delivery schedules[6]. The Change Dimension is designed to achieve earlier and cost-effective development of well-defined change initiatives. The returns on investment in Incubation become evident during the subsequent Delivery stage. That is when the costs and risks of initiative failure are the highest. Proper Incubation reduces the risks of over expenditure and prolonged schedules in the Delivery stage.

Incubation creates and accumulates value

Following the five stages of the Change Dimension will help you to increase added value prior to 'go-live' as well as reduce the time to prepare for the initiative to 'go-live'. In Figure 11.3 the solid line illustrates the time you could save and the value you could add to an initiative by using the Change Dimension. This time saving and added value are compared to how change initiatives are ordinarily conducted (dotted line). Note how you can realise superior value by investing earlier in the Pre-Life-Cycles of initiatives, long before major resources are committed for the Delivery stage. Time and resources spent during the early proactive stages in the Change Dimension are only a fraction of resources spent after the initiative is launched.

Time and cost savings combined with the additional alignment achieved

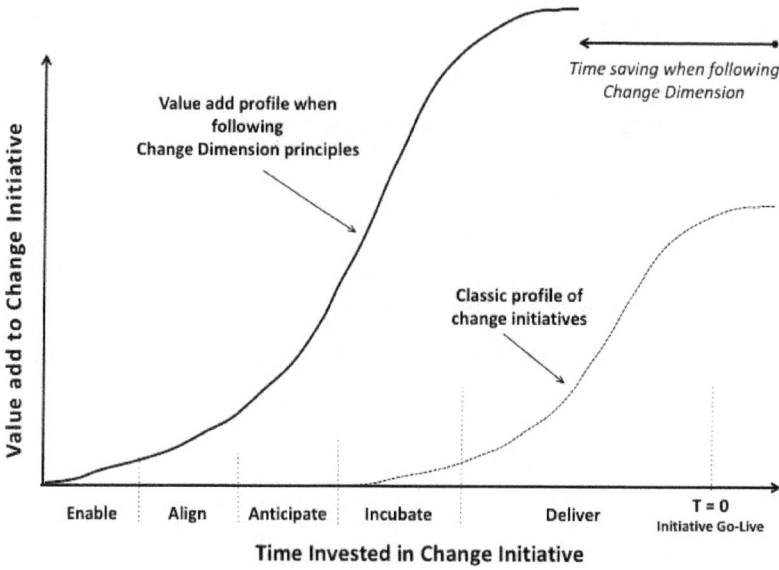

Figure 11.3. Change Dimension Adds Value and Reduces Time

in the early stages translate into significant value creation, before substantial resources are spent.

Entities that emphasise aligned change portfolios, realise cumulative returns on investment (ROI), that are on average 49% higher than the ROI of entities that implement misaligned portfolios[7].

The ROI for individual change initiatives that are correctly aligned with their entity's mutual purpose and strategy is as much as 40% higher when compared to initiatives that are misaligned[8]. Misaligned initiatives realise negative returns—in other words they simply fail and they waste scarce resources. Refer to my discussion on change deficits in Chapter 1.

A word of caution about reactive change initiatives

Leaders must be particularly cautious about any 'Re-'type change initiatives that are recommended for consideration—those are initiatives that begin with *'Re-'* in the name, such as Re-structuring, Re-engineering, Re-organisation or Re-covery.

Be watchful for any proposal that is a *'Re-action'* to change drivers that have been overlooked for some period. These initiatives are notoriously called 'strategic initiatives'. They are often a sign of a leadership team or an entity that has been caught fast asleep—one that did not anticipate a plateau or decline in their S-curves (Chapter 6).

'Re'-type initiatives are infamously 'strategic', secretive, fast tracked, exclusively planned and are consequently not incubated effectively.

'Re'-type initiatives that show characteristics like the following are predisposed to failure:

- The initiative is exclusively conceived behind closed doors with little, if any, inclusion of the rest of the entity.
- The focus of the initiative is almost always on changing the entity's current short-term financial problems, through cost reductions, financial engineering, lay-offs and restructuring of commercial and financial relationships.
- The emphasis is on the short term: The next quarter's results are the main objective, while the long-term implications on the entity are vague.
- Financial investigations and naive financial measures dominate the case. Little else is deliberated in any significant detail.
- The costs and delays that are caused by the disruptions of the *Re-initiative*, and the loss of focus in the entity, is ignored with contempt.

- Lofty forecasted outcomes of the Re-initiative are resourcefully sculpted with clever modelling and zealous sales pitches.

- Implications on customers, clients, stakeholders and employees are superficially addressed, if at all.

- Lack of active engagement and commitment from management and employees is ignored.

- The change initiative is announced with immediate effect and implications for the entity. No room is left for testing the viability of other options.

- The Delivery stage commences immediately after announcement of the *re-initiative*, with unrealistically short turn around targets. Note that proactive initiatives with similar objectives, take much longer.

- At best the *re-initiative* is 'sold' to the entity, stakeholders and the shareholders. At worst, an exclusive leadership team dictates the initiative. People are compelled to 'buy-into' the change initiative.

Gary Hamel has said that, "Too often the strategic planning process ends with the challenge of getting 'buy-in' (from the entity), of getting what is in the heads of the bosses into the heads of the worker bees. But when several hundred employees share the task of identifying and synthesizing a set of unconventional strategic options, the conclusions take on an air of inevitability. In such a process, the leader's task is less to 'sell' the strategy than to ensure that the organization acts on its convictions."
Gary Hamel in 'Strategy as Revolution'[9]

I agree with Gary Hamel (see the box). When leaders diligently follow the principles in the *Change Dimension*, decisions about change initiatives would become inevitable and you would not have to 'sell' them (to people) to get 'buy-in'. In fact, you might have to put brakes on the process, because your entity may likely push for more change initiatives, and sooner.

Successful application of the Change Dimension would mean that you have also created an inclusive change-oriented culture. Change-initiatives that pass successfully thorough the Incubate step would present manageable behavioural resistance and adaptable entity barriers.

The good news is that when you follow the principles of the Leadership Framework (Chapter 3) and the Change Dimension you will be able to prevent scenarios like these occurring in your entity.

Summary

In the Incubate stage we foster dedicated, suitable conditions to support successful selection, implementation and integration of change initiatives. Our prioritised shortlist of change initiatives, generated in the Anticipate stage, is further nurtured and developed. We add significant improvements and value; we identify areas that will save time and expenses and we set the initiative up for success.

Incubate is a crucial step in the Change Dimension. In this stage, we enhance alignment and prepare the change initiatives for delivery. We determine the kinds and amounts of resources needed that will make the initiative a success. We ensure the right conditions are established for viable change initiatives. We make them ready to launch in the next Deliver stage.

A well incubated initiative will have accomplished the following aspects:

- The case for change is complete and ready to be delivered.
- The people who are impacted by, and involved in the initiative are fit for change.
- The entity (its systems, capacity, capability, resources) is fully equipped, aligned and ready to deliver the change initiative.

To ensure successful incubation: diagnose the readiness and alignment of proposed initiatives with a preliminary change fitness assessment. When this diagnosis for change fitness fails: stop, hold or cycle the initiative back to previous stages in the Change Dimension, such as Anticipate, Align or Enable. Finalise the Incubate stage with a comprehensive readiness review before moving forward to the next stage—Deliver.

Notes

1. Beckhard, R., & Harris, R.T. 1987, Organizational Transitions, Addison Wesley, Reading, Massachusetts.

2. Beer, M. 1992, Leading Change, in *Managing people and Organizations, ed.* J.J. Gabbarro, Harvard Business School Press, Boston.

3. Stevens, G. 2003, 'Piloting the Rocket of Radical Innovation', *Research Technology Management*, vol. 46, no. 2, pp.16-25. See Merrow, E. W. 2011, *Industrial Megaprojects – Concepts, Strategies and Practices for Success*, Wiley, New Jersey.

4. Cooper, R.G. & Edgett, S. J., 2005, *Lean, Rapid and Profitable New Product Development*, Product Development Institute, Canada.

5. Cooper, R.G. & Edgett, S. J., 2005, *Lean, Rapid and Profitable New Product Development*, Product Development Institute, Canada.

6. Merrow, E. W. 2011, *Industrial Megaprojects – Concepts, Strategies and Practices for Success*, Wiley, New Jersey.

7. Corporate Executive Board, 2013, 'Breaking Through Indecision for Breakthrough Growth', 2013, https://www.cebglobal.com/blogs/breaking-through-indecision-for-breakthrough-growth/.

8. Corporate Executive Board, 2015, 'Growth Unlocked: Closing the Strategy to Execution Gap', *Corporate Executive Board's Guidance for 2015*.

9. Hamel, G. 1996, 'Strategy as revolution', *Harvard Business Review*, July-August, pp. 69-82.

12. **The Change Dimension - Stage 5**

DELIVER

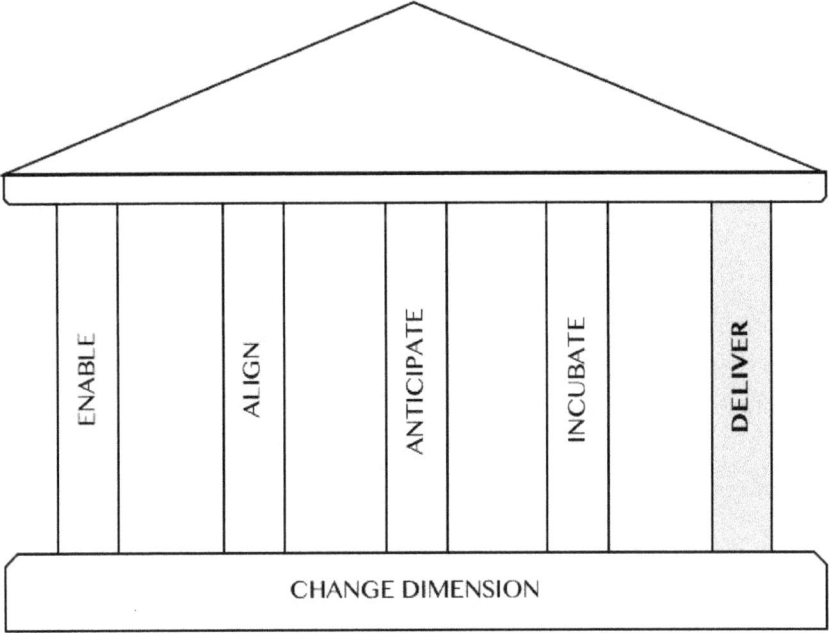

The Deliver stage is the final crucial stage at the end of the Pre-Life-Cycle and the beginning of a new life cycle. It is therefore crucially important to get this right. After the Delivery of a change initiative, it 'goes live'. It starts its own S-curve. After an initiative has gone live, it enters normal operational execution—the topic of the next chapter—that is, the Execution Dimension of leadership behaviour.

The Deliver stage in the Change Dimension is a set of leadership behaviours that integrates the change initiative's new desired behaviours, with the implementation and integration of new systems, structures, processes, new ways of work, and so on, into the entity, so that the initiative's value propositions are realised successfully.

Leaders must lead change!

Leaders must lead change! I don't mean that you should take over the role of your change managers. On the contrary, change managers are necessary to ensure the smooth implementation of change initiatives. Change managers play a vital role.

Reconsider the definition of what leadership is (Chapter 2):

Leadership is a trust relationship among leaders and followers who execute actions and perform change initiatives aimed at achieving mutual purposes.

The last part of the definition says that leaders are the main change agents. Therefore, you should play a highly visible role, from a central position, and reach out to the rest of the entity—not from an ivory tower in a commanding and controlling way, but inclusively—so that your entity can mutually realise successful change initiatives.

Leaders are often very vocal and highly visible during the initial stages of change initiatives, mainly because they are often the main change initiators. Yet, from the launch event onwards, many leaders tend to withdraw from the scene—to attend to 'more urgent and more important' matters, leaving the entire delivery of change initiatives to the change managers.

What could be more important than change initiatives that are delivered to shape the future or direction for your entity?

From your leadership perspective, to ensure successful Delivery, there are three areas you should lead during the Deliver stage. They are depicted in Figure 12.1.

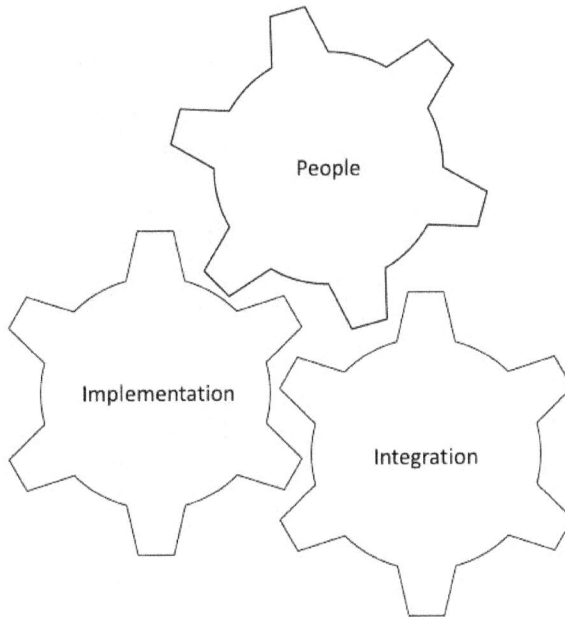

People

Implementation

Integration

Figure 12.1 Focal Areas that ensure successful Delivery of Change Initiatives.

Table 12.1 expands on the three leadership focus areas during Delivery. When you focus on those topics in Table 12.1 in an integrated way on the desired behaviours, you can expect to achieve successful Delivery of the change initiative.

Table 12.1 Leader's focal areas during Delivery stage	
Area	**Leader's focus**
People involved and impacted by initiative	Role modelling Collaborative relationships Recognition and rewards Symbolic events Support personal transitions Resistance resolution
Implementation of the initiative	Implementation plans Accountabilities Launch Monitor progress and performance Course corrections Speed & Timing Change Governance Reallocate resources Risk review
Integration of the initiative within the entity	Drive continual improvements Ensure changeovers Reallocate resources Roll-out initiative Reinforce behaviours

People involved and impacted

You are the role model

Proper role modelling of your behaviours to influence cultural change, in fact any change, is a responsibility you cannot delegate to anyone.

To be the central role model for change, it is necessary that you lead with the behavioural changes you want. Your emotional intelligence is invaluable, especially your self-awareness. Knowledge of your values, principles, habits, preferences, strengths, weaknesses and personality are essential to play an authentic role. The amount of time you allocate to certain issues, your priorities and who you spend time with, are clear nonverbal signals of what you value, and what is important to you. These are highly visible behaviours that people constantly observe and examine. You may also exhibit some obstructive leadership behaviours that you may not be aware of, such as arrogance, aggression, narcissism, an autocratic style, not listening or exclusion, that will stand in the way of successful change initiatives.

Several methods are available to start your journey of self-discovery and behavioural renovation—for example, a 360-degree review of your leadership behaviours. I recommend that you use a 360-degree review to compare and contrast your current leadership behaviours, with your expected leadership behaviours that will ensure the success of your entity and your change initiatives. Also use behaviour reviews and feedback methods that include your personal performance on cultural values, required behaviours, as well as the tangible performance objectives. Beware, this may be a humbling exercise—you must be brave. Denying the validity of personal leadership reviews is almost always a sure sign that you have quite some way to go with your own behavioural transformation.

Any misalignment between your current and required behaviours indicates areas for personal development and behavioural corrections. Subsequently leadership teams should openly, and jointly discuss their individual leadership development needs and solicit development support from their colleagues and coaches.

Sometimes, when there is a significant behavioural misalignment it could mean that the leader who continually exhibits misalignment, has to be dismissed from the entity. Jack Welch of General Electric typifies this kind of misaligned leader as the 'Type 4 Leader'[1]. For example, when a leader who delivers on his performance targets, but disregards the entity's values, principles and behaviours necessary for success, is kept on board, he will harm the entity in the longer run. In GE's vocabulary, the 'Type 1 Leader' is the star leader. He lives by the entity's values and achieves his performance objectives. The 'Type 3 Leader' who lives by the entity's values but doesn't yet completely achieve his performance objectives, is given another chance to improve. The 'Type 2 Leader' who neither lives by the entity's values nor achieves his performance targets is excused from the entity.

Collaborative relationships

The main reason for forming third party collaborative relationships is that your entity may realise it cannot achieve certain objectives on its own. Not all your change initiatives would involve alliances or relationships with external parties or stakeholders. But, if your change initiative relies on the creation of new, or the use of existing relationships, then the following discussion is important when you move into the Deliver stage of a change initiative.

Collaborative relationships or alliances are relationships formed between entities to add value for all parties in the relationship. Alliances are essentially about combining specific strengths to create an entity that will deliver superior value. Robert Lynch[2] says that alliances are often formed because of the weaknesses, and not necessarily the strengths that exist between the joining entities. Instead, Lynch says one would realise more successful associations when the allying entities combine each other's complementary strengths that would also cancel existing weaknesses. Forming allies in this way creates collaborative entities that are stronger than the joining collaborators.

The many objectives for forming collaborative partnerships can be summarised under two headings: Risk Reduction and Co-developing Opportunities.

Risk reduction includes:

- Cost reduction and capacity rationalisation.
- Reduction of exposure to capital expenditures.
- Reduction of exposure to operational risks.
- Access to essential equipment, feedstock, technology, or intellectual property.
- Overcoming barriers created by e.g. nationalisation of private entities, legislation, or import duties.
- Access to financial and other scarce resources.
- Reducing time-to-market.

Co-developing opportunities means:

- Access to new growth opportunities.
- Complementary market channels or products.
- Faster entry into new regions, markets, or capacity.
- Acquisition of technology to support new growth.
- Achieving economies of scale.
- Acquiring new capabilities and knowledge.

Collaborative relationships are inherently unstable. Consequently, the success record of formal alliances is not that bright. Numerous studies put the failure rate of business alliances between 60 and 70 percent and the average lifespan of business alliances around 7 to 8 years. The main reason is that the collaborative forces that promoted the collaborative relationship often shift and the relationship's advantages start to fade. For example, one of the partners could commence some of the activities that were meant to be performed by the collaborative relationship. This type of behaviour if continued will cause stress in the relationship, and could lead to a breakdown of the alliance.

Because collaborative relationships are an important means for entities to achieve some objectives, yet they are unstable, leaders should be on the lookout for relationship deviations that could occur during the life cycle of a third-party relationship.

Deviations in collaborative relationships are typically caused by:

- Risk drift
- Strategy shift

Risk drift and strategy shift occur because of:

- Significant changes in the other associate's strategic context, such as changes in their technology or competition.
- Changes in the other party's leadership that lead to changes in their strategies.
- Negative changes in the other party's financial performance, leading to operational issues and suboptimal cost structures—potentially damaging the joint activities of the alliance.
- Changes in the other party's ownership structure, e.g. the acquisition by another entity may change existing relationships and induce the relationship to dismantle.
- Changes in national or international rules, legislation and regulations.

Be especially vigilant about risk drift or strategy shift before and during the Deliver stage. If you detect them early, you can strategically address the causes or outcomes, and change the course of your initiative. When risk drift and strategy shift are not proactively attended to, they will cause misalignment in the relationship. This normally causes the failure of many change initiatives.

You can make the following provisions to manage risk drift and strategy shift in your third-party relationships:

- Foster stronger personal relationships with important leaders and other key people in the alliances. Do not leave this task solely to your alliance managers. Seek and promote open, honest and timely sharing of information and events that may cause your collaborative partnerships to drift apart.

- Ensure that your anticipation process (Chapter 10) includes your collaborators as important sources of intelligence. It is highly embarrassing to discover that critical information has gone unnoticed or ignored by your entity. Often though, critical alliance information should be methodically pursued. Collaborative entities are often embarrassed to share information that may blemish their reputation. Close relationships with key people in your alliance entities are invaluable. Trusting relations will disclose valuable information, long before it becomes official, and well in time to make proactive strategic course corrections.

- Continuously update your internal risk and performance reviews of collaborators, alliances and partners.

- Collaborative relations have their own life cycles—such lifecycles may not necessarily coincide with your entity or initiative's life cycle. Because these life cycles may differ, you may have to grow or regress the scope of your collaborative relationships. Ensure that there are appropriate plans in place to address such scope and strategy changes.

Recognise, Reward and Remunerate

A powerful behaviour you can use advantageously to change and align your team members' behaviours and the success of your entities' initiatives is to recognise your people for work well done with the three R's; Recognition, Reward and Remuneration.

The main purpose of recognition, reward and remuneration systems is to recognise and reward your team in authentic ways for their positive performance contributions and engaged behaviours. Make effective use of recognition, reward and remuneration as often as possible to change behaviours, reinforce wanted behaviours, and build momentum.

A detailed discussion of recognition, reward, and remuneration systems is beyond the scope of this book. The differences between recognition, reward and remuneration are often blurred and consequently their effectiveness to promote the implementation of change initiatives are lost.

Suffice to say, I view the main differences as follows:

- Recognition for good work is the least expensive, (recognitions are mostly for free), yet it has immediate positive effects. It is mainly non-financial, positive reinforcement of behaviours linked to the values, objectives and culture. Giving recognition is one of the most effective leadership behaviours to achieve change success and to change a culture.
- Rewards are based on agreed performance targets or milestones and are usually awarded financially. Rewards can be a useful mechanism to change cultures, and to embed new behaviours. They carry a substantial cost but can be very effective.
- Remuneration is usually based on objective and equitable market related compensation for different categories of work and responsibilities. It is the costliest method to reinforce

change initiatives or to change behaviours. It is an ineffective mechanism to embed new behaviours, other than initially using it to attract or recruit new members with prerequisite skills and cultural values. When remuneration is however below the equitable market levels, it will in time negatively affect desired behaviours and the entity culture.

Throughout the Deliver stage, the purpose of the recognition, reward and remuneration system is to reinforce new required behaviour patterns. It is an important system that helps to align your entity's mutual purposes, values, and culture, with new behaviours and desired performance outcomes. Your entity probably already has a reward and remuneration system that has been developed and improved over a long period. Often though such mature systems become highly inflexible. For change initiatives to be implemented effectively your entity's recognition, reward and remuneration system must be flexible and able to encourage the behavioural changes you want, otherwise implementation will fail.

Before and during the Deliver stage, ensure that your entity's recognition, reward and remuneration system, can do the following:

- Reinforce and encourage new required behaviours of leaders and people.
- Reinforce new performance standards and objectives intended by the change initiative.
- Include new or revised metrics that can demonstrate when new behaviours are aligned, and when change initiatives meet performance targets. Metrics should be properly defined, and measurable. Behaviours that can't be measured should be qualitatively appreciable.
- Be redefined and allocated to correspond with new behaviours and measures.

Reward and recognition will encourage and solidify new values, new culture and new ways of doing things. As new behaviours are positively recognised and rewarded, you will create positive emotions in recipients and create advocates of the new customs that are valued. When you continue to reinforce the recognition – reward – behaviour cycle, the momentum of your initiatives will build. New behaviours will proliferate through the entity, leading to successful change, and building a change-fit entity.

Be very mindful never to combine a public act of recognition with an act of criticism—whether it is constructive or negative. Constructive criticism, though well meaning, is best left for private conversations with the member or team concerned. Besides, the worst you could do to destroy positive engagement with new change initiatives, is to publically reprimand members about mistakes or slip-ups when they implement an initiative.

Symbolic events

Symbolic events are very useful and are effective recognition and reward methods. You should use them infrequently but with thoughtful effect. When you use symbolic events effectively, you will create significant momentum behind new behaviours and a new culture, by for example:

- Recruiting, selecting, or promoting prominent change agents that are recognised for demonstrating the desired new behaviours.
- Publically announcing rewards of large bonuses or symbols of recognition to people who have demonstrated specific desirable behaviours or cultural values.
- Destroying large piles of old equipment or bureaucratic procedures, to signify the beginning of an era of innovation, and the end of an era of disempowerment.

Symbolic events are good to indicate a fork in the road, yet they are insufficient to galvanise new behaviours. Reinforce the change of direction and behaviours by frequently, and publicly, using a variety of recognition and reward methods to emphasise new behaviours.

Support personal transitions

Change initiatives can cause negative psychological, and emotional transition cycles in people. I have discussed this in some detail in Chapter 7. Reactive change initiatives that occur in the 'Transform' or 'Survive' zones of the *Change Continuum* are especially notorious for causing negative transition cycles in people. Negative transition behaviours become obvious from the moment these initiatives are announced, as well as during subsequent implementation stages. Negative transition behaviours are mainly exhibited by people who were not inclusively involved through the whole Pre-Life-Cycle. Those who may stand to lose something valuable, because of reactive change initiatives, experience the worst negative psychological transitions.

If you have implemented the principles of the Change Dimension you would have improved the level of engagement in your entity to become more inclusive. You would have removed the 'surprise factor' of change to a large degree and the associated negative psychological reactions as much as possible. Many of the negative psychological and emotional transitioning behaviours that are provoked by 'unanticipated' and 'surprise changes' would be circumvented. It means that your entity has become fit for change. There is a culture in your entity that is comfortable with change and pushes change to occur. Shocks of unpleasant changes occur infrequently. Unpleasant changes that do occur unexpectedly, are psychologically and emotionally more tolerable for the few people that are unpleasantly impacted.

As the leader, it is your duty to determine who the people are that will be negatively affected by change initiatives, and ensure they get proper psychological and emotional transitioning assistance. Bridges[3] recommends that entities create transition-monitoring teams to observe peoples' transitions during and after major change initiatives. Psychological transitions normally take considerably longer than the implementation of change initiatives. When you observe a regular recurrence, or a growing need for psychological transitioning assistance, several aspects of your change initiatives are not effective and need to be fixed, starting with the Enable stage of the Change Dimension.

Immediately deal with emerging resistance

Be continuously alert for signs of emerging resistance, especially when change initiatives struggle through the Deliver stage. You have to deal with emerging resistance and systemic barriers before they become substantial forces that threaten the success of initiatives.

Emerging and residual resistance and barriers to change rear their heads throughout the change cycle. During the earlier stages of change initiatives, you would identify, diagnose, and address resistance and barriers to create alignment between the change initiative, people and entity (Chapter 11 – Incubate). However, when a change initiative is implemented, the nature of resistance and barriers changes too.

During the Deliver stage, unforeseen events will occur that may cause strain on capacities, capabilities and resources. Unplanned events cause new forms of resistance and barriers to emerge. An entity that has become fully inclusive and has transitioned into a change-oriented culture will be fit to deal with many unforeseen events. You may typically find one or more of the following sources of resistance and barriers emerge during implementation:

- **Members become disengaged**

Some members can become disengaged with a change initiative. They may have been omitted from the inclusive process around a specific initiative or they may not yet be aware of how an initiative would impact their work. This often happens with people who were not part of the Pre-Life-Cycle and must adapt to the outcomes of a change initiative. If their needs and concerns are not addressed early, they may become a source of increasing resistance.

- **Engagement is misinterpreted as resistance**

When members become truly engaged in their entities and change initiatives, they may often question and probe many aspects of change initiatives. Leaders unfamiliar with, or unsupportive of inclusive behaviours could perceive this kind of behaviours as a source of resistance and regard the members' behaviours as negative. The contrary could however often be true—members are genuinely concerned and want the best for the entity. You must be able to clearly recognise differences between concerned inclusive behaviours and negative resisting behaviours. Recognise and reward members for being open, honest and engaged.

- **Resources and entity capacity become overburdened**

Without proper change portfolio management, your change initiatives may run into work overloads, and resource and capacity restrictions. Be watchful for scope creep within initiatives and for proliferation of initiatives.

Change overload often happens when some initiatives take long to implement, say over several years, while others take a short time, say months. The extra burden caused by overlapping change initiatives are often misunderstood and unaccounted for during planning or implementation. As the strain on the entity and its people start to show, resistance and barriers will raise.

- **Middle management is excluded**

I have often found that the middle management levels of entities are not fully engaged. They are often not informed about their roles, or expected critical contributions to ensure the success of change initiatives. The middle management level is normally in control of short- to medium-term resource and capacity allocation, yet they are often not included in the development or implementation of a change initiative. Because they have been excluded, they may therefore not accurately know when and how many resources under their control are committed to change initiatives. They would therefore resist shifting and reallocation of necessary resources and capacity at critical stages in the implementation process—causing delays and work overloads. Middle management must be included.

- **Legacy behaviours resurface**

Old legacy behaviours resurface when initiatives are struggling to get implemented for many reasons. Legacy behaviours are exactly the behaviours the new initiative wants to replace. Members attempt to make the new initiative work by applying old 'proven' behaviours, 'because they worked so well in the past'. When you spot this kind of resistance pattern, your journey to a new culture is still some distance away. The suggestions I made above on role modelling, recognition and rewarding correct behaviours to embed new behaviours, will suppress legacy behaviours.

- **Yes-men**

Yes-men are particularly hard to identify as potential resistors. Twofaced compliance is a covert form of resistance that is not easy to identify, because presumably yes-men are doing what is expected of them. On the surface, they appear to be supportive and committed. Yet, they may not actually be engaged nor committed to it. To 'comply' and not be perceived as resistant, they just go along or quietly sit on the fence. Beware, if you are a leader that likes your ego to be stroked, or one who dislikes honest critique, yes-men will become your Achilles-heel.

Dealing with emergent resistance and barriers require that you maintain positive momentum created by inclusive engagement during the earlier stages of the Change Dimension. Be alert for signs of emerging resistance, and take immediate action to prevent growing resistance from becoming the cause of initiative failure.

Implementation

Without Implementation, there won't be any Change

At this point, considerable effort has gone into the preparation of the case-for-change, alignment of your people and the entity.

Before launching the initiative, ensure that the following items are in place, and pay attention to several essential areas, particularly:

- A detailed plan of implementation has been drawn up. The implementation plan is firm and any gaps identified during Incubation reviews are closed.
- Role expectations, allocation of accountability and responsibility are clear.
- The launching brief and launch process is in place.

After the launch event, and depending on the type of initiative, implementation of the initiative occurs through several implementation stages and there would be numerous key milestones and decision points along the way. The initiative is reviewed and adjusted when necessary, at several intervals through its implementation process.

During implementation, leaders should focus their attention on:

- Performance and progress of implementation
- Course correction triggers
- Optimisation of speed and timing
- The health of alliances and relationships
- Known and emerging risks
- Reallocation of resources
- Tracking desirable behaviours

Implementation Plan

The implementation plan of an initiative is the detailed actions necessary to ensure successful delivery of the change initiative. It clearly states the need for the change initiative and the value adding deliverables. It details the how, who, when and the what—the necessary resources that are required to achieve the initiatives' deliverables.

The implementation plan must address several critical areas *before the launch*, notably:

- Have any key assumptions changed?
- Have we dealt with the important issues raised during the Incubation readiness reviews?
- Does the implementation plan clearly define what constitutes success and failure?
- Is the implementation plan separated into stages with key milestones, to allow for critical reviews and course corrections?
- When the initiative is implemented through its stages, does every stage have clear thresholds (or triggers) for failure to initiate corrective action or trigger an exit?
- Have the necessary resources, capacities and capabilities been allocated and committed to the initiative?
- Has the plan for change transition been addressed in the implementation plan—a transition plan that bridges the situation between the current state and the new state?
- Has the integration plan been addressed? How will the new actions, behaviours, values, systems and processes be integrated into the normal business as usual operations of the entity (either during, or after the initiative has been implemented)?
- Are the necessary performance metrics and monitoring systems in place to measure the performance of the initiative?

- Does the implementation plan include risk management?

Accountability and responsibility

In the next chapter on the Execution Dimension, I explain delegation of accountability and responsibility and the definition of role expectations in some detail. As the leader, the ultimate responsibility for an initiative's success ends with you. You are the final accountable person. Accountability means ultimate responsibility. You must therefore ensure that the change implementation team has the correct delegated accountabilities, within a suitable structure, to effectively perform the necessary tasks. Ensure that the correct role expectations are defined, are clear and fit the change initiatives' team members. Take care to ensure that:

- The right leaders have delegation of key parts of initiatives—leaders who demonstrate the desired behaviours, perform as role models, include team members and build a change-oriented culture.
- Proper lines of authority and responsibility are designed and in place for all team leaders, including milestones for deliverables of the initiative.
- Authority and responsibility delegations follow clear lines of sight between the initiative objectives and the performance measures of the individuals and teams involved in the initiative.

Revisit the delegation of authorities and responsibilities at every milestone review session. The initiative might change its course, and consequently delegations of responsibility may have to be revised too.

Mutual accountabilities

Many change initiatives may occur across departments, units or divisions. The question often arises: Who is accountable for the success of implementation, and who is responsible for individual milestones and deliverables? In these situations, leaders often struggle with proper delegation of accountability and responsibility.

Holding your individual leaders and units exclusively accountable for the success of their individual parts of initiatives, diminishes the impact of mutual efforts necessary to achieve entity-wide success. Tension develops due to the stresses connected to individual leaders' performance and the collective entity's performance. An example of an approach to bridge this tension is to ensure that unit leaders, working together as a team on initiatives, are collectively responsible to achieve successful implementation.

Mutual accountability assists the creation of collaborative and inclusive cultures. Unit leaders are assigned individual performance targets as well as collective performance targets—both reflect the performance targets of the whole initiative. The weight of the unit leaders' portfolio of collective performance targets for change initiatives, should be higher than the weight of his individual performance targets. Skewing performance weights towards mutual accountability, will favour the success of the initiative.

The effect of creating mutual accountability is that cross-functional initiatives stand a better chance to be implemented on time, teams work more closely, and they eagerly share information, best practices and resources. Mutual accountability and performance is an effective silo breaking mechanism. Potential synergies between units or divisions will be enthusiastically identified and collaboratively realised.

The Launch

The old way

Traditionally the launch event occurs on the moment when change initiatives start their lives in entities. That is when they 'go live'. The launch of an initiative is then often a surprise to many people in an entity—only a few people may have been included in its conception, design or planning.

The launch occurs in the form of a top-down decree or announcement and the leaders' expectation is that the initiative will be implemented quickly and it will deliver extraordinary performance improvements. People are 'sold' on how the initiative is the best thing for everyone. An extensive selling pitch is usually followed by an elaborate communication campaign. A persuasive case and burning platform is created to sell to and shape everyone into understanding.

Usually, after an intense communication program, a sequential change management process is rolled out, commencing with numerous activities to address and reduce resistance and prepare the entity to be ready for the change.

Launch—The new way

Change-oriented leaders, on the other hand, are inclusive and launch change initiatives at the correct point in the Pre-Life-Cycle. In a change-fit entity with an inclusive culture, where change is part of normal life and not perceived as a surprise, the launch of a change initiative is a celebration, not a surprise.

Though the launch is not used as a 'sales' event, it is nonetheless a very important symbolic event. The launch is the first real formal public expression you would deliver on the change initiative. It is a highly visible opportunity to engage with the people, stakeholders and third parties in implementation.

Use the launch event as an opportunity to cement in the course for the future, align the initiative with your entity's vision, give recognition to those who deserve it and demonstrate the new desired behaviours that would make the change successful.

Note that the launch event of a change initiative is not the same as the kick-off of the initiative. The kick-off involves the commencement of the detail work of the implementation team who will also integrate the initiative in the entity. Depending on the scale of the change initiative you may have to launch it several times in several locations. During launch events, the leader would:

- Reinforce how the initiative intends to achieve the mutual purposes, vision and strategy of the entity.
- Ensure that the launch events allow open dialogue with people and stakeholders.
- Engage team members, stakeholders and third parties to contribute during the launch events on important aspects of the initiative.
- Demonstrate how the initiative is a result of a combined endeavour by members of the entity.
- Use memorable symbols to introduce the initiative—symbols that signify the end of an old era and the beginning of a new one.
- Announce key appointments of leaders or members that will drive important aspects, people that have shown the desired behaviours and cultural norms that support the success of the initiative.
- Firmly indicate which old legacy behaviours will no longer be rewarded and that they are being replaced.
- Introduce the new desired behaviours, cultural norms and performance that will be aimed for.
- Demonstrate the behaviours that would be rewarded.
- Publically recognise and reward people who have contributed significantly to the mutual development of the initiative.
- Announce that anyone who has concerns is welcome to engage in an inclusive dialogue about the initiative.

Progress and Performance

"The art of progress is to preserve order amid change
and to preserve change amid order"

Alfred Whitehead

After the launch, the change initiative has entered its Delivery stage. Your change managers are accountable for the smooth implementation of the change implementation plans. The change managers have vested interests in the successful Delivery of the initiative. They will focus on just that—which is what you would expect from them.

Without removing any delegated accountability from your change managers, I would like to reiterate:

Leaders must lead change!

Your objective is to actively lead performance and progress reviews and to meticulously keep change initiatives on course and when necessary, change course and reallocate scarce resources and capacity. Leading performance and progress reviews in a disciplined way, ensures that resources and entity capacity are optimally allocated to the most deserving initiatives in your change portfolio.

There are two types of performance and progress reviews:

Scheduled reviews that coincide with predefined milestones and intervals, and ad hoc reviews used as and when necessary. Use both to gauge performance, progress and speed of implementation of initiatives.

You have to continually steer a number of key areas to ensure performance and progress of Delivery is on target. Your change managers can easily prepare answers to the questions below, nevertheless I recommend that you study the feedback and lead the initiative to stay on course. Essential performance and progress indicators you need to review during initiative implementation are:

- ## Quality of interim and final deliverables

Is the initiative progressing to deliver the defined requirements as per the case for change? An initiative that does not achieve its necessary requirements, products, solutions or services as defined in the case for change is a failure.

- ## Customer and stakeholder satisfaction

Your customers, stakeholders and end-users ultimately determine whether the change initiative is a success. To what extent are they involved during implementation, and are their views considered?

- ## Budget and schedule

Are the budget and schedule as defined for the initiative still realistic? Is the schedule too tight, or does it allow too much slack and extended deadlines?

- ## Resource burn-rates

Is the initiative burning through more cash, resources and capacity than anticipated? Why? Are the implementation requirements more than anticipated? What can you do to stem the burn-rate?

- ## Scope and schedule creep

Are the change managers of the initiative attempting to implement more, or less than the requirements in the definition? If there are discrepancies, are those deviations the cause for variances in the budget, spent resources and schedule?

Course corrections

Consider the following performance metrics and dashboards to inform whether you should correct the course:

- Do the metrics and performance dashboards satisfactorily

measure the performance of change implementation, as well as the performance of the initiative itself?

- Do you employ the correct leading or predictive indictors to make timely strategic course corrections to the initiative?
- Are the leading measures suitable to reveal course corrections and exit triggers? Are the triggers linked to the thresholds of failure as defined in the case for change?
- Are the measures suitable to indicate effective use of resources, capabilities and capacity?
- Do you need to revise the measures to be more relevant in the next stage of implementation?

Speed and timing

In Chapter 13 on Execution, I explain the 'Speed vs. Experience' matrix. I explain that speed always comes at a price. The same principle applies when you implement change initiatives. Speed of implementation is about the correct timing of actions and decisions and the rate at which those actions and decisions are taken. Both speed and timing must be optimised to achieve successful change implementation.

Critically ponder the following questions:

- Are you implementing the initiative at optimal speed?
- Which elements of the initiative need to accelerate and which elements need to slow down?
- Are the schedule and completion dates realistic?
- If you must slow down, which aspects need more time?
- Have you missed critical schedule milestones? Does that warrant exiting, or to correct the course?
- Are resources and capacities overloaded to rush the initiative? What is the effect on the engagement of teams due to the overloads?

- Is change fatigue emerging?
- Does a sense of urgency cause mistakes, breakdowns, delays and blame?
- Do you need to adjust the schedule for subsequent stages?

Change governance

Your change governance team is accountable for monitoring the staged implementation progress and performance thresholds. Change governance takes early, quick and decisive action when they diagnose poor implementation results and when performance thresholds are triggered. Poor interim performance could be due to incomplete Incubation, poor implementation during Delivery, invalid case assumptions, or behaviours that resist the progress.

The change governance team must ensure:

- Course correction thresholds and exit triggers are collectively defined and recalibrated at the start of each implementation stage.
- Roadblocks to efficient implementation are defined. They decide collaboratively whether to correct the course by reallocating resources, postponing or exiting initiatives.
- That decisions on initiatives that show mediocre performance, drain resources and waste capacity without delivering expected value, are made promptly.
- No tolerance for poor interim results beyond two scheduled reviews. If remedial course corrections do not deliver expected outcomes, implement a predetermined exit plan.
- Action is taken the instant thresholds are triggered. Initiate course corrections, accelerate the initiative or exit, depending on the indicated direction of the trigger.

Reallocate resources

- A continuous resource and capacity reallocation process ensures that the entity's scarce resources are transferred to and absorbed by the most promising initiatives in your portfolio.
- The resource allocation process should prompt reallocation when course corrections or exits are triggered.
- It protects the entity against resource and capacity peaks and troughs and prevents organisational restructuring or rightsizing.
- Beware of the 'sunk resources' barrier to reallocate resources. The sunk resources argument is often made to justify continuation of initiatives, especially when they perform poorly. (Chapter 6). In such cases, clear evidence that an unsuccessful initiative is being developed, is being ignored.

Review risks

Risk management and review is a vast subject on its own and is crucial to the success of any change initiative. From your leadership perspective, you should review risks during the implementation of initiatives. The principles discussed in Chapter 11 also apply here during the Delivery stage.

Integration

Integration follows Implementation

Integration of a change initiative occurs when the new preferred ways of work and new behaviours that permanently reinforce the success of the initiative are embedded.

Integration is the grand finale of the Deliver stage and concludes the

Pre-Life-Cycle and the Change Dimension. It is the goal everyone has been working so hard for—that is to see all the benefits and value of the change initiative.

Integration is when the people, systems, structures and processes of the change initiative become part of the normal execution system. It is the final crucial step that determines the success of your initiative and deserves you full leadership attention.

Successful integration is achieved when the intended and expected objectives and milestones, as defined in the case for change are consistently demonstrated and delivered.

An initiative is completely embedded in your entity when:

- Continual improvements and knowledge transfer from the initiative to the rest of the entity (and where applicable, to stakeholders and third parties) occur seamlessly and effortlessly.
- New capacity and capabilities are created that can leverage in future initiatives. Because new capacity and capability have been created, new wealth resources are created.
- The required behaviours are presented continually—they reinforce performance, new values and a new culture.

When you have achieved these integration objectives, the initiative has been a successful change that will deliver value for the long term.

To clinch the success of your change initiatives it is essential that you focus on a few key integration drivers:

- Continual improvement
- Changeovers
- Resource and capacity reallocation
- Initiative roll-out
- Reinforcement of new behaviours

Continual Improvement

One way to boost the momentum created by a recently implemented initiative is through continual improvements that leverage its value. Successful continual improvement occurs when feedback about the implementation—whether good or bad—progress and lessons learned are shared continually and inclusively with the rest of the entity. This practice guarantees knowledge transfer to the rest of the entity. Best practices are recorded and shared so future initiatives can leverage from the experience gained with each initiative.

If stakeholders and third-party relationships are involved, timeous feedback and knowledge sharing with them is essential.

Changeover of systems, structures and processes

Often during the excitement of a new initiative that performs as expected, temporary and legacy effects are ignored. Former and temporary systems, structures and processes are useful during implementation, to support the implementation process. However, they can become crutches for the entity during integration—reducing the value of the change initiative and allowing legacy behaviours to continue. Make sure that all temporary and transitioning supports are removed as soon as possible, so that integration of the new initiative occurs completely.

Resource reallocation

Diligently keep a close watch on expenses and allocation of resources and capacity near the end of implementation. Resources are often locked in beyond effective integration. People and capacity involved in the integration of the initiative are commonly engaged unnecessarily for extended periods after integration. Especially when the initiative had some rough patches during implementation.

The contrary is often also applicable. Members of implementation teams and essential capacity are withdrawn too early. Integration pauses, adopters and users of the initiative struggle to realise the expected value, and the initiative therefore may wither pre-maturely or deliver poor results.

Initiative rollout

Change initiatives are often developed over several stages. The first stage of an initiative could be for example, a small-scale conceptual experiment, pilot study, or a simulation on a dedicated site. Before rolling out the initiative to other locations, units, or the whole entity, it is essential that you test and verify performance metrics, test behavioural aspects, obtain best practices and learn as much as possible about its scalability and transferability. Contextual differences will determine the success or failure of such rollouts. Understanding the contextual differences of other locations, where an initiative will be rolled out, is as important as successful intermediate development stages. The fact that an initiative proved to be successful in one location is no guarantee that it will be successful in another. Put successive rollouts in other locations through the same disciplined change initiative stages as advocated in the Change Dimension—through the Anticipate, Incubate and Deliver stages.

Reinforce new behaviours

A very effective way to integrate an initiative and maintain momentum is by celebrating the successes, during, but most importantly, at the end of full integration. Celebrations, rituals, symbolic events, recognition and rewards of various forms are very beneficial to embed successful initiatives.

Most importantly, reinforce required behaviours inclusively and publically:

- Celebrate successes frequently
- Recognise the performance of valued contributors
- Recognise expected new behaviours.

Summary

The Deliver stage is the crucial stage at the end of the Pre-Life-Cycle and it begins the life cycle of a completely integrated change initiative. This stage in the Change Dimension embeds a set of specific leadership behaviours. It integrates a change initiative's new desired behaviours into the entity, with the implementation and integration of new systems, structures, processes and new ways of work. The initiative's value propositions can then be realised successfully.

During delivery, leaders should focus on three areas to ensure the success of change initiatives. The three leadership focus areas are:

- The people involved in and impacted by change initiatives
- The implementation of the initiative
- Integration of the change initiative into the entity's day-to-day operations.

Within each of the three focus areas there are several specific issues leaders must lead to ensure successful initiatives. After the Deliver stage of change initiatives, they 'go live'. They begin their own life cycles or S-curves. After initiatives have gone live, they enter the normal operational execution system of the entity. Execution is the topic of the next chapter—the Execution Dimension of leadership behaviour.

Notes

1. Krames, J. A. 2002, *The Jack Welch Lexicon of Leadership*, McGraw-Hill, New York.

2. Lynch, R.P. 1990, The Practical Guide to Joint Ventures and Corporate Alliances, John Wiley, New York.

3. Bridges, W., & Bridges, S. 2009, *Managing Transitions*, DeCapo Press, Philadelphia.

13. **The New Execution Dimension**

'Leadership is about Execution'—is a favourite expression. That is true, but up to a point. When execution fails, leadership has failed. However, it is critical that you distinguish between your behaviours—between leadership behaviours and operational behaviours

Introduction

The Execution Dimension of leadership is about proper strategic governance of your entity's execution system. In many contexts, an entity's execution system is also known as its 'operations'.

Execution is the performance of millions of coordinated tasks and activities, in a systematic way to implement the strategy and initiatives that are aimed at achieving the entity's mutual purposes. Ultimately you must ensure that your entity achieves what it set out to do. When execution fails, your leadership has failed.

The importance of leaders' execution behaviours has been underemphasised in most popular leadership literature in the period between the 1950s and 2000. The focus was predominantly on developing leaders' relationship-oriented behaviours, or so-called 'people skills'. However, since the late 1990s, which is around the same time when the major inflection occurred on the Mega-S-Curve, fresh new interest occurred to develop leaders' execution behaviours. Since this inflection occurred more attention is focused on how leaders can improve the leadership of execution so that entities can improve their performance.

During the past two decades, we have seen pressure mounting on leaders to deliver extraordinary performance results. This rising pressure must be seen against a backdrop of many entity failures that were triggered by several financial and political crises globally. The reasons for the failures are many. I have reflected on the context of the age of change in Chapter 1.

Judging by the literature and common wisdom, one may certainly get an impression that we need to develop leadership behaviours that focus predominantly on improving trusting relationships. I have also emphasised in Chapter 4 about the Relationship Dimension, that trustworthy relationships are the foundation of leadership. However, I am of a firm opinion that we should reconsider our thinking about other behaviours leaders need for the age of change. Leaders should spend about equal attention on each of the three leadership dimensions—Relationships, Change and Execution, to be effective leaders in the 21st century.

Execution systems

Every entity, whether it is a team, organisation, school, political party or country, purposely designs its execution systems so that it can effectively seize opportunities in its unique context and deliver on its purpose, strategy and objectives. External and internal contexts, change drivers and strategies determine how execution systems are designed and reconfigured. The execution system is the vehicle that allows your entity to produce its outcomes and secure its performance and its survival in the long-term.

When an execution system does not produce its intended outcomes, the entity will soon fail and its leadership will be regarded as having failed too. Leaders therefore must be skilful to lead their entity's execution system proactively and flexibly, without sacrificing long-term resilience.

Why does Execution demand so much leadership attention — the 'Spell of Execution'

Three inherent features of execution explain why some leaders can become entrapped and often obsessed with 'commanding' execution.

- Execution is about performing millions of activities. So many things can go wrong—therefore the sheer amount of activities that must be performed correctly have a tangible influence on leaders' attention.
- Most activities should be completed in very short time frames; so, the execution system puts enormous demands of 'urgency' on the entity—seizing another portion of the leader's attention.
- The entity's short- and medium-term survival may depend on the efficiency of the execution system; therefore, leaders may feel compelled to fully concentrate their attention on operational matters.

Many leaders fall into one or more of these traps. I call it the 'Spell of Execution'. No wonder leaders who are entrapped by this spell have so little time to lead essential change initiatives or, even worse, they have little time to build lasting trustworthy relationships.

'Leadership is about Execution'—is a favourite expression. I agree with that, but up to a point. If execution fails, leadership has failed. However, it is critical to distinguish between your execution oriented behaviours. Are your behaviours 'leadership behaviours', or are they short-term oriented 'operational behaviours'?

In the following section I discuss the leadership behaviours that will set you free from the spell of execution.

The new Execution Dimension

When you follow the new Execution Dimension you will be freed from 'commanding and doing' execution activities. You will be set free to lead. Consequently, your people will be better equipped and enthusiastic to add value to their entity. You would provide the guidance, governance, strategic direction, and tangible support to drive your execution system. In the age of change you do not, and should not, command execution to the nth degree. That was the old leadership paradigm: commanding and driving execution from the top. In the age of change, you simply won't have the time, resources or attention span to command and control execution any longer. From now on you must boldly lead execution.

By applying the Execution Dimension systematically, it will help you to:

- Achieve superior outcomes and performance results.
- Improve current and future leadership relationships.
- Effortlessly implement change initiatives in your current execution systems (business-as-usual or BAU).
- Discover new change initiatives that will build your entity's long-term resilience, growth and agility.

The Execution Dimension with six major behaviour elements is illustrated in Figure 13.1.

The Execution Dimension is a set of core leadership behaviours, designed to systematically govern and direct enhanced performance, at optimal speed, while gathering and using essential intelligence. In your entity's execution system, intelligence is gathered on internal and external signals, trends and information, which will drive proactive change initiatives.

The Execution Dimension, like the Change Dimension, is firmly secured

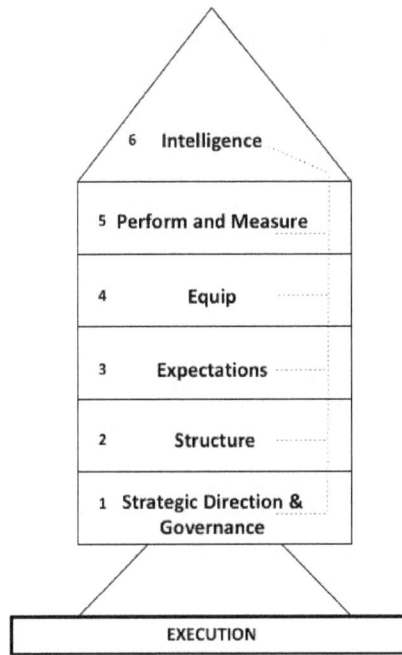

Figure 13.1 The Execution Dimension

on the solid foundation of the Relationship Dimension. The Execution Dimension will only function effectively when excellent leadership relationships exist in your entity.

Each of the six elements should be aligned and systemically integrated so that your entity can achieve its objectives within a continually evolving context.

The elements of the Execution Dimension are:

1. Strategic Direction and Governance

2. Structure

3. Expectations

4. Equip

5. Performance and Measurement

6. Intelligence

Furthermore, the Intelligence element is the main linkage between the elements of the Execution Dimension and the Change Dimension. The intelligence system enables proactive identification, testing and implementation of change initiatives within the execution system. Once all the elements are in place, the Execution Dimension will ensure everyone has clear line-of-sight. Clear line-of-sight begins with the 'Strategic Direction and Governance' element where you direct your entity's mutual purposes and strategies, and it ends with the 'Performance and Measurement' element.

The Execution Dimension is wrapped in a self-learning and a self-reinforcing intelligence system—a comprehensive inclusive system that sustains your entity's execution system to be fully operational. Through actionable intelligence, the intelligence system has the key objective to enable your entity for superior performance in the short, medium and long term. When elements in the Execution Dimension need course corrections, the intelligence system must be able to proactively trigger these changes.

You will be able to strategically govern and direct your entity with the support of the intelligence system. The actual performance of thousands of tasks and responsibilities are left to your capable people who are appointed with proper skills, accountabilities, and equipped with the right resources to achieve their expectations.

Each element is explained in more detail below.

1. Strategic Direction & Governance

Strategic Direction and Governance is the first element in the Execution Dimension. The main purpose of this element is to align the mutual purposes of your entity, its strategies and objectives, with each member's objectives, from the top to the bottom, from the bottom to the top, and across the entity. It creates clarity and unity of purpose throughout the entity. Clarity and unity of purpose and a thorough understanding of the strategic direction significantly build engagement.

Your strategic direction and governance sets the direction of the execution process. In this element, you work inclusively with your entity to co-develop mutual purposes, strategies and key objectives.

The objectives of strategic direction and governance element are to:

1. Direct the entity towards achieving superior, sustainable results in the short, medium and long term.
2. Direct any course corrections in the execution system as and when new intelligence triggers proactive action.
3. Proactively redirect the course of execution in the longer term when change drivers suggest that.

Strategic direction and governance is about creating and maintaining clarity by focusing on a few fundamental aspects of execution. These strategic fundamentals can be expressed by a few key questions:

Why?

Answers to the why question provide the context and the mutual purpose behind execution behaviours. You must clarify the contexts in which your entity is doing the things it does, and the purpose behind those activities. Context provides the background, trends, opportunities, and assumptions, to give the reasons why your entity is following certain directions and not others. It answers why it makes sense what the entity does. Understanding the context of why your entity does what it does, adds significantly to peoples' experience of their personal purpose, meaning and sense of belonging to an entity. Especially when people can clearly see the connections between their roles and the strategic direction of their entity. The mutual purpose describes the enduring reason for the existence of your entity. It is this 'reason for being' that provides the true north on the entity's compass. Everything the entity does must be aligned to that. The strategic governance and direction element of execution is key to creating this alignment in your entity.

Where?

Answers to the where question provide the map to the strategic direction. The map clearly describes the terrain and environment within which your entity operates or competes (scenarios, markets, competition, etc.). Your entity's values and purpose will determine the kinds of endeavours (the routes on the map) it might pursue.

What?

Answers to the what question outline the strategic objectives that support the entity's strategic direction and purpose. The strategic objectives are the landmarks, milestones and destinations, along the selected routes on the strategic 'map'.

Where to?

The routes and journeys to be taken to reach the strategic objectives. It outlines the strategic plans to get to the selected destinations on the map.
  It links the strategic map with specific routes the entity wants to take to achieve its purpose and strategies objectives. Strategic plans are detailed to support each strategic objective or initiative.

Where not?

Answers to the 'where-not' question set and describe the main boundaries within which your entity will operate. Firstly, your entity's values and purpose will set specific boundaries around the kinds of endeavours your entity might pursue. Secondly, it sets the legal, moral, ethical, social, environmental, competitive, regulatory and other boundaries over which your entity may not cross.

When and how fast?

Answers to this question set the schedule and the pace at which execution objectives will be executed.

*Notice the **absence** of who- and how-questions in the element of 'Strategic Governance and Direction'.*

Who?

Questions and answers about who would work on objectives are not asked, nor answered in this element. The who-questions are asked and answered in the Expectations element.

How?

How are we going to execute the entity's objectives? Strategic Direction and Governance is not about giving detailed direction on how your entity should achieve its objectives. The leader does not provide detailed instructions and procedures, but sets key directions and governing guidelines. Your people will be fully equipped (Equip element), and capable to do what is expected of them (Expectations element). You do not have to tell them and control them on how to execute their tasks. When your people are not fully equipped or capable, then it is your leadership responsibility to ensure that they become fully equipped to achieve their accountabilities.

Control

Customarily, Strategic Direction and Governance systems are notoriously labelled as 'command-and-control' systems. The label command-and-control has a bad reputation and is a remnant of the industrial era—of a past when non-inclusive, autocratic leadership and controlling cultures prevailed. Unfortunately, such styles are still highly prevalent in many entities today.

Speed of Execution

Determining the speed of execution is an essential part of strategic direction and governance. It is becoming a major topic for the age of change. A loud chorus seems to encourage leaders and entities to increase the speed of execution and performance. Presumably higher speed equals better performance. Some myths about speed must however be clarified.

Often when an initiative faces headwinds, performance starts to decline, or an execution process produces less than the expected results. At this point executives put their foot on the proverbial pedal and demand even speedier performance to reach set performance targets. When increase in speed does not seem to work, the next port of call is often to restructure or reorganise the complete execution system—often the whole entity. Presumably the restructured entity would move faster and perform better. Often this step does not provide the desired results either... This popular mindset is one of looking at the speed of execution as a singular dynamic. It incorrectly equates higher speed of execution with better performance results.

The truth is that speed of execution has many facets and it does affect performance a lot. The question is though: which of the execution elements do leaders have to lead better so that their entities can increase the pace of execution?

The most important variable that determines optimal speed is the level at which the entity and people are prepared for, and experienced with what they have to perform. Attentive leadership of the Execution Dimension will ensure that your entity is ready to execute at optimal speeds.

The matrix in Figure 13.2 illustrates an entity's Speed of Execution on

---

the vertical axis and it's Level of Experience (or Fitness to execute) on the horizontal axis.

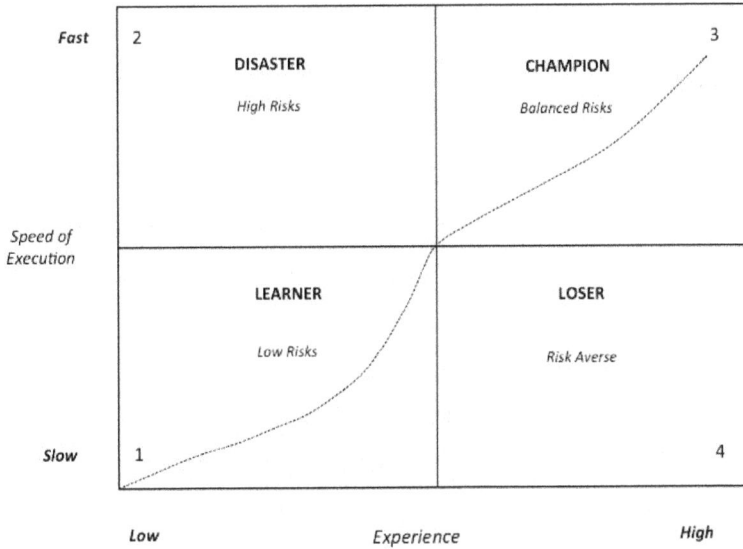

Figure 13.2. Speed at a Price: Speed-Experience Curve

Learners

In quadrant 1—the domain of Learner performers—the pace of execution is slow. The entity is not yet experienced with specific initiatives or new strategic directions. The entity is experimenting, innovating, testing, and gaining knowledge in new fields—at a measured pace to minimise risks.

Failures are expected, but seen as learning opportunities, that occur at low cost to the entity. As the entity builds more knowledge, expertise, and therefore becomes more prepared, it takes more balanced risks because it begins to understand the dynamics of its new endeavours. The pace of execution picks up because the entity is becoming ready and fit to execute a specific initiative. It moves into quadrant 3 to become a Champion performer.

Champions

In quadrant 3, the Champion, clear strategic direction and governance ensure that execution happens at optimal speed. Champions in quadrant 3 are recognised for being:

- Experts in their fields, and when they are not experts yet, they invest the time and necessary resources to gain essential know-how.
- Knowledgeable about the risks involved.
- Focused on long-term viability.
- Agile, to quickly adjust and change course when necessary.
- Able to anticipate change long before their competitors.
- Resilient, because they always keep enough resources ready for lean times, unexpected headwinds, and lucrative opportunities.
- Disciplined when they follow governance frameworks.

Disasters

Execution in quadrant 2 often leads to disaster. Entities who execute in that domain move too fast from the Learner quadrant. They arrive hurriedly in quadrant 2, because they are impatient, overconfident, arrogant or plain greedy. They burn scarce resources unnecessarily and take costly risks to chase their new initiatives. When they do not sensibly reduce the speed of execution, they usually fall into ruin, like the mythical Icarus who soared beyond the altitude his wings could carry him. Q2 performers typically exhibit a combination of the following behaviours:

- Are greedy and overstretch their entity's capability and capacity resources.
- Exhibit extreme pride, arrogance and regard necessary preparatory work to gain experience as pointless.
- Are novices in the field and disregard hard-earned experience.
- Are self-professed high-risk takers.
- Gamble the entity, leaving little resources spare to preserve the entity's resilience.
- Embark too late on the correct strategic direction and must rush to catch up on their rivals. The rush to catch up without the necessary experience causes them to stumble and fall.

Losers

Losers in quadrant 4, on the other hand, are notorious for being too slow, late and low on risk tolerance. Because of their slow speed of execution, Losers can miss perfect opportunities and initiatives, not because they are unprepared or inexperienced. They miss opportunities, or change too slow, because they typically display one or more of the following behaviours:

- Are reactive, instead of being proactive to change drivers.
- Struggle to make decisions in time—and often delay.
- Follow highly bureaucratic, hierarchic and complex decision-making procedures.
- React slowly when facing change.
- Are low on empowerment and inclusion.
- Are highly averse to risk-taking.
- Have a low tolerance for failure and punish mistakes.

2. Structure (and Re-structure)

Structure is the second element in the Execution Dimension.

Metaphorically speaking, your entity's Structure is the physical vehicle in which your entity will travel on the routes of the strategic map as directed by your strategic governance.

Structuring of entities is a major organisational development theme—one that I will only touch on briefly. I will discuss a few areas that I deem vital for leaders, when you must consider appropriate structures (and for that matter, restructuring) of execution systems.

The entity's structure in essence is a formalised decision-making system. It is optimally designed for your entity to proactively execute its activities, and use its resources, to serve its clients and stakeholders within a continually changing environment. It is an adaptable arrangement of decision-making authorities, accountabilities, functions, roles, information flows, and systems, aimed at achieving the entity's purposes and strategic objectives within an ever-changing environment.

An effective structure resembles a system of conduits that allows frictionless flows of decisions, intelligence, feedback, feed forward and learning through the entire entity. It enables the entity to effectively operate and modify the execution elements to deal with changing demands.

Through regular, but optimal modifications, proper restructuring can help to preserve your entity's long-term resilience and agility.

Indeed, the dictum made famous by Alfred Chandler[1] still holds true today. In a nutshell, Chandler said that an entity's optimal structure will be determined by the strategies the entity chooses, within its environment and its stakeholder expectations. The strategy and therefore the structure must correspond with the demands of its different stakeholders. In turn, the strategy of the entity is continually influenced by changes in the contextual environment and changing demands of stakeholders. When your entity no longer serves its stakeholders efficiently and satisfactorily, it should adjust its strategy and corresponding structure (its vehicle of execution).

Chandler's dictum thus forms a circular and systematic argument. For example, it follows this circular pattern:

Strategy → Structure → Performance → Environmental Changes → Revise Strategy → Modify Structure → and so on

It was never Chandler's view that the link between strategy and structure should be short-circuited when major changes occur in the contextual environment.   Yet, especially newly appointed leaders seem to be determined to restructure their entities, the moment they arrive in their new position. Their underlying (and often unarticulated) presumption seems to be one or more of the following:

- They need to be seen making an impact and being decisive about the entity—especially when it has been struggling or in a decline phase for a while. It is a common reflex reaction to poor historical performance. Such apparent decisiveness can also stem from leaders with egocentric characters, who lack the discipline of rigorous assessment before action.
- Restructuring is presumed to be relatively easy and straightforward—and changing the structure is presumably all that is required to redirect the entity onto a new strategic route to superior performance.
- Restructuring will improve the performance, speed, agility or any other desired performance objective. Yet there are many other elements in the Execution Dimension, apart from its structure, that can be changed quicker, cheaper, with better results.

Restructuring decisions that are driven by any of the above presumptions, often have major damaging effects on the entity due to consequent losses of engagement, capability, capacity and resilience. Moreover, any change in structure will have consequential effects on other elements of the Execution Dimension. After modifications are made to a structure, successive changes are necessary to realign the entire execution system. Successive changes can often take years to complete and settle in, especially when they are not expected and planned before the restructuring initiative. In the meantime, lots of energy, talent and resources are wasted, whilst the entity took its focus off its purpose.

Restructuring may be necessary from time to time. But focusing simply on reorganising your entity's structure seldom produces the desired results. There are potentially many other less invasive changes you can make in your execution system, by systematically assessing each element in the Execution Dimension. Applying the Change Dimension, as discussed in the change chapters, will assist you to decide if restructuring is a necessary intervention.

Since the 1960's when Chandler discovered the link between strategy and structure the rate of change and complexity has increased dramatically. Changing an entity's structure every time a major contextual change occurs simply is not feasible. Rather, it would be better to change another execution element first. Changing an element that does not have such a dramatic impact (like restructuring), but renders the entity equally or more effective than an entire restructure, would be better.

Objectives for structuring

The main objectives for structuring are to:

- Position your entity's internal resources, processes and systems such that it can proactively engage with challenges and opportunities in its contextual environment.
- Create a framework that aligns the other elements in the

Execution Dimension (Figure 13.1). It must create clear line-of-sight from the entity's purpose through to everyone's daily activities.

- Facilitate proactive and responsive interfaces between your entity, its clients and its stakeholders within changing contexts.
- The structure supports the desired behaviours you want to reinforce through relationships. The tangible experience of your entity, that is, what clients and stakeholders observe and feel when engaging with your entity, is through key touch points with your structure. For example, it is important that key front-end contact points, those interfaces that deal with clients and stakeholders, are accurately positioned within the structure.
- Produce proactive distribution of intelligence and decisions to enable quick adaptation to changing environmental forces.

Structuring an entity such that power and authority is concentrated in a few key positions is never a good objective. When leaders follow such an objective, the result is often a structure that satisfies the power and political agendas of a few powerful people who want to control key decision areas and therefore limit empowerment. Structuring an entity with the objective to build political power, or an imbalanced base of authority, often creates an entity that produces suboptimal performance. Such structures are inherently exclusive, they stifle proactive decision-making and choke knowledge flows. Concentration of power and authority usually leads to exclusivity—the opposite of inclusion.

The protection and preservation of positions with power should not be a consideration when designing appropriate structures. A structural design that is properly aligned to the purposes of the entity has a balanced allocation of power and authority throughout.

Generic organisational structures

There are many structural forms to choose from. A fundamental consideration is the way in which your entity wants to engage with its contextual environment. Structural forms can be categorised into four generic organisational structures. The four general structures are grouped by the way entities engage with their customers and stakeholders.

Figure 13.3 illustrates the four fundamental ways an entity can choose from to structure the interface with its contextual environment.

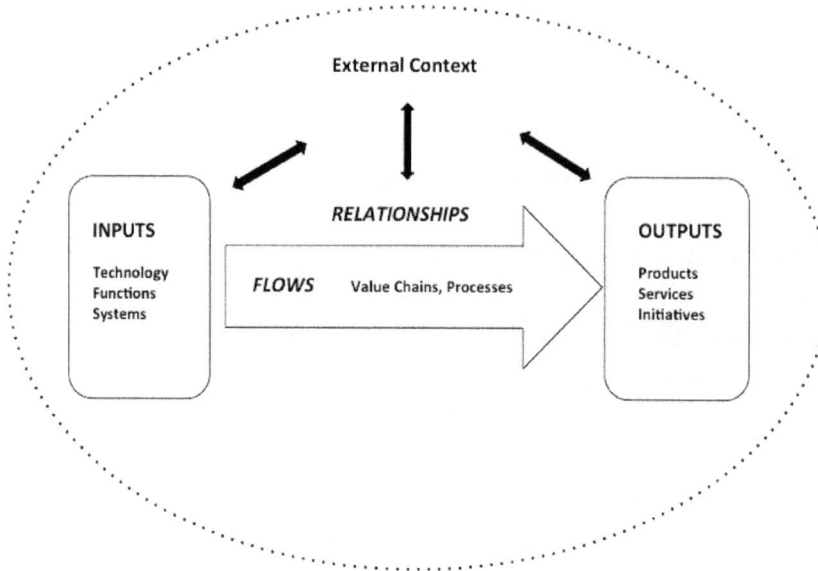

Figure 13.3. Structures are Based on an Entity's Contextual Interfaces.

The four fundamental structural designs are based upon:

- Inputs
- Sequential flows
- Outputs
- Collaborative relationships

▽ Structures based on inputs

Structures based on inputs are most common. They are designed around specific skill sets, professions, systems or technologies. These structures are familiar functional designs. This family of structures is fundamentally inward focused. The structure assists the entity to optimise its internal operations by grouping functional or technological expertise, such as combining all the financial roles into one accounting department.

▽ Structures based on flows

Structures based on flows are designed around sequential actions, processes, and value chains. Many manufacturing process and service entities use this kind of structure because most of their operations are performed in sequential steps. Fundamentally the focus of process structures is to achieve internal optimisation of sequentially connected processes and systems.

▽ Structures based on outputs

Structures based on outputs are based on what the organisation generates, such as its products, services, projects or initiatives. These are the typical divisional structures. Divisional structures have many variants, such as product-, market-, service-, customer- and geographical structures. They are primarily focused externally. The extent of focus on customers, clients and stakeholders can be varied, but the main objective is to align the entity with what the market desires from the entity.

▽ Structures based on collaborative relationships

Structures based on collaborative relationships are designed with the focus on maximising opportunities and minimising threats in the contextual environment through the formation of collaborative structures. Collaborative structures are designed to enhance proactiveness in entities that operate in contexts that require agility, speed, innovation and high levels of customer and stakeholder interaction. Structures are designed such that key relationships are built and maintained in flexible ways. Examples of collaborative structures are self-organising teams, formal or informal groups, remote and virtual teams. They often incorporate a wide diversity of skills sets.

Delivery of unique or innovative offerings to customers ahead of competitors is a common characteristic of collaborative relationship structures. There are many different relationship structures and new designs are continually evolving. Some relationship structures have been around for centuries and can be highly formalised, such as joint ventures and consortiums. Some newer collaborative relationship forms are more informal, more open, and more flexible; such as networks, alliances, virtual organisations and clusters.

Considerations for structures

Leaders are continually on the lookout for opportunities to increase performance, speed of execution, responsiveness to clients' needs and being proactive. Optimal structuring has a major influence on these needs. Before you choose an organisational structure or a combination of structures for your entity, there are a few design aspects you should cautiously consider, especially in this age of increasing change. Table 13.1 lists several considerations for designing an optimal structure for your entity. No single structural design can satisfy all considerations. It will be a case of which considerations carry the highest priority in your context.

Table 13.1 Leadership considerations for structuring

How your entity should preferably connect with its context and customers (Fig. 13.3)

Interfaces and relationships with customers, clients, stakeholders, partners, collaborators and authorities

Products, services and initiatives your entity generates

Diversity of the offerings

Key technologies, professional and technical skills, unique capabilities, processes and systems your entity uses

Resources and capacities currently in use and which may be required in future

Time spans for delivering your offerings (i.e. large projects are delivered over years, versus fast foods are delivered instantly)

Speed and intensity of anticipated changes that may impact your offerings

Levels of proactiveness required to innovate and change your entity's offerings

Intelligence conduits necessary to facilitate decision-making, speed and proactivity

Behaviours you want to reinforce through the choice of structural form

Centralisation versus decentralisation of certain functions, activities or services

Final thoughts on structuring

It is important to realise that it is not necessary to choose only one generic design for your entire entity. Many hybrid designs are practical and potentially superior. The most common hybrid is the project or matrix structure, which is a combination of the generic input and output structures. Matrixes are often temporary structures that are dispersed after the projects or initiatives have been implemented and delivered.

In addition, you may choose to have certain services or systems structured into a centralised functional form, while the main outputs could be designed into a process flow, or a divisional form. No structural design or hybrid will completely satisfy all the considerations I have listed in Table 13.1 and no single design will ensure that the entity will constantly deliver its offerings at peak performance levels. All the structural forms have pros and cons and the pros and cons will vary based on your contexts, engagement with the external world, customers and stakeholders. However, restructuring on every occasion these factors change, will be fraught with danger.

The design of the following elements in the Execution Dimension like Expectations, Equip, Perform & Measure and Intelligence, will help you to maximise the benefits of your structural design and minimise some of its disadvantages.

*

3. Expectations

The third element in the Execution Dimension, after you have made your choice of Structure, is setting the Expectations.

When the Expectations for every role are set clearly and correctly, and the roles are aligned, the entity's structure will function optimally. Every role will be able to achieve its objectives and your entity would achieve its mutual purpose. But from the outset we should ensure that Expectations for every role are set and met.

For your entity's structure to engage proactively and flexibly with challenges posed by its contextual environment, it should be filled with the necessary roles, each with clear expectations.

Proper and clear setting of expectations is a key leadership task that is closely linked to relationship behaviours and it drives exceptional performance. It provides vital 'push energy'. It inspires people when done inclusively. Setting correct expectations shows confidence and trust in your people. Clear expectations form a golden thread between your entity's mutual purpose and strategies, and each member's actual activities.

Expectations are unique for each role. Deficiencies within and gaps between roles result in all sorts of organisational disorders—some of which I will touch on below.

The Expectations for a role is defined by a set of interdependent role characteristics. The role characteristics are:

- **Role accountability** – What should be accomplished by the role, and what are the means necessary to fulfil the role?
- **Role fit** – Who has the correct attributes to fill the role?
- **Role clarity** – Why does the role exist, or why do we need it?

Together the three characteristics; role fit, role clarity and role accountability complete the picture of role Expectation. If any one of the role characteristics are not completely defined, the expectations of the role will not be met. A lack in any one of the role characteristics will result in poor execution and reduced performance.

Note that the role characteristics do not address *how* roles are to be performed. Each role player determines how his role is performed. When role fit and role accountability are correct, every role player will have the necessary skills, capabilities and resources to enable him to decide how to do the tasks he is accountable for.

The interdependent nature of the three role characteristics is shown in Figure 13.4. Together, they create a complete picture of a role's unique expectations. When a role's expectations are incomplete, many kinds of incorrect assumptions about a role's accountability often develop—which will result in suboptimal performance results.

Figure 13.4. Expectations

Accountability

When you are accountable for an outcome you are ultimately answerable to achieve the agreed deliverables to realise that outcome. Accountability answers the what-questions of expectations. It defines the decision-making parameters and boundaries within which a role must achieve its actions and tasks.

Irrespective of your choice of entity structure, each role in it has a set of unique accountabilities. Accountabilities must be agreed correctly and aligned with the rest of the execution system. It is imperative that leaders do this with their direct reports at regular intervals. The principle of alignment of accountabilities applies through the entire entity. Hence, assignment of accountabilities is a process that cascades up and down and across the whole entity. Following the principle of aligning accountabilities, will prevent biased or mistaken expectations and substandard performance.

▽ Setting role accountabilities

Each role has a defined set of delegated accountabilities. For someone to perform his role optimally there needs to be a balance between his role requirements and the resources he needs to fulfil those requirements. A useful instrument to help assign and balance role accountability is an 'accountability balance sheet'. Table 13.2 is an example of an accountability balance sheet. The left-hand side of the balance sheet contains important role requirements, and the right-hand side contains the essentials needed to realise accountabilities. An accountability balance sheet is applied and balanced for every role in the entity. When an accountability balance sheet is not in equilibrium, several performance issues will show up sooner or later.

Table 13.2 Accountability Balance Sheet	
Role Requirements **(Demands of the role)**	**Role Needs** **(Resources to perform a role)**
Scope and type of work	Scope of decisions
Complexity of the work	Decision-making rights
Decision-making and information requirements	Decision-making boundaries and constraints
Impact of decisions on entity Impact of decisions on execution schedules	Delegated power and authority—level of empowerment Allocated resources, budgets and capabilities
Level of problem solving	
Level of collaboration internally	Cross-boundary interface requirements
Level of external collaboration	Shared responsibilities and collaboration requirements
Technology, systems and levels of complexity in the role	
Specific behaviour requirements, internally and externally	

You can use the role requirements in the balance sheet to slice and dice your entity's total scope of decision-making and deliverables into vertical layers (levels) and horizontal layers (roles within levels). For example, levels of complexity, decision-making, problem solving, and collaboration, in your entity will determine the number of leadership and managerial levels. The different types and scopes of work, technologies, resources and required behaviours, will determine the design of unique roles needed to achieve the objectives.

When you do an accountability balance for every role, ask the question: 'Will the accountability parameters for this role, help or hinder the role's expectations and goal achievement?' When a role's accountability is correctly designed, it will have the proper range of decision-making authority within clear boundaries. It will have adequate resources and proper delegated powers.

Every role's accountability differs from the roles above, below and beside it. A role's accountability must be different from those of the roles reporting to it; from those it reports to, and from those with which it collaborates. The uniqueness of role accountability is a fundamental requirement for creating empowerment and inclusion. Any overlaps or gaps in accountability that may occur horizontally, vertically or laterally will lead to less role clarity, duplication and waste of resources. Figure 13.5 illustrates this point. Lower role clarity leads to confusion, disempowerment, lower inclusion and poor performance.

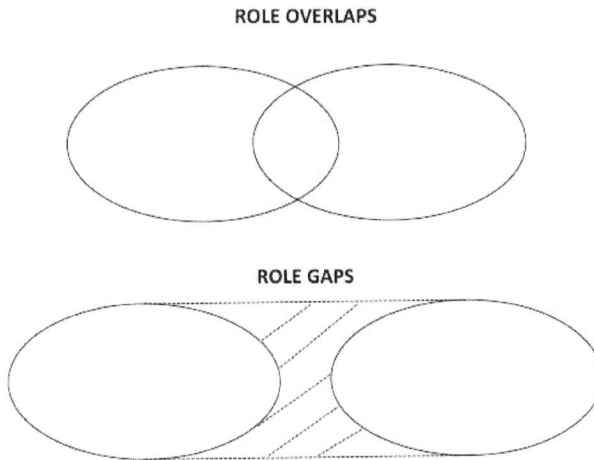

ROLE OVERLAPS

ROLE GAPS

Figure 13.5. Role Overlaps and Role Gaps

∇ Horizontal role overlaps

Unless a deliverable is designed and agreed to be a joint accountability (which is by definition not an overlap) then more than one person could be responsible for a deliverable or parts of a deliverable. Horizontal overlaps lead to turf wars over resources, politicking, silo formation, disempowerment and exclusion.

∇ Horizontal role gaps

Horizontal gaps are not always easily identifiable, especially for new roles. Horizontal gaps become obvious when unexpected execution problems need to be solved and there is no clear identifiable role that is accountable to resolve the issue. When accountability gaps are closed, frustrations will stop, people will not distance themselves from problems, and performance will improve.

∇ Vertical role overlaps

Roles that overlap vertically are the antithesis of empowerment and inclusion. Vertical accountability overlaps occur when more than one person shares the same, or parts of, decision-making rights, authority and power. An example of vertical overlap usually occurs between managers and their subordinates. The manager is unwilling to delegate or share his power, authority and decision-making rights with his subordinate.

Vertical role overlap is probably one of the main causes of disempowerment and disengagement. It diminishes meaning, purpose and value from the person in the overlapped role. Because of the overlap, evidently some parts of either role may be unnecessary, and neither of the roles can fully contribute to their maximum potential. Vertical role overlap not only disempowers, it wastes vast amounts or resources and of human potential.

A positive reason to have some vertical overlap for a period is when the sub-ordinate in the overlapping role does not yet have the necessary skills and experience to fulfil his role effectively. This situation should only continue provisionally until the sub-ordinate has gained the necessary skills. His expectations are then adjusted to include his new capabilities and to remove the overlaps.

▽ Vertical role gaps

Vertical gaps in role accountability often become evident after restructuring exercises when the entity discovers that the capabilities of certain individuals do not match the requirements of their roles. Due to restructuring the entity may have lost capabilities or capacity, or a need develops for certain capabilities or capacities.

▽ Lateral role overlaps and gaps

Lateral overlaps and gaps between roles typically occur within and across project teams, groups, and collaborative relationships, where roles are assembled temporarily to deliver specific outcomes. When role accountabilities in such situations are not clearly defined, lateral gaps and overlaps occur, resulting in many performance disorders, some of which were discussed above.

▽ Do not skip levels or jump boundaries

A related behaviour that results in role overlaps is when leaders skip across authority levels. Resist the temptation to skip levels or jump across accountability boundaries that were defined. Often leaders would skip a level past a direct report or jump laterally across several accountability boundaries. For example, leaders often do this hastily, by delegating to, or asking someone else (without the correct accountability) to quickly do something for them. Such behaviour is indiscrete and violates your delegation of accountability, authority and power. It is rude and disrespectful. It erodes your trust, confuses expectations, and is a primary cause of disempowerment and disengagement. Work within the expectations and structures you have created—this will build your trusting relationships and inclusion.

Role fit

Role fit addresses the who-question of expectations. It clarifies the attributes of the most suitable candidate for a role, such as, the set of skills, capabilities, and level of experience that are necessary to perform the tasks in a role. Ideally there should be more than one person available within an entity that could fit into a role and its accountability profile. However, this is often not the case. You would therefore either develop capable candidates with the potential to fit into the role (with the necessary training, mentoring and coaching), or you would have to recruit candidates with the necessary profile that fits the role.

Role clarity

Role clarity, together with role accountability and role fit complete the picture of expectations. Role clarity addresses the why-questions of expectations. It is a clear and unambiguous description of the reasons why a role player should perform certain tasks to achieve the performance objectives he is accountable for.

Create role clarity through dialogue: First with the individual and if necessary with his team members. Role clarity leads to commitment to mutual objectives. Dialogue about role clarity is not about how the role incumbent must do his job. That is a waste of leadership time. Role incumbents should already have the necessary skills and abilities to fit in the role so they can autonomously decide how to achieve their delegated objectives.

Dialogues that focus on role clarification, address the following topics with each person:

- The specific objectives he is accountable for are clear.
- Objectives are discussed in relation to the entity's context. Discuss the background reasons and rationale why specific actions are necessary to achieve role objectives.

- The incumbents' objectives are clear, realistic, achievable and challenging.
- Show them how their roles and objectives align across the entity with the mutual purposes and strategy.
- Context and alignment give role incumbents a clear sense of how their personal purpose and their roles fit into the mutual purpose. Role clarity results in higher inclusion and mutual ownership of the entity's future direction.
- How the objectives of your direct report interlock with your objectives, and how your direct report's objectives interlock with the objectives of their direct reports. This understanding of how objectives interlock ensures uninterrupted cascading accountability—without overlaps and gaps.
- Mutually commit on accountability parameters. Set clear decision-making rights, authority levels, boundaries and constraints, task scopes, budgets and resources.
- Do an accountability balance check together. Determine if his objectives are achievable with his level of assigned accountability. If not, readjust the necessary accountability parameters to get a balance.
- The objectives are achievable with his skills, capabilities and experience. For example, when a role incumbent does not have the necessary level of skills, plan to develop those skills to close the gaps.
- The necessary intelligence is made available to the role.
- Agree on how performance will be measured: What are the key parameters, the standards of execution and the quality standards for deliverables?
- Determine how achievement will be recognised and rewarded.
- Be unconditionally clear about the consequences that will follow when the role incumbent does not achieve his

accountabilities—the consequences for both his role and the effects on the entity.

Team expectations

Teamwork and team performance often derail because the team's expectations were not determined from the outset or changed when needed.

As a leader of teams, you can use the same principles applicable to individual role expectations. This equally applies to permanent teams, such as executive teams, and to temporary teams, like project teams. A key difference is that role accountability, role clarity, and role fit should be established for a team as a unit, as well as for every team member in the team.

A lack of clarity among team members about team expectations will significantly discourage team performance. Team members are often assigned to a team without clear understanding of their roles and their team members' roles, their accountability and the team's accountability. Often the expectations at the team level are not the same as individual expectations—especially when people are assigned to temporary teams. For example, team members may have specific formal roles in the entity, but other shared roles within a temporary team context. The expectations in the two contexts can be markedly different. Therefore, clear accountability, responsibility, and authority need to be considered and committed. Most importantly, teams need to be clear about their shared purpose and shared objectives.

A key requirement for effective teamwork is that team member expectations must interlock laterally—without overlaps and gaps. An effective way to create an efficient team is to have open and candid dialogue amongst the members about team and individual expectations. The dialogue process will uncover gaps, overlaps, and accountability deficiencies.

Outcomes of open dialogue about team expectations should be:

- The team's objectives and how the objectives align with the entity's purpose are clarified.
- Every member will understand how his individual and the team members' roles contribute and interact with each other.
- Clarity of individual and mutual accountability is established.
- Gaps and overlaps are addressed transparently to reduce potential for disempowerment, turf clashes or unwanted outcomes.
- Possible changes to team members, or their accountabilities, due to role overlaps are implemented.
- Additional members with additional skill sets are invited to join the team to fill accountability gaps.
- Accountability parameters are readjusted to obtain necessary empowerment, decision-making authority and resources.

Final thoughts on Expectations

The usual approach to expectation discussions is the dreaded annual performance review—commonly applied retrospectively in a unidirectional way. The two sides of the coin, expectations and performance, though intricately related, are not the same. Performance follows upon expectations. Hence, setting proper and clear expectations sets the scene for exceptional performance.

Retrospective performance reviews are obviously inadequate, reactive and usually highly overdue. It may suffice for higher echelon roles to have semi-annual or annual expectation review sessions, mainly because the impact of such roles is predominantly in the longer term.

Continual change and the resulting impact on our entities means that we should have dialogues about expectations with direct reports and teams on a much more regular basis. When there are changes in peoples' expectations, for example, when roles, functions, or scopes of work change, dialogue about renewed expectations is instantly necessary. We readjust accountability and role clarity accordingly. Delaying changes to expectations result in widening accountability gaps and overlaps, which would result in performance decline.

---

4. Equip

After establishing the necessary expectations for each role, the next leadership task is to equip each role so that your entity is capable to accomplish its objectives. The forth element in the Execution Dimension is 'Equip'. Effective equipping is the allocation of all necessary attention, time, resources and means to every role so that the entity can execute its tasks effectively and efficiently. Equipping involves your leadership actions such as, providing necessary and sufficient consideration, time, resources, systems, processes, capabilities and capacity so that your entity is able, competent, and ready to deliver on agreed expectations. Equipping to execute is a dual leadership function: On the one hand it involves the allocation (and reallocation) of resources, while on the other hand it is the simultaneous removal of obstacles and barriers that are in the way of wealth creation. Both leadership actions are necessary to enable your people to effectively perform their agreed expectations.

Leaders equip on three levels:

Yourself

Equipping yourself relates to how you allocate your scarcest leadership resources—that is your time, leadership capabilities, and your personal energy. We all have a limited amount of emotional, physical and mental capacity available to complete our daily tasks. Judicious application of your time and energy is key to how you lead. When you properly equip yourself, you will have the means to equip your entity to deliver on their expectations.

Every individual person

When you have determined individual expectations, it is imperative that you provide them (your direct-reports) with the necessary means and resources so they can deliver on those expectations. I have seen countless examples where expectations and necessary resources did not match. Inevitably the results of such mismatches are performance failures, frustration and broken careers. Not surprisingly, the blame for these negative results was put on someone else's shoulders—seldom the leader's.

Your entity

Equipping your entity is about making sure that the allocation and reallocation of resources and means across the entire entity is done efficiently so it can achieve the mutual purpose and strategic objectives. The topic of reallocation of resources is covered in depth in the chapters about the Change Dimension.

Resources needed to equip the entity

The resources we use in Execution can be either sustainable or non-sustainable. Sustainable resources in the context of this book are those resources the entity can use repeatedly to increase the wealth of your entity. Sustainable resources have the largest impact on wealth creation. Non-sustainable resources have a limited lifespan and once it has been used, it ceases to exist. A primary purpose of equipping is to leverage the entity's non-sustainable resources as much as possible, to multiply its sustainable resources.

Figure 13.6 illustrates the range of different resources you may need to properly equip your entity to deliver on expectations.

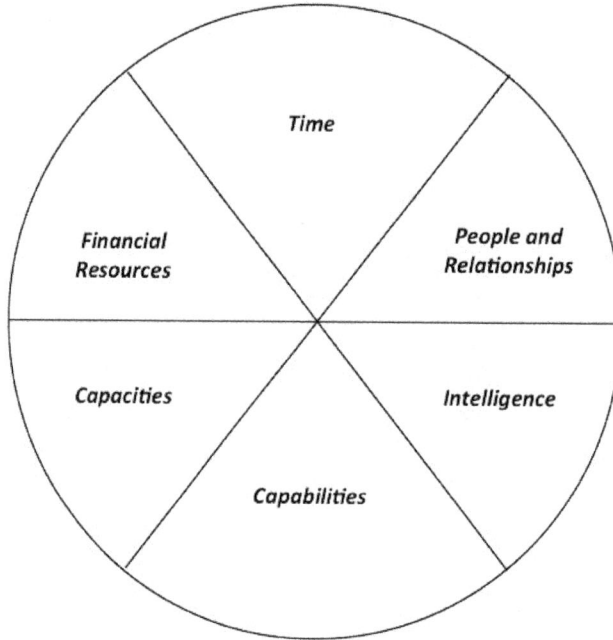

Figure 13.6. Resources Needed to Equip Your Entity

Leaders must Equip their entities with six main resource groups: time, finance, people, capacities, capabilities and intelligence.

▽ Time

Time is the total number of hours available to your entity to achieve its objectives. Time available to the entity is the sum of all your peoples' actual hours available over a specified timeframe, for example, a week or a year, to accomplish specific tasks and goals. Depending on the size of your entity, your total time budget may amount to millions of hours per annum.

▽ Financial resources

Financial resources are all the available financial means available to your entity. This is normally obvious in the entity's balance sheet, and cash flow statement, but it also includes potential new sources, such as equity and loan finance.

▽ People and relationships

As a resource, people and relationships include:

- **Individual human energy:** Our individual emotional, mental and physical energy. Every one of us has a finite amount of human energy available every day to accomplish our objectives.
- **Leadership power and decision-making authority** are important resources you have at your disposal as a leader, and collectively as an entity when you share it inclusively. Your power and authority should be judiciously allocated and shared to ensure better performance results. Hoarding leadership power and authority causes exclusion and disengagement.
- **Relationships and connections** with customers, suppliers, stakeholders, intelligence providers, communities and third parties (i.e. alliances, collaborative networks).
- **Insourced labour** is used to increase human capacity on a temporary basis.

▽ Capabilities

Capability is *the ability and competency* to transform resources with lower value, into resources with higher value (or resources with higher utility), to achieve our objectives. Capability resources are all the abilities, competencies, and technologies we need to perform, produce and deliver inventions, services, products, and offerings to our customers, clients and stakeholders.

Capability resources include:

- Leadership and managerial competencies.

- Professional skills, functional skills and competencies acquired through education, training, experience and on-the-job training.
- Change-orientated capabilities as discussed in the Change Dimension.
- Technological capabilities and intellectual properties that support our ability to innovate and develop new ideas.
- Systems, processes, procedures and methods to produce, innovate or provide services.
- Capabilities that can be acquired, borrowed and insourced from third parties or collaborative relationships.

▽ Capacities

Capacity is a *quantitative or volumetric term* associated with resources. It applies to both tangible and intangible resources. Capacity resources are resources that have limits and boundaries. Examples are: The size of your office building, the capacity of your factory, the size of the property you could use productively, processing capacities, the number of people with specific qualifications or skills, the credit facility you have with your bank, etc.

Note that resources can have both capability and capacity attributes.

Capacity resources include:

- Leadership and managerial capacity—for example, leadership time and attention available to be invested in essential leadership responsibilities.
- Actual human talent and level of competencies available to execute necessary execution tasks. (Note, this is not the same as 'human energy' discussed before).
- Operational and administrative capacities of the entity. For example the physical facilities that produce services or

products. It includes plant, equipment, machinery, land and physical locations.

- The level of access the entity has to raw materials, utilities, logistical infrastructure and other essential resources.
- Technological capacity is the methods, know-how and intellectual property that enable the entity to deliver on its objectives.
- Systems, processes, and procedures that are flexible, and able to be reallocated.
- Capacities that can be acquired, borrowed or insourced from third parties.

▽ Intelligence is a sustainable resource

Intelligence is so important for an entity to function sustainably, that I have created an entire Intelligence element in the Execution Dimension. See the discussion on the seventh element called Intelligence later in this chapter. Intelligence is also a fundamental sustainable resource. I discuss intelligence as a resource first.

Intelligence is:

Advanced Actionable Information

In other words, intelligence is the timely higher value information, knowledge and understanding that is available and applicable to redirect, grow, protect and sustain the entity.

Intelligence becomes a sustainable resource when it is continuously refreshed, enhanced and shared for conversion into solutions, new innovations, competitive strategies, and change initiatives. The aim of actionable intelligence is to ensure short- and long-term viability and resilience of the entity. It is one of the key resources necessary to build the wealth of entities, communities and nations.

Note that in the context of execution, intelligence does not refer to the mental or emotional intelligence of people. Rather the meaning suggests that it is exploitable high value information and understanding. It has a similar meaning to intelligence in a military context.

Advanced intelligence is created through successive conversion steps that normally start with abundant, frequently confusing, and often highly complex data, and end in purpose-oriented applicable intelligence.

$$Data \rightarrow Information \rightarrow Knowledge \rightarrow Intelligence \Leftrightarrow Purpose$$

Data has low value in terms of its cost, high volume, high availability, weak durability and non-sustainability. The process of creating high value actionable intelligence starts with the conversion of data into information, followed by conversion of information into higher value knowledge, which is in turn converted into actionable intelligence. Creation and application of intelligence is purpose oriented. Intelligence supports and follows the entity's strategic objectives towards the entity's purpose.

Principles to Equip

Consider the following principles when you equip your entity:

- Your entity's mutual purposes and strategy should be the main considerations that determine how resources are allocated, and reallocated amongst different initiatives.
- Budget your own and your team's time. Roughly divide your leadership time budget as follows:
    - 15% solitary time (to plan, think, and formulate strategy).
    - 25% on building relationships (internal, external, stakeholders, members, clients, etc.).
    - 25% on change and strategic initiatives.
    - 25% on execution and operational issues (including your digital communication).

    — 10% of time on urgent and unexpected issues.

- Budget your entire entity's time (not in excessive detail). Start with priority initiatives and projects. There are hundreds of courses on individual time management. Yet it is 'high time' that this competency is elevated to the organisation and executive team level. It is not a foreign concept—project managers perform scheduling on a routine basis. Why can't it be done for entire entities? Be particularly vigilant about proliferation of initiatives and projects. An organisational disease, common in many entities, is called initiative overload. It occurs when time is implicitly regarded as an infinite resource.

- Investigate the life stages of your entity and its various offerings on their lifecycles (the concept of S-curves is discussed in depth in the Change Dimension). Identifying the life stages will help you to determine when, where and how much resources should be reallocated.

- Use predetermined and agreed resource allocation criteria. Without definitive resource allocation criteria, you will spend resources inconsiderately, leading to mediocre performance.

- Prioritise. When there are not enough resources to reallocate to preferred initiatives, prioritise. Highest priorities are equipped first. Other worthy priorities remain on the back burner until your entity has the necessary resources to attend to them too.

- Budget and allocate resources. Following prioritisation, allocate (or reallocate) the necessary time, finances and other resources.

- Ensure everyone in the entity is equipped satisfactorily, across the full range of necessary resources.

- Reduce unnecessary work, complexity, procedures, systems, decision layers and controls. Unnecessary barriers consume scarce resources, cause inefficiencies, stifle performance and cause disengagement. Run periodic audits to sweep out unnecessary bureaucracy and reduce resource wastage.

- Be on the lookout for people who hog power, authority and information. People who show hogging behaviours restrict access to important relationships, key connections and critical intelligence. People who hoard resources prevent the entity from meeting its expectations effectively, if at all. Results will be delayed, restricted or off-target. Confront power hogs and restore sharing of power, authority and information.

- Recalibrate role expectations. Recalibration is a vital principle but is often neglected. Yet we expect that the entity and individuals will deliver on expectations without recalibrating the link between expectations and equipping. Whenever expectations for roles change, necessary resources to adequately equip roles may also change. Hence the need for recalibration. Recalibration of the expectation-equip link, leads to organisational effectiveness, better aligned expectations, improved engagement, performance, resource savings and successful initiatives.

*

Resource Sustainability

The concept of resource sustainability is illustrated graphically in Figure 13.7. For example, on the left-end of the scale, time is the most unsustainable resource. On the right-hand end of the scale, wealth is the most sustainable resource. Wealth means different things to different entities. Wealth includes resources such as tangible assets, intellectual property, important long-term relationships, etc. For the sake of the argument, I have put financial resources, at the central pivotal point of the resource continuum.

When we apply resources, our main objective should be to multiply the value of the resources we use and create new resources of higher value. Therefore, it makes sense to apply the scarcest and non-sustainable resources as judiciously as possible to create higher value sustainable resources. Sustainable resources can be used and leveraged repeatedly. Moreover, when you leverage higher value wealth resources, such as key relationships, or intelligence, you can create additional wealth resources like new capabilities or innovative intellectual property, and ultimately multiply exceptional wealth.

Sustainable Wealth Resources

On the positive end of the sustainability continuum in Figure 13.7 are the wealth resources. Sustainable resources form an entity's 'Wealth Portfolio'. The wealth portfolio includes your entity's net financial worth, tangible assets, intellectual property, intelligence, capacities, capabilities, and very importantly, the relationships with stakeholders, employees and third parties.

Wealth resources are:

- Resources your entity creates and builds painstakingly over long periods of time.
- Not limited to the net financial worth of the entity—that assumption can be very misleading.
- Not easily copied.
- Slow to depreciate; and
- Not easily substituted.

Wealth resources shape your entity's unique characteristics, help to provide distinctive offerings, create competitive advantages, new innovations, and sustains the brand. Wealth resources form the core of your entity's resilience when you need it most in dire times. Your entity needs wealth resources to grow and survive. And, when your entity has the need to be agile in favourable times it will rely on its wealth resources to seize opportunities.

Financial resources

There is no doubt that financial resources are very important in any entity, but as a resource it is not as sustainable as the 'wealth' resources. In Figure 13.7 financial resources is in the central pivotal position. When the financial resources that are at an entity's disposal are not managed well its value become less sustainable (the value moves to the left on the scale), while the opposite equally applies, when finances are managed well. Of all the resources at our disposal, money in all its different forms gets the most leadership attention when it comes to resource planning, allocation and budgeting. The systems and processes for managing financial resources are often very sophisticated. But, is it correct to focus so much leadership attention on this resource alone? What about the other resources?

Time

Time as a resource, is unsustainable. One cannot create time. Once a second has past, it is gone forever. Time is the scarcest resource we have at our disposal. Mismanaged time equals lost opportunities and reduced performance, period. Yet time is the most leverage-able resource. Regard the time available to your entity like a forward contract. The price you pay for this forward contract is equal to the cumulative salaries and benefits of your entity's people. The value you will get from the forward contract is entirely up to you. Your leadership determines the upside value of the time forward contract. So, it would make sense to budget and manage the time your entity buys on a forward contract with equal, if not more care, as you would manage its financial resources. Yet, only a small sector of entities regards time budgeting as a serious resource matter. Leveraging your entity's time—the scarcest non-sustainable resource—as best as you can, and you would multiply the cumulative value of sustainable wealth resources.

Other non-sustainable resources

Other resources on the non-sustainable end of the scale are; data, information and human energy.

Data and information

Data and information must be continually refreshed to sustain their exploitable value. In today's contextual environment, we are flooded with data and information, but data's exploitable lifespan is becoming shorter and shorter.

Human energy

The human energy (our individual emotional, mental and physical energy) every person brings to the entity is only sustainable for one workday; then it must be replenished sufficiently—or else human exhaustion, stress, and even burnout will set in. Somehow some leaders seem to miss this very normal point about the people who work for them (including themselves). People get overworked and change-fatigued when they are pushed beyond their sustainable energy capacities. The result is disengagement, performance losses, increased absence from work and increased workforce turnover.

*

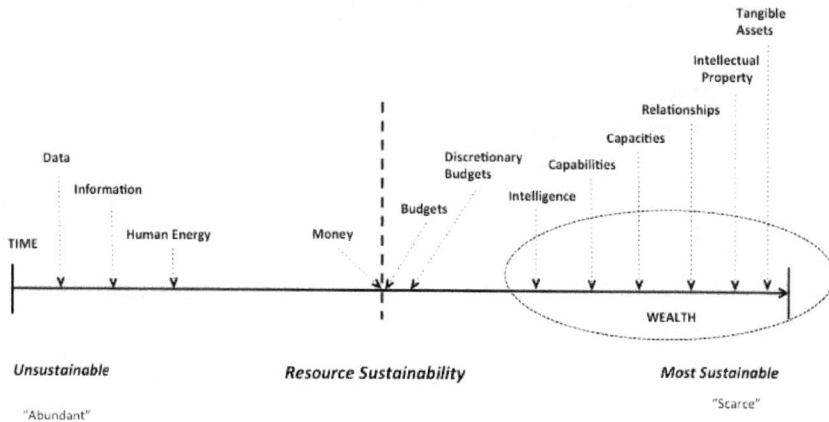

Figure 13.7 Resource Sustainability

---

5. Performance and Measurement

The fifth element in the Execution Dimension is 'Performance and Measurement'.

By this point of the Execution Dimension, you have governed your entity's strategic objectives, put the necessary structures in place, clarified and agreed expectations, and equipped everyone to deliver on their expectations. The entity is ready to move into the final stage of the Execution Dimension. It is ready to perform and be measured on outcomes and results.

Performance is the actual accomplishment of all the necessary tasks to deliver on agreed expectations, strategic objectives and mutual purposes. Performance and Measurement is where the rubber hits the road. Achieving exceptional performance is undeniably a condition that determines your success and the entity's. Performance is often too narrowly defined in terms of an entity's financial or economic results. For-profit organisations, almost universally have a singular focus on short-term financial metrics that focus on profitability and share price. Such a fixation on financial results and metrics often harms the long-term future of entities.

Your entity's performance must be achieved in alignment with its mutual purpose. Broadly, performance is the sum of all outputs and results, in terms of the value, satisfaction, quality and compliance your entity delivers to your customers and stakeholders, while it maintains and improves its agility, resilience and wealth in the short- and long-term. Your entity's good wealth and wellbeing guarantee that it will be able to perform continually, in good and bad times.

Exceptional short-term performance that weakens your entity's long-term wealth, resilience and agility is poor performance.

Measurement

On the flip side of the performance coin is measurement. Performance measurement is the act of comparing an execution system's outputs and results against set objectives, targets, standards, baselines, benchmarks, values and principles.

Deming, the famous quality management guru, once said:

"You can expect what you inspect" and "You get what you measure"

Measuring your leadership performance

For leaders, performance measurement of their leadership serves important but sometimes less obvious objectives. Deviations from predefined behaviour indicators, either positive or negative, are valuable signs for your personal development and changing your behaviours. Many outcomes in your entity are the direct result of your leadership behaviours. Often these outcomes can range from highly valuable to highly detrimental to your entity, its reputation, its relationships and your peoples' engagement. The consequences of your leadership behaviours may only become obvious at a much later stage, often long after you have departed. Sometimes the consequences of your behaviours are only observable years after you have taken an action.

George Pickering once said:

"Not everything that counts can be counted, and not anything that can be counted, counts"

To become a better leader and to ensure that your entity performs at its best, you should design leadership performance metrics that measure the effects of your leadership behaviours on the performance of your entity—directly and indirectly. It is essential for effective execution and building trusting relationships.

Measuring and evaluating the relationships between your leadership behaviours and resulting outcomes, will inform you when your behaviours were successful, or when they need modification. Many outcomes of your leadership behaviours can only be measured indirectly. For indirect measures, you can use entity measures as proxies. The measures will assist you to learn and improve on your behaviours.

Performance measurement at the entity level

At entity level, it is obvious why we need performance measurement. Without it we would be at a loss to know if the entity is meeting its execution targets, and to what extent we are meeting, exceeding or missing our performance targets. Performance measurement serves important objectives, such as:

Transparency and accountability

Performance measures must enhance the shared picture of how the execution system currently performs and how it could likely perform in the future. It highlights where performance issues are created. Everyone should be able to see this clear picture through open and honest presentation of performance facts. Transparency on performance helps everyone to focus proactively on solving problems, collaborate, re-allocate resources and change priorities. Transparency about performance issues helps to correct execution issues in time to recover lost performance, and to engage new opportunities. Transparency builds better accountability—everyone becomes more willing to readjust their objectives, resources or priorities for the entity can meet its mutual objectives. With transparent measures, you can resolve conflicts of interest constructively and uncooperative people will become highly noticeable. People who display non-transparent behaviour will either have to behave more collaboratively, or they will leave the entity when the level of transparency makes them uncomfortable.

Alignment

Performance measurement is the final test of entity alignment. Issues with alignment with e.g. the strategic objectives, expectations or equipping, will become clear with accurate and sufficient measures. Performance measures will help to indicate where misalignments are, and where broken connections with the entity's strategy exist. You may need to interpret a combination of different measures to pinpoint alignment issues. You can then take the necessary proactive steps to realign.

Behaviour modification

Design and track specific performance measures that will indicate when behaviours are in line with the purposes of your entity. Use the feedback from such measures to readjust behaviours or to change the culture of your entity if necessary.

Change and learning

When you combine performance measures with intelligence from the external context, it creates opportunities for learning and change. Learning created through performance feedback is used to improve and readjust elements in the Execution Dimension.

Entity future and wellbeing

Fortunately we can now use the power of Predictive Business Analytics (PBA) to forecast future-oriented measures. With PBA, we can create measures that provide intelligence on possible future initiatives one might consider. Wellbeing measures will tell you how agile and resilient your entity is to withstand future change and seize opportunities.

Which performance measures should you use?

In Figure 13.8, there are three focus areas we must consider when measuring performance: leadership behaviour, execution, and change.

Performance measures in execution systems

Performance measures and metrics in execution systems focus on effectiveness, efficiency and compliance.

Effectiveness

Effectiveness reflects the degree to which objectives and standards have been accomplished. Effectiveness demonstrates if your entity's actions were sufficient to accomplish its objectives, and produce the intended results. For example, your entity may have reached its target to make a specific number of products, or to reach a specific quality target.

Typical examples of effectiveness measures are:

- Project milestones.
- Employee, customer and stakeholder satisfaction measures.

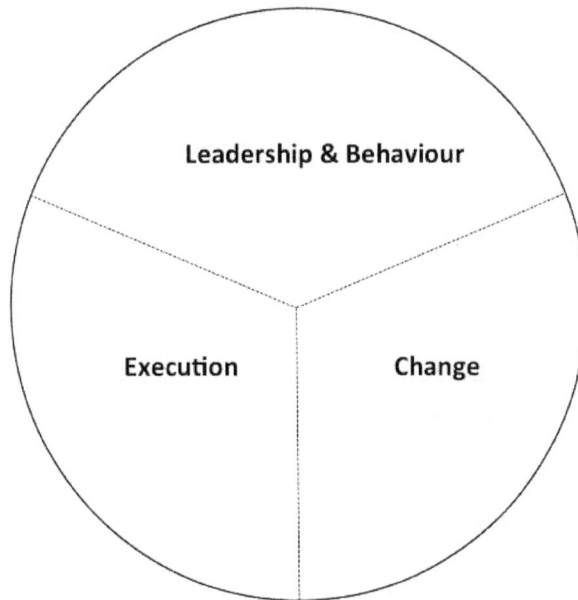

Figure 13.8. Performance Measurement Focus Areas

- Organisation culture measures.
- Share price and dividend growth.
- Quality measures for services and products.
- Time-to-market.
- Levels of customer service and product customisation.

Efficiency

Efficiency defines ratios (or percentages) of resources used (inputs) to outputs produced, to achieve predefined objectives. For example, expressing the efficiency of product development can be something as follows:

The value of revenue earned through sales of the new product, expressed as a ratio to the resources spent to develop such new product, for example: $ Revenue / $ Development. The higher the efficiency ratio, the better the utilisation of resources for this example.

For-profit entities, typical use efficiency measures like:

- Financial and economic ratios that measure the entity's operating performance, such as: return on assets, return on equity, margins on sales, and sales to assets ratio, etc.
- Shareholder return ratios: dividends per share, market to book value, earnings yield, price-to-earnings, etc.
- Productive efficiency: ratios of product or service outputs to the amounts of resources used.
- Utilisation Ratios: ratios of product or service outputs to the levels of capacity utilisation, for example, revenue per unit of plant capacity.

It is important to use efficiency and effectiveness measures in combination to get a complete picture of your entity's execution performance. Effectiveness measures do not provide information on how productively or economically resources were used to meet defined targets. For example, your entity may have reached a targeted number of products, but with unproductive resource utilisation. The target may therefore be achieved quite effectively, but not efficiently.

Compliance

Compliance can be broadly defined as adhering to the requirements of laws, regulations, industry and organisational standards and codes. It includes common law obligations, fiduciary obligations, and contractual obligations. Compliance performance measures are important to guide leadership behaviour because you may be initiating and driving initiatives that are regulated by compliance instruments—often compliance requirements that were unknown to you or your entity.

Most compliance measures are like light switches—either on, or off. You comply, or you don't. Some compliance requirements are mandatory, while others are less stringent. Because of the proliferation of compliance requirements, it is prudent that you design compliance measurement systems that adequately gauge how your entity responds.

Compliance measurement systems should include early warning mechanisms, so you can avoid potentially severe penalties.

Your entity's specific area of conduct may have various regulations that could differ between jurisdictions. You should be specifically attentive of compliance measures in the following areas:

- Health and safety management standards.
- Financial and fiduciary codes.
- Taxation rules and regulations.
- Employment laws and regulations.
- Environmental management practice codes and standards.

The levels of accuracy, frequency and reporting requirements on compliance metrics are usually stipulated in regulations. Stakeholders will scrutinise your entity's performance on compliance measures. Often non-compliance is followed by detailed scrutiny, audits, legal prosecution, and in severe cases, imprisonment of the responsible leadership.

Irrespective of your compliance requirements, your performance measurement system must be able to alert you in advance of issues that could lead to non-compliance. You want to log and investigate near misses. Pay close attention to near misses—identify them and do root cause analyses as you would for non-conformances. Address the causes immediately and thereby reduce potential non-compliance and potentially serious legal action in the future.

Leadership Principles of Performance Measurement

Entities are flooded with too many performance measures. The blame for that is partly due to the sheer power and ability of analytics to analyse almost any activity in our entities. Yet leaders have limited time to interpret too many performance measures and act on them. These principles will help you to design performance measurement systems that drive proactiveness, save time and resources:

Align measures with the purpose

At the leadership level performance measurement systems should mainly report on how the entity is tracking towards its mutual purpose, its strategic objectives and key initiatives.

Focus on less-is-more to improve accountability

Build your performance measurement system in a hierarchical pattern. A hierarchy of performance measures ensures that performance is measured where it counts and where the action takes place. For example, your R&D division deals with innovation measures on a divisional level. The same principle applies to other divisions, for example, human resources. Performance results for each division are rolled-up into a smaller number of Key Performance Indicators (KPIs), intended for leadership governance. Each division will have appropriate measures to be managed at the respective organisational level. Hierarchical designs prevent the proliferation of measures at the leadership level and push relevant measures down the levels of accountability. At each level, accountable leaders will have their specific sets of measures that gauge their performance.

Advance inclusion

Formulate and design performance measures at every level of the entity in an inclusive manner to build mutual ownership and accountability for initiatives and objectives.

Collaboration versus control

Tracking performance through measures should not be used as another form of command-and-control. Use a transparent performance measurement system to encourage collaboration, as a tool to proactively solve problems, to identify resource pinch points and to identify opportunities for change.

Use different kinds of measures

Use qualitative and quantitative, predictive and historical, lead and lag metrics.

Most performance measurement systems are designed to use historical (lagging) and quantitative data (numbers) as inputs and outputs. It is much more powerful and value adding to also use qualitative and predictive (leading) performance measures. Now, with the enormous power of data analytics we can enhance performance measurement with higher confidence levels. Entities can now proactively revisit and change product and service offerings by using predictive measures. Behaviour modification, a key component of leadership and cultural change is heavily reliant on qualitative data. Predictive measures are crucial when you want to determine your entity's wellbeing.

Continually refresh the measures

Periodically refresh your performance measurement system. Check if your baselines, benchmarks, KPIs, scorecards and dashboards still represent best practice for your entity and industry. Do your measures assist alignment of your entity's objectives with its purpose? Regularly remove redundant

> measures and improve the predictive power of your leading
> measures.

*

---

6. Intelligence

The final element in the Execution Dimension is 'Intelligence'. As discussed above, Intelligence is *both a sustainable resource, and a key element* in the Execution Dimension.

Intelligence is:

Advanced Actionable Information

Intelligence is the timely higher value information, knowledge and understanding that is available and applicable to redirect, grow, protect and sustain the entity.

In their report *"The Digital Universe by 2020"* John Gantz and David Reinsel[2] state that only three percent of data that is created in the digital universe is captured, while only half a percent of the data in the digital universe is analysed. It means that 99.95 percent of useful data available is not being analysed. By 2020, they estimate that there will be a 67 percent increase in data available for analysis. This fact presents an enormous opportunity that is ready to be harvested if we can create actionable intelligence from this vast source of data through analytics. These are the real opportunities presented in the new era of big data and analytics—and the amount of data available will only increase—exponentially.

Because of the sheer power of analytical software and the immense amounts of data available, big data and analytics are in vogue. The digital fraternity emphasises the vast opportunities of big data and analytics, while entities are drowning in information overload. On top of that is a pressing need for more accurate real time information so entities can remain competitive.

Intelligence does not start, nor end with big data or analytics. These wonderful innovations do not solve execution problems nor do they create intelligence. They have their proper place in an intelligence ecosystem. Yet too much emphasis is placed on them—biasing the subject of intelligence towards data sources, data itself, and the analytical methods to process data.

So, what do leaders have to do?

- First ask the key question: For which specific strategic execution aspects do we need intelligence, and why do we need that?

- Followed by: How do we gather, analyse, add value, distribute and apply that specific intelligence to our entity's advantage?

Asking the strategic questions upfront is much more valuable than analysing loads of potentially irrelevant data and creating intelligence that might not address key execution issues. Secondly, when you apply other mental models, such as, creative, strategic, systems, synthesis, and scenario thinking in addition to analytical thinking, you will create high value actionable intelligence. Chapter 8 discusses different mental models.

Analytics is good at answering pre-formulated questions. However digital algorithms are not effective when decisions need to be based on human creativity and judgment. Creative mental models that do not solely rely on analytical thinking are necessary. The leadership skill that integrates diverse demands from different contexts and a variety of mental models will become a most valuable leadership capability in the age of change. This ability to integrate creative mental models and analytics will significantly differentiate leaders and entities, and provide huge competitive advantage.

Intelligence systems that run on a common integrated platform facilitate inclusive and transparent execution since all users obtain the same intelligence from a single platform. Such integrated intelligence systems feed forward, feed back, and cycle actionable intelligence. Integrated intelligence systems assist course corrections and continuous improvements on any execution element quicker and easier. Because the system is more transparent and it feeds off an integrated platform it breaks down silos that exist to protect exclusive turf.

An integrated intelligence system enables you to see what expected future performance might look like, how the entity performs currently, and how it performed in the past. It also indicates which execution elements need improvement to advance performance. Everyone can 'read from the same page'—there is little room for ambiguous decisions.

An integrated intelligence system enables your people to continuously improve their performance. They have access to a wide selection of relevant intelligence that enables them to achieve and alter their expectations. Because they have open access to intelligence, decentralisation of accountability and control is much easier.

Transparency of intelligence makes everyone able to clearly see the performance of everyone else. Transparency of intelligence enables inclusive collaboration processes. People can work on impending performance problems and generate solutions across functional boundaries.

Leading intelligence

The ability to lead execution with proper deployment of integrated intelligence is a vital skill in the new age of change.

Intelligence is created in three time frames: the past, real-time and for the future. Figure 13.9 shows three kinds of intelligence—each created within a different time frame.

- **Historical intelligence.** Intelligence created by past performance is called historical intelligence.

- **Operational intelligence.** Intelligence created in real time is called operational intelligence.

- **Anticipatory intelligence.** Intelligence created to anticipate how future operations might unfold is called anticipatory intelligence.

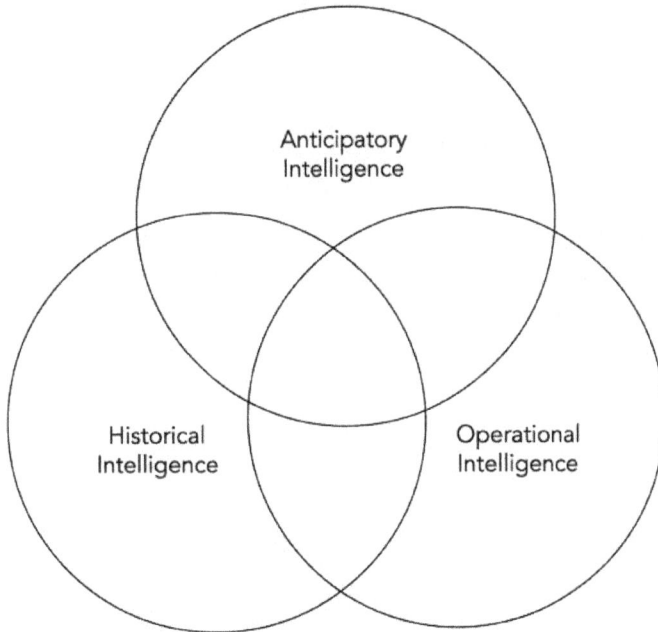

Figure 13.9. Leading Intelligence

Leaders play the central role in leading the integration and dissemination of intelligence from the three different contexts or time frames. Governing and directing intelligence also means that you should resolve the different and often contradictory demands and conflicts that are presented by intelligence from the three timeframes. For example, historical intelligence may suggest that your entity is doing just fine in terms of its resource utilisation and revenue. Real-time operational intelligence may suggest that pinch points exist with the allocation of certain resources, for example, capacity constraints. This may suggest that the execution system is not operating as efficiently as it could. However, anticipatory intelligence may suggest that you might have to reallocate resources to entirely new lines of services or products. Forecasts and trends may indicate that the current line is showing a decline in demand.

Historical Intelligence

Historical intelligence is gathered and created by past execution activities. It is closely linked to the execution and compliance performance measures discussed before.

Sources of historical intelligence are mainly internal and usually date back a month, a quarter or a year. Sources include, for example, financial, market, behaviour and compliance inputs and outputs of the entity. External sources such as benchmarks, codes, and standards are obtained for comparative purposes.

Historical intelligence assists answering questions such as:

- How did we perform?
- Did we comply?
- Did we reach our goals and objectives?
- How do we compare to competitors?

At best historical intelligence assists reactive responses to change certain elements in your Execution Dimension. Depending on the speed and complexity of the necessary change, reactive responses are often too late to have the required effect.

Operational Intelligence

Operational intelligence is created in real-time from direct customer, human and process interfaces. Real-time operational intelligence sources, such as sales, online polls, automated manufacturing, and online surveying is now commonplace. For decades already, technologies in automated process manufacturing have generated this kind of intelligence. This same ability is now available to capture almost any human behaviour in digital code. By gathering such human behaviours, mining and reprocessing the data through analytics, we can almost instantaneously model future behaviours. Such real-time intelligence, when integrated with historical intelligence is a powerful tool for correcting execution systems. With real-time operational intelligence entities we can now proactively identify immediate, and short-term continuous improvements in execution systems.

Operational intelligence assists with answering questions such as:

- Are we deviating from our agreed expectations?
- Is the execution system performing as intended?
- Which of the execution elements must be improved?
- Are we allocating our resources efficiently?

Anticipatory Intelligence

Anticipatory intelligence is the creation of intelligence that can suggest how future events might unfold and how future operations might be improved. We know that we can't create intelligence about the future—but we can anticipate what might happen in the future. Thanks to the digital power of predictive and prescriptive analytics we are now able to mine and analyse vast historical and real-time data sources and forecast potential future ways of execution.

Anticipatory intelligence can suggest proactive change initiatives so we can redirect execution activities timeously. Sources of anticipatory intelligence are mainly external.

It is essential that entities integrate anticipatory intelligence with operational and historical intelligence to make timely and accurate change decisions. When you also apply creative mental models that do not solely rely on linear analytical methods, you will add significant value to anticipatory intelligence. I have discussed anticipatory intelligence in more detail in the Change Dimension – Anticipate stage.

Anticipatory intelligence assist by answering questions such as:

- Do we need to change the execution system entirely, or only certain execution elements?
- How much life is remaining in the life cycles of our entity and our offerings?
- What changes to the execution system are likely?
- Are we prepared to make those changes and are we resilient against adversarial changes?

Principles for integrated intelligence systems

Priorities and objectives for integrated intelligence systems vary. Below are principles that will assist you to design and lead intelligence systems that are suitable for the age of change.

Transparent

The intelligence system must create transparency across your entity to enhance inclusion and accountability. The intelligence system enables everyone to openly and freely share information with others, including information about their own performance. Intelligence clearly shows causes and effects of every individual's actions. Everyone has the necessary intelligence, in time, to control and improve their own performance in collaboration with other people to the benefit of the entire entity. Intelligence enables everyone to hold each other accountable, across departmental boundaries, for agreed expectations—mutually and individually.

Consistent

Intelligence is built on a platform of common integrated sources of data. It works from this integrated platform that spans across boundaries and helps to build a culture of collaboration and trust.

Reliable

The intelligence platform is a trusted sustainable resource that is not disputed, unless intelligence quality and reliability seems questionable. Nor can it be manipulated by biased approaches or methods. The reliability and quality of a common execution intelligence platform must be continually verified, audited and refreshed to avoid second-guessing and decision stalling. Segregated, unilateral and non-integrated intelligence systems (for example, individual or departmental spreadsheets) that do not feed off, and feed into the integrated platform are discouraged. External sources are continually reviewed for quality, relevance, reliability and credibility.

Current

Intelligence is a sustainable resource that can deteriorate quickly in value. Operational intelligence has the shortest life span. Intelligence therefore must be kept current and available on time. The currency of intelligence must align with the requirements of the three intelligence time frames. Your intelligence system must provide quick dissemination and free flow of intelligence through the entity.

Improve decision-making and accountability

Specific intelligence is served purposely to specific decision nodes for early problem identification and opportunity realisation. Everyone gets the intelligence suitable to their contexts to support their decision-making and accountability. Timely and accurate intelligence significantly improves delivery on expectations. Instead of waiting for execution disturbances to have their full effect across the execution system, accountable people can make proactive course corrections immediately.

Security of intelligence

Sensitive intelligence usually resides inside Anticipatory intelligence (such as strategic, competitive and change intelligence). Highly sensitive intelligence often occurs within normal operational execution systems, such as for example, confidential personal information about customers. Cautiously determine the balance between the preservation and availability of sensitive intelligence to specific roles. Security of intelligence is not the same as hogging information. Hogging information is a closefisted behaviour, often used by individuals as an excuse to install exclusive behaviours as an alias for intelligence security. Hogging intelligence leads to silo formation, exclusion, disempowerment, loss of trust, reduced performance and lost opportunities.

Control and governance

Open and integrated intelligence systems encourage self-control and mutual accountability. It reduces the need for old-style unidirectional command-and-control mechanisms. The principles listed here promote enhanced transparency, decentralisation of decision-making, empowerment and inclusion.

An integrated intelligence system provides real opportunities to strengthen your leadership, but it also allows tightening of controls over entire execution systems. However, rather focus on the improvement of effective leadership, enhancing decentralised decision-making and inclusion, than tightening controls. Like the topic of security discussed before, be extra cautious to protect the positive aspects of governing intelligence against a control mentality. Using integrated intelligence to enforce tighter control can achieve lasting negative behaviour effects—destroying the constructive objectives envisioned by integrated intelligence.

Creating intelligence for Execution systems — The Process

To create actionable intelligence, your intelligence system should follow an iterative and systematic process. I have developed such an intelligence gathering and generation process that is easily applicable in a wide range of contexts. The process—which I call the *Anticipate Change Funnel*, is described in detail in Chapter 10 about Anticipation in the Change Dimension. With few adjustments, the *Anticipate Change Funnel* can be readily applied in the Execution Dimension.

Summary

The Execution Dimension describes the leadership behaviours that are necessary to strategically govern your entity's execution system. In many contexts, an entity's execution system is also known as its 'operations'. Execution can be defined as the performance of millions of coordinated tasks and activities, in a systematic way, to implement the strategy and initiatives that are aimed at achieving the entity's mutual purposes. The actual performance of these tasks and responsibilities are left to your capable people who are appointed with proper skills, accountabilities, and equipped with the right resources to achieve their expectations. However, ultimately the leader must ensure that his entity achieves according to its agreed mutual purpose. When the entity's execution fails, the leadership has failed.

From your perspective, there are a few key Execution Elements you should lead attentively to ensure successful performance of your entity. The elements of the Execution Dimension are:

1. Strategic Direction and Governance
2. Structure
3. Expectations
4. Equip
5. Performance and Measurement
6. Intelligence

The elements are aligned and systemically integrated so that your entity can achieve its objectives within its continually evolving context. The Execution Dimension, like the Change Dimension, will be firmly secured when excellent leadership relationships exist in your entity.

Notes

1. Chandler, A. D. 1962. Strategy and Structure, MIT Press, Cambridge.

2. Gantz, J., & Reinsel, D. 2012, The Digital Universe 2020 - Big Data, Bigger Digital Shadows, and Biggest Growth in the Far East, https://www.emc.com/leadership/digital-universe/index.htm.

14. Applying the Leadership Framework

We all like change as long as it is not us who need to change

In this final chapter I will show you how to apply the concepts and principles of the Leadership Framework, by illustrating a few practical examples.

In Chapter 3, I have introduced the Leadership Framework. As you will recall, the framework (Figure 14.1) is based on the Three-dimensional theory of leadership. In Chapters 4 and 13, I introduced the Relationship and Execution Dimensions respectively, with specific supplementary frameworks.

A large part of this book covers the third dimension about change-oriented leadership. Chapters 5 to 12 discussed the Change Dimension—designed for leadership of change in the 21st century. Combined, the three leadership dimensions are designed to easily apply appropriate leadership behaviours in your everyday leadership.

When you apply the Leadership Framework and its three dimensions, they will help and encourage you to become a leader for the 21st century. This is an age that is renowned for extraordinary change. It is an age where change is experienced and appreciated as being continuous and a natural part of our lives.

There are literally thousands of applications and contexts within which leaders can apply the Leadership Framework and the underlying principles in my book. I chose three examples to illustrate how you can start to apply the principles you have learned in previous chapters. The examples relate to these questions:

- **How can you apply the Leadership Framework to yourself?** This is a useful application if you would like to fix, change or develop your personal leadership behaviour.
- **How can you apply the Leadership Framework to your entity?** This example is related to contexts where it may be necessary to make changes in the **execution system** of an entity. There may be some performance issues, or you should deal with a 'broken' entity that needs to be fixed. Where do you begin?
- **How do you lead change using the Change Dimension?** This example illustrates how one can apply the Change Dimension and S-curves to lead change initiatives.

Example 1:

Apply the Leadership Framework to develop your leadership

The example that follows shows you how you can personally use the Leadership Framework with its key component—the Three-dimensional leadership model. (Figure 14.1). You can apply the principles of the third dimension, 'Change', integrated with all the facets of the leadership framework that you have mastered while reading this book.

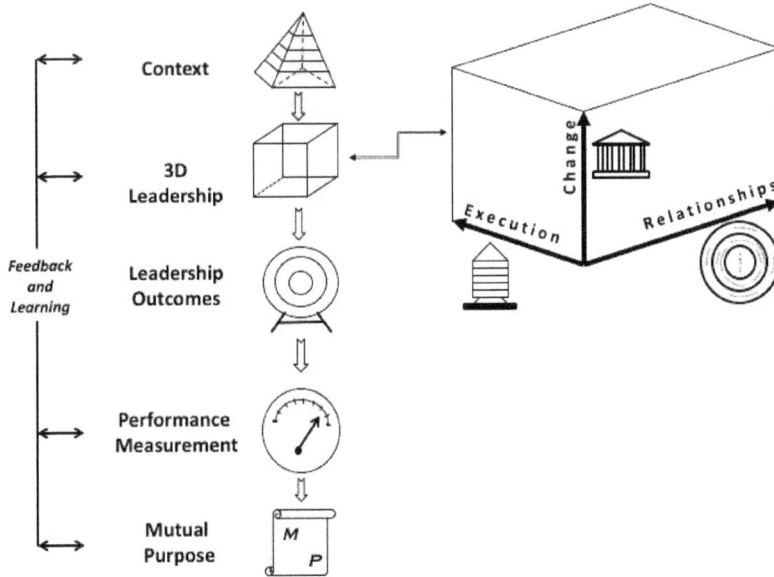

Figure 14.1. The Leadership Framework

Your journey starts with forming and appreciating an accurate context of your personal leadership. Courage is the main requirement for you to embark on a journey of changing your leadership behaviour (and perhaps your leadership team's). Sometimes it will require extraordinary courage. As you will discover, you may need to set aside your ego as best as you can, to become truly honest with yourself, to ask tough questions, to listen without criticism, to accept honest feedback, to desist blame and to be highly alert to self-deception.

I have seen many leaders with exceptional success records who find such courageous moves most difficult. Therein is the rub—relying on your past successes and entrenched behaviour won't guarantee the course of future success. But being courageous to make behavioural changes, to act on them, and to learn from them, will put you on the next wave of success.

Applying the Leadership Framework to your own behaviour will have the following benefits:

- You will get a clear picture on how your behaviour influences and affects your people, the culture and the performance of your entity.
- You can start small, but where you will have most control.
- You will see the benefits first-hand and personally.
- You set the tempo and extent of the changes you wish to accomplish.
- You can easily make mid-course corrections.
- You get to know how the framework works and where you may want to tweak it for your context.
- You can set a perfect example of how it gets done.

First understand your leadership context

The objective of determining your leadership context is to get to a point of clear awareness and accurate self-knowledge about your leadership behaviour in the setting you work in.

An accurate context of your leadership behaviour is best obtained through using information from a combination of the following sources:

- Review the leadership behaviour discussed in the Relationship, Execution and Change Dimensions.
- A set of tough and open questions about your leadership behaviour (see guidance further down).
- Feedback you receive from your team, coaches, mentors, members and third parties about your leadership.
- Your emotional intelligence—particularly the self-awareness, self-control and empathy dimensions of EI.
- Analysing favourite role models you have elected to follow.
- Behaviour reviews such as 360-degree surveys.

- An accurate cross verification of your feedback results obtained by methods such as the above.
- Honest self-reflection.

Use as many of these methods as possible. In that way, you would be able to verify your leadership context, identify your behaviour baselines and set appropriate targets for leadership improvement.

Start by asking tough questions

The more successful you have been as a leader, the tougher these questions will be—to ask them, and to heed the feedback. Remember when you were still a novice; you knew what needed fixing and you did so promptly and with success. As you become more successful, the margins for improvement get thinner and, oops—you become the biggest stumbling block to your own improvement.

Also, as you become more successful it gets increasingly difficult to observe how you contribute to your inertia against improvement. Therefore, courage is so important—courage to face your own questions. So, you need to be open to see yourself from different perspectives.

Questions like the ones below will get you started. Take the time to write the questions and your answers to the questions down, so that you can later reflect on them.

- Do I really want to make necessary changes to my leadership behaviour? Why?
- Am I, or my behaviour, the cause of or contributing to the lack of engagement, the high level of risk averseness, the lack of innovation or resistance to change in my entity or personal life environment?
- Are any of my behaviours not truly in line with the mutual purposes of our entity? What are those behaviours?

- Can I say with confidence that my people can trust me and that I do not go back on my word?
- Do I habitually shift the blame for my faults and the entity's failures to other people or circumstances?
- Do I struggle to face the music and come out in the open when my entity or I have made mistakes?
- Does everyone in my entity know, understand and own our mutual purposes?
- Do I set clear expectations for everyone to follow? Do I set clear expectations for myself?
- Are those expectations in alignment with our mutual purposes?
- Do I make sure that everyone in the entity (including me) is sufficiently equipped to be able to fulfil his or her expectations?
- Do I lead change initiatives on an inclusive manner or do I tend to dictate changes exclusively?
- Do I listen more than I talk to my members?
- Do I overrule my people's accountability to do their jobs, or do I empower them to handle problems and opportunities on their level?

Self-awareness and self-control

Obtain answers on your tough questions from your team, coaches, mentors, members and others about behaviours you need to change or new behaviours you might want to introduce. This is an excellent opportunity for you to practice your emotional intelligence skills, particularly your self-awareness and your self-control.

A list of tough questions and answers can create an honest account of situations where your behaviour was not conducive to leadership for the age of change, and help you to learn new approaches to monitor yourself and substitute better behaviour. With honest reflection, you will perceive and understand your own underlying values, purposes, motives, strengths and weaknesses.

Self-awareness is not solely about ourselves! It is primarily about understanding others' emotional reactions to our behaviour. It is being attentive of the impact we have on others and taking responsibility for our behaviour.

Emotional self-control will help you to manage your emotions, feelings and moods. This is especially important during personal interviews about your behaviour when you may perceive some feedback as downright unpleasant or incorrect. Self-control will help you to suspend judgment, to reflect logically, and think before you act. You will control emotional impulses and channel them positively. You will be able to control your own disruptive tendencies and deal with negative feedback in constructive ways.

Ironically, those tough questions often reveal the lack of emotionally intelligent behaviour as a focus area for leaders to develop or change. This may look like the typical chicken-and-egg conundrum. Which one comes first—the EI skills, or the behavioural changes? Both EI and behaviour skills can be acquired. If you have the courage, and the will to make behavioural changes, you can improve your EI too. The more you improve your EI the easier it will become to improve any other leadership behaviours.

After you have gathered different sets of feedback to your tough questions, and you have verified the answers by applying a number of the different methods I mentioned above, it is time for critical self-reflection. During self-reflection, be especially conscious of behaviour you may have espoused from favourite role models and the assumptions you may have made about leadership. Maybe it is time to change your role models too.

Which of my behaviour dimensions need more work?

Your questions, feedback and self-reflection will reveal certain behaviours in the three dimensions that would need more work on your side.

For example, in the Relationship Dimension you may have to work on being more inclusive, or become better at conflict resolution. In the Execution Dimension, you may have to work on setting Expectations or providing Strategic direction, instead of dictating the way work gets done. In the Change Dimension, you may have to work on expanding your own mindsets and allow your people to make mistakes without fear of being reproached.

Act, model, measure and learn

Pick two or three of the behaviours you identified to improve. If there are many, leave some for later. Rome was not built in a day. Focus on a manageable number. In that way, you can keep track of your progress and not lose heart—some behavioural changes can be quite challenging.

Share, clarify and declare your intentions to make changes to the chosen behaviour. Declare what you expect to achieve with your behaviour. Set bold objectives with challenging targets and design your own performance measures to keep track of your improvements.

When people know, and perceive that you are honest and serious about changing your behaviour they will help you along the way. Don't hesitate to ask your people how you are tracking. Share this with trusted members of your leadership team, mentors, coaches and trusted others. Ask them for options and alternatives.

Start to model your actions to change your behaviour. Measure the outcomes and effects at regular intervals—again using the methods you used to determine your leadership context. Share, discuss and learn from the feedback you obtain, readjust your actions where necessary, and repeat the process on another set of behaviours. Reward and celebrate the new behaviours you have conquered. After a few rounds of applying the Leadership Framework on your own behaviour, the process will become natural to you.

Your willingness and demonstration to make behavioural changes and include others along the journey serves as an excellent opportunity to demonstrate that you are serious about being an inclusive leader. You will be a perfect role model on how everyone in the entity should approach his or her behavioural changes. It will start to build a new culture that is open to change—laying the foundations for a change-fit entity.

Example 2:

Apply the Leadership Framework to fix an entity

This example is about applying the framework and its dimensions in contexts where it may be necessary to make changes to the entity, and more specifically, to its execution systems.

The generic principles of the Leadership Framework apply (Figure 14.1), but with specific reference to the Execution Dimension as discussed in Chapter 5. The Execution Dimension is shown in Figure 14.2 further down in this chapter.

The Execution Dimension and Change Dimension have many important interfaces. You will recall from Chapter 5 that your entity's Execution Dimension should be hardwired into the Change Dimension to enable you to effectively lead change in the entity's execution system (or its operations).

After you have determined the necessary solutions, the execution elements should be realigned and solutions implemented. This will ensure that your entity continues to achieve its objectives within constantly evolving contexts.

Develop the context for change

One of the examples below could be a situation you are facing:

- You have been appointed as the new leader or a CEO to fix a broken entity, that may have been through several changes already, or
- Your entity's performance is in a steep decline, or
- After using the Change Dimension, a need for significant changes has been identified for the entity, or
- All the above applies.

An accurate appreciation of the context sets the scene for your leadership choices to direct necessary and timely solutions to execution, change and relationship issues.

Like in the previous example, start asking tough questions and conduct open discussions in inclusive ways, before you launch into a change initiative. It is crucially important, for an inclusive entity, that your people are included in formulating these tough questions.

Questions need to be wide-ranging and pointedly specific. The following list is a good start:

- Do we really understand which of the seven elements in the Execution Dimension is the cause of the problem and why it/ they needs to change? (Figure 14.2) Perhaps this is your key question.
- Do we consider whether our performance decline is due to structural change drivers, mature S-curves, or due to leadership failures, to properly define and align the execution system?
- Are we convinced that we have fully engaged the Change Dimension, its process, and principles in an inclusive manner to identify the needs and correct initiatives for change to the execution system? (The application in example 1 above may serve as a starter).
- Do we use a disciplined methodology such as the Change Dimension to distinguish between daily operational problems

and contextual change drivers that could redefine the future of our entity?

- Do we have accurate and current baselines for our capacities, capabilities and resources?
- Does our intelligence system give us early warnings and observations about internal execution issues as well as external change drivers that might impact the daily operations?
- Do we allocate sufficient time and attention to correctly define and align the execution elements? (See Figure 14.2)
- Does our leadership team spend most of their time fighting operational fires, or do we focus on the strategic direction and governance?

Where do we begin to make necessary changes?

As the example suggests you may have inherited a broken entity. When entities are in a crisis there could be many causes—so where do you start?

Many new leaders and CEO's attempt to 'fix' a problematic entity or declining performance by launching a new structure, often within months after arrival in their new roles. This obviously has a highly visible effect. Restructuring signifies that the new leader is serious about taking tangible steps to alter the course of the entity.

Other leaders dive right into changing the strategy first—which may be a better place to start than changing the structure. Others start by changing the entity's culture, and simultaneously launch a new structure and vision. Those leaders often announce such changes exclusively (or with the help of a closed-knit team at the top).

Unless you are sure about the context and the facts, and if you have arrived at solutions mostly inclusively, initiatives like the above can be a recipe for disaster. Such change initiatives will not necessarily turn around the decline in performance. In fact, it often accelerates the decline because the entity loses focus. It takes excessive energy to implement fundamental changes and simultaneously keep the entity focused on daily performance. These initiatives eventually land on the same pile as so many other failed attempts that make up the horrible 70% failed-change-statistic (Chapter 1).

You may be facing a similar situation; and you may not have the advantage of fully functional Execution and Change Dimensions. If you did, you would have been able to pinpoint what and where the problem elements are in your execution system—and duly fix them. However, a situation like this provides an ideal opportunity to start applying the principles of the Leadership Framework.

Accurate appreciation of the context and clear mutual understanding of what needs to be fixed will help you to direct and govern the choice of necessary interventions. After you have gathered feedback on the tough questions, and the answers have been verified through inclusive discussion and dialogue, you will pinpoint where the problematic execution elements are, and identify what needs to get fixed.

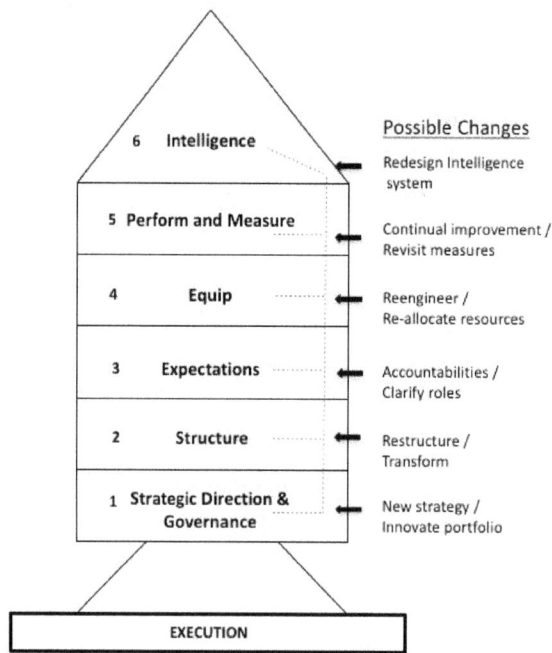

Figure 14.2 Execution Dimension paired with Change Initiatives

You will recall that Chapter 13 illustrates the Execution Dimension and how an entity's execution system can be explained as a sequence of elements. The sequence ranges from the general to the specific. At the bottom of the Execution Dimension is the element of Strategic Direction and Governance (i.e. the strategies, vision and mutual purpose of the entity). This fundamental element sets the scene for designing the appropriate Structure, which in turn forms a template for the correct Expectations, followed by Equipping of the entity. When these elements are sequentially balanced and aligned, the entity can perform according to agreed performance measures.

Any changes to the base elements, for example changes to the Strategic Direction and Structure, will cascade into substantial changes further up the Execution Dimension.

Figure 14.2 is an illustration of how the Execution Dimension can be coupled with possible solutions and interventions, shown on the right-hand side under 'Possible Changes'. Note that the extent and extensiveness of the solutions in this example increase from the top to the bottom of the dimension.

For example, performance issues at the level of Perform and Measure can generally be addressed with interventions such as continual improvement and incremental change. Further down, if Expectations are not met, perhaps the entity needs to revisit the accountabilities of specific roles.

Let's say that to fix a performance problem in your entity you decided to implement a new strategy. If the new strategy deviates substantially from the existing strategy, the chances are good that you would also have to make structural, changes. Structural changes will usually mean that adjustments to some peoples' expectations are necessary (and often many roles will need their expectations to be reset). New Expectations, element 3 in the Execution Dimension, will require reallocation and changes of budgets, resources, systems and processes. Thus, a large part of Equip (element 4) would possibly have to be reset and realigned also.

By now a picture probably starts to take shape. Too often, new leaders reason that when they change the Strategy or Structure, the rest of the execution elements will quickly fall into line and performance issues will be a thing of the past. When you deal with a broken entity and large performance declines you should take a holistic approach across the entire Execution Dimension. If you make changes to some elements and those changes are not aligned across all elements, the performance problems may worsen, or you may not obtain the complete result you expected.

Changes in Strategic Direction often means changes in Structure would be necessary, which would lead to changes in Expectations, Equipping, and so forth. In complex cases, several iterations between elements may be necessary to arrive at optimal solutions.

An important point is that you should be especially careful when changing the fundamental execution elements of an entity, i.e. the Strategy or Structure. Those changes may be necessary, but may not need correction as often, or as extensive as you might think. The argument is that change initiatives should commence in the right element in the Execution Dimension. To illustrate this point: If the performance issues are due to Expectations that were set incorrectly, fiddling with the Structure or the Strategy won't solve the problem. Figure out why Expectations have been skewed and help your leaders to realign Expectations with the rest of the dimension. The same principle applies to all other elements, like Equip. If your people are not empowered to do their jobs with suitable systems, processes, accountabilities and resources, a restructure or new strategy will not solve that issue.

Applying the Execution Dimension in this example

Always ensure that the Intelligence element (element 6) of the Execution Dimension (Figure 14.2) is intact. If you have identified performance problems to be addressed at your leadership level (and not at operational levels), it is most probably an indication that the right intelligence did not reach the right people, at the right time, to make the right decisions. If your intelligence system proactively did its work, performance issues would not have escalated to your level to demand significant leadership attention. Thus, start with a detailed scrutiny of your Intelligence element.

If indeed the Intelligence element functioned as it should and it indicated timeously where exactly the problem was, you would have known at what managerial level the solutions had to be applied. It would have indicated which of the execution elements needed changes.

It might be that the next element down, the Perform and Measure element, is no longer adequate and effective. Some performance measures could be misaligned or not transparent enough. Or, it might be that your measurement system focuses too much on historical performance measures, instead of a balanced view that includes anticipatory and real-time measures.

Fix the Measure element and it might not be necessary to change any other element, because the entity is then able to measure proactively that which really indicates performance.

Performance issues that originate in the Equip element could relate to misallocation of resources, inadequate systems and inefficient processes. The entity is not adequately equipped to deliver on the Expectations that were set. The cause may not be as obvious as the misallocation of budgets, capacities or capabilities.

The less obvious misallocations can come from for example, spending too much or too little time on issues that are key factors in your entity's performance. Or, the correct amounts of intelligence or human energy are not available to ensure proper delivery of products or services. When you make necessary changes in Equip remember to make changes in the Perform and Measure, and the Intelligence elements too, to realign. Ensure that you have equipped everyone according to his or her Expectations.

Next up is the element of Expectations. Many causes of losses in performance originate from skewed or inaccurate Expectations. It often occurs when there are many movements of people in an entity, or when an entity is in a steep growth phase, or during a restructure. The three role expectations; role accountability, clarify and role fit, can easily get neglected and become misaligned with the presumed performance expectations.

Expectations is an element that needs continuous managerial attention to ensure everyone is aligned with the entity's strategy, mutual purpose and performance expectations. The usual problems in this element that need fixing are inadequate decision-making powers, insufficient intelligence, lack of role clarity and non-inclusive leadership. After a restructure for example, many people's role expectations would have shifted—often dramatically. Accountability, fit and clarity must be rebalanced as soon as possible to ensure the entity is back on track to perform effectively.

Because restructuring has such a pervasive effect on all the Execution elements, only make changes to the entity structure where it is really necessary. With a seamless intelligence system connected to the Change Dimension, the structure can be tweaked continually as and where needed. Adjusting the structure incrementally and proactively will prevent the need for massive transformations that are often too late.

Consider changing your entity's structure when the contextual feedback clearly indicate that the entity can no longer engage proactively with the challenges in its external environment, or when you should make a strategic shift from a mature S-curve to new initiatives on your portfolio. If your existing structure cannot facilitate effective responsive interfaces between your entity and your clients any longer—you should restructure it accordingly.

A decision to restructure the entity is often caused by a decision to change its Strategic Direction. When one or more of the answers to the fundamental questions on Strategic Direction changes (Chapter 13), a new strategy is required. The fundamental questions are 'Why', 'Where', 'What', 'Where to', 'Where not to' and 'How fast'.

A new strategy could mean that some changes to the current structure are necessary, with subsequent cascading effects across the entire Execution Dimension. Successful strategy implementation goes beyond the formulation of strategy and the rollout of strategic plans. Strategy implementation means every element in the Execution Dimension needs to be revisited, changed where necessary, aligned and implemented.

Example 3:

Lead Change using the Change Dimension

This example shows how you can apply the laws of S-curves and the Change Dimension to start leading a change-oriented culture in your entity. It illustrates how you can identify which areas need change and when to consider new change initiatives.

Create a context for change

If you haven't yet created a change-oriented culture in your entity—one that follows the five pillars of the Change Dimension, you can start by gradually and incrementally introducing a context for change. Creating a context for change does not happen by a singular massive transformation, but by fostering a change-oriented culture, one that demonstrates a habit of continuous reinvention.

You can create such a context by introducing change as a regular agenda item to engage in dialogue with your direct reports. In the beginning have it as a weekly item, and then more frequently expanding it to a complete change agenda until it becomes a habit. Ensure ample time is allowed for a change agenda, and include everyone on your team. Then gradually spread this habit outwards into the entire entity.

A context for change must consider both the current set of S-curves, as well as potential future initiatives—those that could replace and renew your current offerings.

Change-oriented leaders push their teams to consider factors that cause the entity and its offerings to slumber into a comfortable equilibrium. For example, growing revenues may be very comforting to a business entity, but when the underlying margins are starting to thin, it is a sign of competitive pressure and perhaps a maturing S-curve. A comfortable equilibrium is almost always the forerunner of an S-curve that is about to turn its direction toward decline. Change-oriented leaders are continuously on the lookout for factors that would interrupt the upward performance momentum of S-curves.

As the leader, it is your duty to consistently and continuously introduce discomfort with the current state of affairs. But not to the point where everyone gets nervous, confused and loses sight of their daily Expectations. A healthy discomfort with the status quo breads a culture that is fit for change.

Create a context for fresh thinking and inclusive contribution. Setting the context for change creates an environment for learning and generation of novel solutions, it stimulates continuous reinvention. Once everyone in the entity realises that they also own the changes, they will include themselves to co-create new initiatives, they will go after initiatives faster, and more creatively, and implement those initiatives in a fully engaged manner.

Regular questions to help frame a context for change

Repeatedly use questions like the following to frame a context for change in your entity:

- Do we see the real opportunities that lie on the long-term horizon—opportunities to reinvent our current S-curves and opportunities that would potentially mean totally new (or related) initiatives?
- Do we see the major trends that could potentially undermine the ways we execute our current S-curves in unexpected ways?
- Do we know how our S-curves are driven by larger contextual

trends (or macro S-curves), for example, how does the economic cycle or demographic trends influence this S-curve?

- Do we know whether execution problems are caused by internal misalignments in the Execution Dimension or are they signs of imminent structural changes that threaten our entity?

- Do we know how our capacities, capabilities, resources, systems and processes that support S-curves follow their own inherent life cycles? Each element needs to be revisited regularly to prevent premature losses in performance. Are you aware of any shortening life cycles of capabilities, advantages or resources?

- Do we balance our resource spread across current activities as well as initiatives that would sustain the future?

- Do we have the necessary resource resilience to withstand disruptions, counter uncertainties and seize new initiatives?

- Do we know what would potentially disrupt the natural growth cycles of our S-curves? Do we have exit plans or alternative options available in the event these disruptions occur?

- Is there a sudden sense of urgency in our leadership meetings to plan for change – but we don't know what it means yet? Are there performance declines due to shifting trends?

- Can we implement change initiatives at optimal speed when necessary? (Refer to the Speed vs. Time matrix in Chapter 13)

- Is everyone in our entity included in the change agenda?

- Is my entity psychologically and emotionally fit to engage change initiatives on a continuous basis?

- Do we follow a systematic set of behaviours and principles, such as the Change Dimension, to help us answer questions like these on a continuous basis?

Examine your entity's S-curves

The natural laws of life cycles or S-curves do not only apply on the entity level. The laws also apply to macro trends such as the economy, technologies and demographics. The laws further apply to the things that support your entity's life cycle, such as its systems, processes, structures, capabilities, technologies, and business or operational models.

So, when you determine the positions of your entity or your offerings on their respective S-curves, consider the following characteristics:

- The ultimate level of growth potential in any S-curve is finite.
- What are the macro trends that support the S-curves? Are they strengthening or are they fizzling out? Are they replaced by other macro trends?
- Several key items support the growth and performance of your S-curves, i.e. technologies, resources and capabilities. Which of those supporting elements are reaching their plateaus? E.g. if you are supporting an offering with outdated technologies—be very cautious about disruptors that could come from left field. So often does the financial performance curve of an entity grow solidly, while it masks the deterioration of the very things that support the growth. By the time the financial curve shows a decline in performance, it is too late to refresh the supporting elements.
- S-curves are timing and context sensitive. For example, the same business or entity in another context, e.g. a first world vs. a third world setting, will be on a different position on the curve.
- The position on the S-curve is influenced by the amount of competition. Normally the higher up the S-curve, the more competition you would expect. Many newcomers would have detected the growth opportunity and clamber onto the S-curve

too, with competing offerings. The closer you get to the top of the S-curve (of the original offering), the more competitive it becomes and shakeouts become common. S-curves of competing offerings become shorter (shorter lives), signifying a limited amount of remaining growth (for the underlying or original offering).

- As the growth curve rises, often unpredictable competitors arrive with innovative and disruptive business models, or technologies, or new capabilities. This may curtail an S-curve to a sudden death, or remove slow changing competition, leaving most of the growth potential available to competitors with superior offerings. A counter attack is ill advised unless you have a more superior disruptive innovation ready to launch against your competition.

- Having determined the positions of your entity and its offerings on their respective S-curves and taking cognisance of competitors' positions and disruptive moves, how much growth potential is left in each? Can we still compete on these curves? What is required to successfully ride out the wave? Or, do we need to move onto brand new S-curves to secure our entity's long-term sustainability? When is the most opportune time to exit from the current S-curves?

Engage the Change Dimension to renew the entity and its offerings

Starting a habit of regular change agendas and focused dialogues about change, as I suggest above, will create a context for building the first stages of Enable and Align in the Change Dimension. Ensure that this change-oriented habit is formed inclusively, with a continual focus on mutual purposes.

To constantly have fresh ideas for new S-curves, and to be proactive about threatening change drivers, use the *Anticipate Change Funnel* (Chapter 10), and follow through with Incubation (Chapter 11). It is essential that you provide enough suitable resources to keep the *Anticipate Change Funnel* full and deliver fully incubated future initiatives. Fully incubated initiatives are those that are ready and viable to replace mature and declining S-curves, before they start to erode your entity's resilience.

Quo Vadis?

In this final chapter I presented a few examples to show how you can apply the Leadership Framework to develop your leadership behaviour, how to fix an entity with execution and performance issues and how to lead change initiatives.

The concepts, frameworks and principles were designed and integrated around your comprehensive role as a leader. It does not matter what kind of entity you are leading and what the continually changing context is that you lead in. *Leadership for the Age of Change* will serve you with practical guidance. You can apply the framework at any level and in many contexts. Apply the Leadership Framework whether you lead a country, a government, a global organisation, a team, a school, a sports organisation or a political entity—the principles in *Leadership for the Age of Change* are universal.

The occasions in which you can apply what you have learned in *Leadership for the Age of Change* are innumerable. I would encourage you to refer to this book again and again as you progress through your career. Make it a desktop companion you would use in everyday situations and for the complex leadership contexts you will face in the age of change.

Enjoy being a successful leader in the 21st century—the age of hyper-change!

References

Adams, J., Hayes, J. & Hopson, B. 1976, *Transitions: Understanding and managing personal change*, Martin Robertson, London.

Aguirre, D., Finn, L. & Harsak, A. 2007, Ready Willing and Engaged, Booz&Co, Chicago.

Anderson, D. & Anderson, L. A., 2010, *Beyond Change Management, 2nd Ed.* Pfeifer, San Francisco.

AON Hewitt, 2013, *Managing Engagement During Times of Change, White paper by AON Hewitt.*

Argyris, C. 1977, 'Double-loop learning in organisations', *Harvard Business review*, Sept-Oct, pp.115-124.

Arvonen, J. 1995, Leadership Behaviour and Coworker Health – A study in Process Industry, Department of Psychology, Stockholm University, Sweden.

Bandura, A. 1977, *Social Learning Theory*, Prentice-Hall, Englewood Cliffs.

Banmen, J. 2002, 'The Satir Model: Yesterday and Today', Contemporary Family Therapy, vol. 24, no. 1, pp. 7-22..

Barassa, A. 2006, *Integrating Leadership behaviour and climate perceptions in teamwork*, PhD thesis, Universidad Complutense, Madrid, Spain.

Bass, B. M. 1990, *Bass & Stogdill's Handbook of Leadership. Theory, Research, and Managerial Applications.* 3rd Ed. The Free Press, New York.

Beckhard, R. F. & Harris, R. T. 1987, *Organizational Transitions: Managing complex change,* Addison-Wesley, Reading, Massachusetts.

Beddington, J. *The 2030 Perfect Storm Scenario*, Population Institute.

Beer, M. 1992, Leading Change, in *Managing people and Organizations, ed.* J.J. Gabbarro, Harvard Business School Press, Boston.

Blake, R. & Mouton, J. 1964, *The Managerial Grid: The Key to Leadership Excellence*. Gulf Publishing Co, Houston.

Bridges, W. 1991, *Managing Transitions: Making the Most of Change 2nd edn.*, Perseus Books, Cambridge.

Bridges, W., & Bridges, S. 2009, *Managing Transitions*, DeCapo Press, Philadelphia.

Carmeli, A. & Sheaffe, Z. 2009, How Leadership Characteristics Affect Organizational Decline and Downsizing, *Journal of Business Ethics*, vol. 86, no. 3, pp. 363-378.

Chandler, A. D. 1962. *Strategy and Structure*, MIT Press, Cambridge.

Collins, J. 2001, *Good-to-Great*, HarperCollins, New York.

Conklin, J., Basadur, M. & VanPatter, G.K. 2007. Rethinking Wicked Problems: Unpacking Paradigms, Bridging Universes, *NextDesign Leadership Institute Journal*, vol. 10. pp. 1-30.

Cooper, R. K., & Sawaf, A. 1997, *Executive EQ: Emotional intelligence in leadership and organisations*. Grosset/Putnam, New York.

Cooper, R.G. & Edgett, S. J., 2005, *Lean, Rapid and Profitable New Product Development,* Product Development Institute, Canada.

Corporate Executive Board, 2013, 'Breaking Through Indecision for Breakthrough Growth', 2013, https://www.cebglobal.com/blogs/breaking-through-indecision-for-breakthrough-growth/

Corporate Executive Board, 2015, 'Growth Unlocked: Closing the Strategy to Execution Gap', *Corporate Executive Board's Guidance for 2015*.

Covey, S. R. 2005, *The 8th Habit*, Free Press, New York, 2005.

Dobb, R., Manyika, J. & Woetzel, J. 2015, *No Ordinary Disruption,* PublicAffairs, New York.

Dulewicz, V., & Higgs, M. 2000, 'Emotional Intelligence: a review and evaluation study', *Journal of Managerial Psychology*, vol. 15, no. 4, pp. 341-372.

Ekvall, G. & Arvonen, J. 1991, 'Change-centred leadership: an extension of the two-dimensional model'. *Scandinavian Journal of Management,* vol. 7, pp.17-26.

Ekvall, G. & Arvonen, J. 1994, 'Leadership profiles, situation and effectiveness'. *Creativity and Innovation Management,* vol. 3, no. 3, pp. 139-161.

Ekvall, G. 1991, 'Change-centred leaders: empirical evidence of a third dimension of leadership', *Leadership and Organization Development Journal,* vol. 12, pp. 18-23.

Employee Engagement Trends Report, 2011, *Report by PeopleMetrics,* Philadelphia PA.

Fleishman, E. A., Harris, E.F., & Burt, H. E. 1955, *Leadership and Supervision in Industry.* Ohio State University, Columbus.

Fleishman, E.A. 1957, 'A leader behaviour description for industry', In R.M. Stogdill & A. E. Coons (Eds.), *Leader Behaviour: Its Description and Measurement.* Ohio State University, Columbus.

Gantz, J., & Reinsel, D. 2012, *The Digital Universe 2020 – Big Data, Bigger Digital Shadows, and Biggest Growth in the Far East,* https://www.emc.com/leadership/digital-universe/index.htm

George, J. M., 2000, 'Emotions and Leadership: the role of emotional intelligence', *Human Relations,* vol. 53, no. 8, pp. 1027-1056.

Gil, F., Rico, R., Alcover, C. M. & Barrasa, A. 2005, 'Change-oriented leadership, satisfaction and performance in work groups, *Journal of Managerial Psychology,* vol. 20, no. 3, pp. 312 – 328.

Goethals, G. R., Sorenson, G. J. & Burns, James M. 2004, *Encyclopedia of Leadership,* Sage Publication, London.

Goleman, D. 1996, *Emotional Intelligence: Why It Can Matter More Than IQ.* Bloomsbury Publishing, London.

Goleman, D. 2004, 'What makes a Leader?', *Harvard Business Review,* vol. 76, no. 6, pp. 93-104.

Hamel, G. & Prahalad, C.K. 1989, Strategic Intent, *Harvard Business Review,* July-August, pp. 148- 161.

Hamel, G. 1996, 'Strategy as Revolution', *Harvard Business Review*, July-August, pp. 69-82

Harbour, J. L. 2009, *The Performance Paradox*. CRC Press, New York.

Holman, P. & Devane, T. 1999, *The Change Handbook*, Berrett-Koehler, San Francisco.

Hoyle, J. R. 1995, *Leadership and Futuring: Making Visions Happen*. Corwin Press, California.

Hughes, M. 2011, 'Do 70 percent of all organisational change initiatives really fail', *Journal of Change management*, vol. 11, no. 4, pp. 451-464,

IBM, 2013, *Making Change Work, Report by IBM*.

James Canton, J. 2006, *Extreme Future – The top ten trends that will reshape the world*, Penguin, New York.

Johnson, B. Polarity Management, in Goldsmith, M., Govindarajan, V., Kaye, B., & Vicere, A. A. (2003). *The many facets of leadership*. FT Press.

Kast F.E. & Rosenweig J. E. 1985, *Organization and Management – A Systems and Contingency approach*, 4th Ed., McGraw-Hill, New York.

Kast, F. E. & Rosenweig, J. E. 1972, 'General Systems Theory: Applications for Organization and Management', *Academy of Management Journal*, vol. 15, no. 4, pp. 447–465.

Kelley, D. & Conner, D. 1979, The Emotional Cycle of Change, in *The Annual Handbook for Group Facilitators*, eds. J. Jones, J. & J. Pfeiffer, University Associates, San Diego.

Kiel, F. 2015, *Return on Character*, Harvard Business Review Press, Boston.

Kotter, J. P. 1996, *Leading Change*, Harvard Business School Press, Boston.

Krames, J. A. 2002, *The Jack Welch Lexicon of Leadership*, McGraw-Hill, New York.

Kübler-Ross, E (1969) On Death and Dying, Macmillan, New York.

Lewin, K. & Cartwright, D. 1951. *Field Theory in Social Science*, Tavistock Publications, New York.

Lewin, K. 1951, 'Frontiers in Group Dynamics,' *Human Relations,* vol.1, pp. 5–41.

Lewin, K. 1952, *Field Theory in Social Science,* Harper and Row, New York.

Loughman, A., Bowman, K. & Kalia, C. *Leadership Styles amongst the Emergency Services,* UWA School of Medicine and Dentistry, Perth, Australia.

Lourens, J.F. & Boshoff, A.B. 2001, 'The Change Centred Leadership behaviour dimension in the South African context', *Proceedings of the 8th International Conference on Advances in Management,* vol. 8, pp. 74.

Lourens, J.F. 2001, *Change Centered Leadership and Various Correlates,* PhD thesis, University of Pretoria, South Africa.

Lourens, J.F., Boshoff, A.B. & Van Wyk, R. 2002, 'Change Centered Leadership and various Correlates', *Proceedings of the Pan Pacific Conference XIX,* 28 – 31 May 2002, University of Nebraska-Lincoln, Lincoln, pp. 251-253.

Lourens, J.F., Boshoff, A.B. & Van Wyk, R. 2003, 'Relationships between Emotional Intelligence and the Three-dimensional leadership Behavior Construct', *Proceedings of the 1st International Conference on Contemporary Management,* 1-2 Sep. 2003, The University of Adelaide, Adelaide, Australia, pp. 49-55.

Luecke, R. 2003, *Managing Change and Transition,* Harvard Business School Press, Boston.

Lynch, R.P. 1990, The Practical Guide to Joint Ventures and Corporate Alliances, John Wiley, New York.

Manz, C. C., & Sims, H. P. 1986, 'Self-leadership: Toward an expanded theory of self-influence processes in organisations'. *Academy of Management Review,* vol. 11, pp. 585-600.

Manz, C. C., & Sims, H. P. 1989, *Super Leadership: Leading others to lead themselves.* Prentice-Hall, New York.

Manz, C.C., & Sims, H. P. 1987, 'Leading workers to lead themselves: the external leadership of self-managing work teams', *Administrative Science Quarterly,* vol. 32, pp. 106-128.

Marx, E. 1999, *Breaking Through Culture Shock.* Nicholas Brealey Publishing, London.

Mayer, J.D. & Salovey, P. 1993, 'The intelligence of emotional intelligence'. *Intelligence,* vol.17, pp. 433-442.

McShane, S & Von Glinow, M. 2010, *Organizational Behavior, 5th Ed,* McGraw-Hill, New York.

Merrow, E. W. 2011, *Industrial Megaprojects – Concepts, Strategies and Practices for Success,* Wiley, New Jersey.

Mintzberg, H. 1989, *Mintzberg on Management – Inside our strange world of organisations,* Collier Macmillan, New York.

Nadler, D. A. & Tushman, M. L. 1977, 'A diagnostic model for organisational behaviour', in *Perspectives on behaviour in organisations,* eds. J. R. Hackman, E. E. Lawler & L. W. Porter, McGraw-Hill, New York.

Nanus, B. 1992, *Visionary leadership – Creating a Compelling Sense of Direction for Your Organization.* Jossey-Bass, San Francisco.

Norris, E. A. 2005, *An investigation of the leadership styles and change styles in a high quality manufacturing organisation,* PhD thesis, University of Phoenix, Arizona.

Obeng, K. 1960, 'Culture Shock: Adjustment to new cultural environments', *Practical Anthropology,* vol.7, pp. 177 – 82.

Obolensky, N. 2014, *Complex Adaptive Leadership, Embracing Paradox, and Uncertainty,* 2nd Ed, Gower, Surrey, England.

Ohmae, K, 1983, *The Mind of the Strategist,* McGraw-Hill, New York.

Prochaska, J.O., Redding, C. A. & Evers, K.E. 2008, 'The Transtheoretical Model and Stages of Change', in *Health Behavior and Health Education,* 4th ed., eds. K. Glanz, B.K. Rimer, & K. Viswanath, Jossey-Bass, San Francisco.

Revans, R. 1982, *The Origin and Growth of Action Learning,* Chartwell Bratt, London.

Rimanoczy, I. & Turner, E. 2008, *Action Reflection Learning,* Davis-Black, California.

Rittel, H. & Webber. M. 1973, 'Dilemmas in a General Theory of Planning', *Policy Sciences,* vol. 4, pp. 155–169.

Rost, J. 1991, *Leadership for the Twenty-first Century*, Preager, New York.

Rost, J. 1993, 'Leadership Development in the new Millennium', *The Journal of Leadership Studies*, vol. 1, no. 1. pp. 91-110.

Sargent, C. 1970, *Psychological Aspects of Environmental Adjustment*, Unpublished manuscript.

Satir, V., Banmen. J., Gerber. J, & Gomori. M. 1991, *The Satir Model: Family Therapy and Beyond*, Science and Behavior Books.

Schein, E. H. 1985, *Organisational Culture and Leadership*, Jossey-Bass, San Francisco.

Senge, P. M. 2004, *The Fifth Discipline – The Art and Practice of the Learning Organization*, Currency Doubleday, New York.

Shockley-Zalabak, P. S., Morreale, S. P. & Hackman, M. Z. 2010, *Building the high trust Organization*, Jossey-Bass, San Francisco.

Skogstad, A. & Einarson, S. 1999. 'The importance of a change-centred leadership style in four organisational cultures', *Scandinavian Journal of Management*, vol. 15, pp. 289-306.

Smith, M. 2002, 'Success rates for different types of organisational change', *Performance management*, vol. 41, No.1, pp. 26 – 33.

Stevens, G., 2003, 'Piloting the Rocket of Radical Innovation', *Research Technology Management*, vol. 46, no. 2, pp.16-25.

Swieringa, J. & Wierdsma, A. 1992, *Becoming a learning Organization – Beyond the learning curve*, Addison-Wesley, New York.

The State of the Global Workplace, 2013, *Report by Gallup Inc.*

Van Der Heijden, K. 2005, *Scenarios – The Art of Strategic Conversation*, John Wiley, West Sussex, England.

Volckman, R. 2005, 'A Fresh Perspective: 21st Century Leadership – an interview with Joseph Rost'. *Integral Leadership Review*.

Wack, P. 1985, 'Scenarios: Uncharted Waters Ahead', *Harvard Business Review*. September-October.

Williams, D. 1999, 'Human Responses to Change', *Futures*, vol. 31, pp. 609-616.

Yukl, G. 2003, 'Tridimensional leadership theory: A roadmap for flexible, adaptive leaders'. In R. J. Burke & C. Cooper (Eds.), *Leading in turbulent times*, pp. 75-92, Blackwell, London.

Yukl, G. A., Gordon, A. & Taber, T. 2002, 'A Hierarchical Taxonomy of leadership behaviour: Integrating a half century of behaviour research', *Journal of leadership and organisational Studies*, vol. 9, no. 1, pp. 15-32.

Acknowledgements

This book has been in the making for more than thirty years. Ever since I started my career I have been interested in the subject of leadership. Many people have influenced and honed my thinking and knowledge. Writing *'Leadership for the Age of Change'* would not have been possible if it were not for them.

Firstly, I would like to give the honour and glory to my Almighty God and Father, and Jesus Christ my Saviour and the Holy Spirit for giving me the understanding and strength to complete this work.

I cannot sufficiently express my gratitude to my wife Annelie, for her enthusiasm and commitment as main editor of this book and for her endless patience to create a work that reads easily. Thank you from the bottom of my heart!

To my family and friends, very special thanks for your unceasing encouragement and love to make this work possible. Thank you for believing in me.

This work would not have seen the light if it were not for the dedication of Prof. Adré Boshoff, who was my PhD supervisor and who led my study in the field of Organisational Behaviour. Adré has taught me the immeasurable value of scientific inquiry, rigorous research and the process of following structured methods to advance the theoretical into practical application. I will forever remember our many stimulating and refreshing intellectual deliberations. Thank you Adré.

To Chalette Brown, our daughter, who took it upon herself to proof read the entire book. I cannot express my gratitude enough.

To Ernest, our son, who has a keen eye for the logical flow of concepts and the presentation of images. Thank you for your priceless input.

I want to specially express my gratitude to the people listed below for their willingness to spend so much of their time reading my advance copy and who have written the testimonials in the front of this book. In no specific order, they are:

Cedric Johnson, John Howard, René van Wyk, John Munro, Rina Visser, Tobias Hills, John Doughty, Theo Veldsman, Edgar Johnson and Anton Visser. Your words of endorsement and validation of the concepts, frameworks and principles in this book are priceless. Thank you for your valuable feedback and all the discussions we had.

About the Author

Jannie Lourens is the co-founder of *IncludeChange,* a company that consults and coaches in the fields of leadership, strategy, performance and commercialisation of large industrial ventures. He coaches leaders to excel in leading change. His purpose is to help leaders and their entities to become pre-prepared and change-fit for the challenges and vast opportunities that are presented by the age of change.

Jannie's core values centre on his passion to be excellent at what he does, to include people in decisions, to build trustworthy relationships and to collaborate towards achievement of mutual purposes. His varied education and experience across many countries provide him with a rich resource to follow his passion—to add value and encourage leaders who want to lead proactively into a future that holds significant change, challenges and opportunities. He firmly holds to the view that change follows natural laws—laws one can easily understand and apply inclusively through new leadership frameworks towards a better future.

Currently Jannie is chief financial officer (CFO) for a mega-project to build a sustainable eco-industrial complex aimed to serve the growing industrial and energy markets in Southern Africa. Previously he held many senior leadership roles in strategy, new venture commercialisation, technological innovation, project management, international energy markets and consulting. His career spans across the fuels, chemicals, power generation, energy, steel, military and education sectors, among others.

Jannie completed a doctoral program in Organisational Behaviour with a honourable distinction. The research for his doctoral dissertation focused on the integration of the recently discovered theory of three-dimensional leadership behaviour, emotional intelligence, leadership visioning, and organisation citizenship. He has presented several papers and presentations on the results of his research.

Jannie also holds a Masters in Business Administration. His Masters dissertation focused on the application of artificial intelligence in strategic management. Prior to that, Jannie obtained two tertiary qualifications in Chemical Engineering.

He is a co-author of 'Management for Engineers, Technologists and Scientists', first published in the year 2000. It has subsequently been published in its 3rd edition. He is the author of the parts on business and technology strategy.

Jannie is married to Annelie. They have two children, both married, and one granddaughter. They live in Adelaide, in the state of South Australia.